Empire to Umpire

Canada and the World
to the 1990s

Empire to Umpire

Canada and the World to the 1990s

Norman Hillmer

J.L. Granatstein

Copp Clark Longman Ltd.

Toronto

ISBN: 0-7730-5439-1

Executive editor: Jeff Miller
Editor: Camilla Jenkins
Proofreader: Robyn Packard
Cover cartoon: Aislin
Typesetting: April Haisell, Carol Magee
Printing and binding: Metropole Litho Inc.

Canadian Cataloguing in Publication Data

Hillmer, Norman, 1942–
Empire to umpire: Canada and the world to the 1990s
Includes bibliographical references and index.
ISBN 0-7730-5439-1

1. Canada - Foreign relations - Great Britain. 2. Great Britain - Foreign relations - Canada. 3. Canada - Foreign relations - United States. 4. United States - Foreign relations - Canada. 5. Canada - Foreign relations - 1867–   .*
I. Granatstein, J.L., 1939–   . II. Title.
FC242.H5 1994   327.71'009'04   C94-931911-2
F1029.H5 1994

Copp Clark Longman Ltd.
2775 Matheson Blvd. East
Mississauga, Ontario L4W 4P7

Associated companies:
Longman Group Ltd., London
Longman Inc., New York
Longman Cheshire Pty., Melbourne
Longman Paul Pty., Auckland

Printed and bound in Canada

1 2 3 4 5   5439-1   98 97 96 95 94

For Ian M. Drummond
and
John T. Saywell

CONTENTS

Contents

PREFACE

Foreign policy is the face that Canada presents to the world, and foreign policy to a substantial extent is what the world uses to define Canada. Our politics, culture, institutions, material well-being, defence, and national self-esteem have been influenced, and frequently shaped, by our dealings with other nations.

What was the face Canada presented to the world? What is it today? In the early years of the Dominion of Canada, we were part and parcel of the British Empire. In great measure, Canadians took their personality and their confidence from belonging to the greatest empire the world had ever seen. A century later, that empire long vanished, Canadians increasingly define their nation as a mediator, a middle power, an adjudicator, or an umpire, as we try to teach the rest of the world the rules of the game as we wish it to be played. As our title suggests, this book is an attempt to chronicle Canada's passage from Empire to Umpire.

We have been assisted by a number of friends and colleagues. Gabrielle Nishiguchi, Greg Donaghy, Angelika Sauer, and Susan Villeneuve commented on large portions of the manuscript to our great benefit. Roger Sarty was enormously stimulating on questions of defence policy. Carman Bickerton, Carl Christie, Rich Gimblett, Cheryl McKinnon, and Vincent Rigby intervened at critical points. William Kaplan provided the title for the last book we did together; this time he merely approved the suggested title, but that was important, and so too was his enthusiasm for the project. This book's title belongs to Jeff Miller of Copp Clark Longman, who was far more helpful and understanding than any publisher has a right to be. Camilla Jenkins edited the book superbly, while Barbara Tessman and Andy Carroll put it through the press with despatch and competence. We are most grateful.

Finally, we have, as ever, been supported in all the important ways by Anne Hillmer and Elaine Granatstein.

NH
JLG
June 1994

A Subordinate but Still a Powerful People, 1867–1896

CANADA WAS BORN in ambiguity. The British North America Act, 1867, united Canada East, Canada West, New Brunswick, and Nova Scotia, but this law of Britain's Parliament placed important restrictions on the independence of the fledgling state, particularly in the arena of external affairs. It could run its own domestic business for the most part, but it had no foreign policy of its own, no international status, no standing. Like the former British North American colonies of which it was constituted, the new Canada was wrapped snugly within the British Empire. The imperial crown was indivisible, the Queen-Empress Victoria ruling over all her domains, Canada included. It was against natural law to contemplate one part of the empire having a different policy from another on a matter of importance. Britain was superior—legally, constitutionally, diplomatically. As a future prime minister would put it, Canada was a nation that was not yet a nation.

The Queen's British ministers thus established the foreign policies of the British Empire and all its components. Canadians simply had to await decisions from across the Atlantic. Requests for information or advice could be sent to the bureaucratic centre of the empire in Whitehall, but only through the agency of the British-appointed governor general of Canada, "the human link in the imperial chain."

Replies would come back to him from Britain's colonial secretary, and the governor general then transmitted them to "his" government. If Canada wished to talk to or deal with any other country, it was understood that this would be done by or through the Foreign Office in London and British representatives around the world. This had tangible advantages for the smaller power. Parochial Canadian concerns undoubtedly carried more weight in Washington and other capitals if they were presented by Her Britannic Majesty's ambassador. The arrangement was also economical. British consulates and embassies handled Canadian questions without charge, gladdening the heart of the minister of finance in Ottawa. The prime minister said in 1882 that being forced to use the country's own resources "would be an injury, a destruction, a ruin of Canada."

When Canadian politicians were fashioning their Confederation, they wanted to call the union a "kingdom" or "viceroyalty" in order to underline the distinctiveness of their experiment, as well as their allegiance to Britain and rejection of the United States. The authorities in London, however, were concerned about the American reaction to an ostentatious reminder of royalism: "a monarchical blister" on the side of a country that had rebelled against King George III during the American Revolution a century before. Canada had to settle for "dominion" as a self-description, a term still suggesting British control but apparently not nearly so offensively. It was a small thing, but revealing. Anxious to limit their commitments in North America, the British cared more about harmony with the ever more powerful United States than they did about Canada's needs or wishes. That was to be a consistent theme in the history of Canadian diplomacy.

Canadians took great pride and comfort in the British connection. As the BNA Act made its way through the Parliament at Westminster, John A. Macdonald, the first prime minister and the country's leader for most of its first quarter-century, told Queen Victoria, "We have desired in this measure to declare in the most solemn and emphatic manner our resolve to be under the Sovereignty of Your Majesty and your family for ever." British values, institutions, and power were seen as a bulwark against the excesses of the United States, real and potential. In 1871, the Toronto *Globe* warned, "we are divided only by an imaginary boundary . . . from a people . . . [who]

have before now proved themselves aggressive—a people who believe in 'manifest destiny,' 'universal sovereignty,' and other ideas not very re-assuring to their neighbours." By that year Britain had removed most of its army from Canada but was pledged to defend "every portion of the Empire with all the resources at its command." The Royal Navy controlled the seas, and the British maintained substantial fortified garrisons at Halifax, Nova Scotia, and nearby Bermuda.

Yet there was every expectation that Canadian freedoms would grow as the country grew. Macdonald predicted in 1865 that "a different colonial system" would gradually be developed, "and it will become, year by year, less a case of dependence on our part, and of over-ruling protection on the part of the Mother Country, and more a case of a healthy and cordial alliance. Instead of looking upon us as a merely dependent colony, England will have in us a friendly nation—a subordinate but still a powerful people—to stand by her in North America in peace or in war." Both an anglophile and a nationalist, Macdonald understood not only the importance of Britain's support but also the benefits of developing a distinctive international personality. With Confederation, the Canadian government immediately began to carve out an autonomous niche for itself in diplomacy, albeit very slowly. The process was especially evident in the crucial relationship with the United States, where British and Canadian interests were apt to clash.

The American Civil War, which raged between the northern Union forces and the Confederate states of the South from 1861 to 1865, had strained relations between Great Britain and the United States and between the United States and Canada. Confederate ships were built in British ports, and southern raids were surreptitiously launched from Canada against the Union, the perpetrators returning to sanctuary in British North America. On one occasion Union naval vessels stopped a British mail ship, the *Trent*, in neutral waters and removed two Confederate diplomats at gun point. War was barely averted. Against this background, the Union took steps to abrogate the Reciprocity Treaty of 1854, which provided for free trade in natural products between the United States and the British colonies and which was widely thought to have brought great prosperity to the Canadas, New Brunswick, and Nova Scotia.

Tensions continued after the war. In 1866 the Fenian Brotherhood, strengthened by Civil War veterans and American cash and political support, tried to advance its cause of Irish independence from Britain by launching attacks on the Canadian colonies from U.S. soil. The loss of reciprocity and the Fenian threat contributed mightily to Canadian Confederation and to reinforced distrust of the Americans. When the United States demanded in the late 1860s that Britain hand Canada over in compensation for sins against the Union during the Civil War, that was just what was to be expected from the grasping Yankee.

The wounds had to be bound up. In 1871, representatives from the United States and Great Britain sat down in Washington to negotiate solutions to their differences. Because Canada was involved directly in so many of the issues, Macdonald attended as a member of the British delegation. In itself, this was a historic event; the prime minister was the first Canadian and the first representative of a British dependency to be given such a key role in negotiations affecting his country.

Macdonald wanted to settle the question of the inshore Atlantic fisheries, where the United States had gained rights under the 1854 reciprocity treaty. When the Americans had scuppered the accord in 1866, they had lost those rights, but their fishers paid no attention and came anyway. Increasingly stringent measures to stop the fisher-pirates only provoked the Americans. They complained bitterly that Canada, a "semi-independent" and "irresponsible" part of the British Empire, was acting with little regard for international friendship. Canada's aim was to get reciprocity once more in exchange for the fisheries but Congress was protectionist, as so often in the future, and unwilling to allow products to enter the United States unless and until a high duty was paid.

The British sought tranquillity, not tough bargaining. They might have hoped a decade before that the United States would be divided in two by the Civil War, but the Union had triumphed and reintegrated the South into the greater whole. Now London saw only an opportunity to make amends, to set relations on a promising course for the future. Over Macdonald's protests, the British government gave the Americans unrestricted access to the inshore fisheries.

Canada received some valuable fishing concessions and the promise of a cash payment, but the dream of reciprocity turned to dust and the United States refused to pay compensation for the damage done during the Fenian raids. Britain was simply unprepared to allow a narrow political huckster like Macdonald to derail its efforts at reconciliation with the Americans. British negotiators, the sadder but wiser Canadian moaned, had "only one thing on their minds—that is, to go home to England with a treaty in their pockets, settling everything, no matter what the cost to Canada."

Macdonald had little choice but to go along with the 1871 Treaty of Washington. If he refused to sign, a course of action he considered, British–American relations would remain at the boil. The clear-eyed Canadian leader recognized that the best guarantor of his country's security was Anglo-American amity. Should the United States lash out at Britain, Canada was the closest and most convenient part of the empire to attack. Britain would come to the defence of its colony if politics and budgets and the state of its military permitted, but in the interim Canada would be swallowed whole. As Macdonald put it in arguing for approval of the treaty in the House of Commons, "Canada would be, as a matter of course, the battleground of the two nations. We should be the sufferers, our country would be devastated, our people slaughtered, our prosperity destroyed."

Macdonald realized right from the start of Confederation that some form of representation at the heart of the empire was necessary. The various British North American colonies had immigration agents and other officials in Britain before 1867. The dominion consolidated representation in a single immigration office in 1868, and similar offices soon opened in Europe and the United States. In 1869 Macdonald placed his former finance minister, Sir John Rose, in London as "a gentleman possessing the confidence of the Canadian Government with whom Her Majesty's Government may properly communicate on Canadian affairs." Rose was a proto-diplomat; he acted on instructions from Ottawa, promoted trade and immigration, exerted informal influence on British politicians and officials, lobbied to achieve Canadian ends, and reported on the state of affairs and opinion in London. Rose's main contact back home was Macdonald, contributing to a trend towards prime ministerial dominance over external affairs.

Macdonald's Conservatives fell from power in 1873 and the Liberals under Alexander Mackenzie took office. Rose's position was formalized and raised in status; he became financial commissioner for Canada. When Mackenzie decided to renew the push for reciprocity with the United States, he sent a major Grit figure, the Toronto newspaper publisher George Brown, to Washington to negotiate in tandem with the British ambassador. Those discussions failed, but they reinforced the concept that Canadians had to be involved with the British in dealings directly affecting their country. The original reciprocity talks in the early 1850s had been handled by the governor general alone; little advice was sought from the colonies. By contrast, Mackenzie went so far as to ignore the ambassador in Washington entirely on occasion, transacting business directly and causing British officials in the Colonial Office much annoyance.

Returned to power in 1878, Macdonald took further initiatives. He dispatched Alexander Galt, another former finance minister, to negotiate trade pacts with Spain and France, unsuccessfully, as it turned out. The British were not wholly pleased at this assertion of independence, and nor were they happy when Macdonald decided that he needed a "resident minister" to be his envoy to London, a title that smacked of diplomacy carried out by foreigners. The British nevertheless compromised on the question of representation, agreeing that Canada could station a "high commissioner" in their capital. Galt was appointed to the post in 1880 to give, in Macdonald's words, "a higher status to Canadian commerce and more direct means of communication with the various nations." He was also named chief emigration agent, a position that was in fact his top priority.

Galt stayed only three years. He was irked by London's reluctance to grant him diplomatic status and by Ottawa's unwillingness to give him sufficient resources to make a splash in a profession still for the most part reserved for the wealthy. Because the governor general was entitled to know what the government was telling its high commissioner, Galt also discovered that British officials sometimes knew his instructions on specific matters well before he opened his mouth. Galt's successor, Sir Charles Tupper, a Cabinet minister and future prime minister, stayed much longer and made a greater impression, establishing such a reputation for himself that in 1890 Macdonald claimed the British "have begun to treat the colonial representatives as diplomatic agents rather than as subordinate executive officers, and to consult them as such."

The dominion's presence in London was matched by one in Paris. In 1882, Quebec sent French-Canadian senator Hector Fabre to France as a representative, or agent, for the province. Ottawa immediately announced that the federal government would employ his services as well, "only due to that portion of the population of Canada who speak the French language." The agent, later called commissioner, was charged with giving "to his compatriots on the other side of the ocean all possible information about Canada, the French Canadians, and the institutions and lands of that Province." Fabre was meant in addition to promote immigration and trade for Canada, but his successes in those realms were meagre. He prospered instead as an emissary of culture and publicity, cultivating high society and literary folk, advertising the country in speeches and tracts, and publishing a newspaper, *Paris–Canada*, largely at his own expense. Not until 1912 did the commissioner in Paris cease to represent Quebec and become solely the agent of Canada.

When the important matter of a trade agreement with France came up, the Canadian government called not on Fabre but on Sir Charles Tupper as its negotiator. No doubt because he was placed in London and had the confidence of the prime minister, Tupper had become a kind of roving unofficial ambassador for the government, attending international conferences and at least once taking great pleasure in pursuing a very different line from the British. He was able to hammer out the details of a commercial understanding with France, and he and the British ambassador in Paris signed it in 1893 in the Queen's name. The precedents were piling up. Canada could now negotiate trade accords independently and have them ratified by its Parliament. The British signature on these documents was vital, however. London retained the authority to make international treaties and agreements of all kinds on behalf of the empire or any of its parts.

The search for commercial opportunities and the manipulation of tariffs were an important part of Canada's early external life. In 1879, Macdonald instituted the National Policy, a program of increased duties on manufactured imports designed to encourage the flagging industrial sector, to keep at home young Canadians who might be attracted by jobs in the United States, and to fight the natural north-south pulls that detracted from the development of a national economy. Beginning as a fiscal measure, the National Policy became synonymous with the new nation. It evolved into a broader expression of the intention to build up the Canadian economic structure by means of tariffs, railways, and immigration and to take aggressive stands on important issues in Canadian–American relations, such as the fisheries. The National Policy, in short, was a conscious act of foreign policy, a statement of Canadians' insistence on protecting themselves from and grappling with the United States.

Willson, 1879

Public Archives, Ottawa

UNCLE SAM: "National Policy! British Connection! Protective Tariff! Canada Pacific Railway! Colonization! And this is your 'friendship', Sir John! Pshaw!"

(National Archives of Canada)

Yet through it all shone a desire to emulate the expansion of the United States and its economy. Branch plants of American firms sprouted in Canada, a way for u.s. entrepreneurs to circumvent high duties by doing business behind the tariff wall. It may have been a deliberate goal of policy to bring business and development north in this way: to seduce, in other words, as well as to compete. Nor did nineteenth-century Canadian administrations ever stop searching for a new reciprocity deal with the United States. Even so, politicians knew that those who went too far in advocating closer north–south trading relations were susceptible to the "loyalty cry" that they were damaging the British connection and turning the country over to the Americans. Macdonald masterminded just such a strategy to defeat the Liberal platform of "unrestricted reciprocity" in the election of 1891, his last campaign.

Like the National Policy, national defence was seen as an instrument of survival and identity. As George-Étienne Cartier, Canada's first defence minister, explained in 1868, military force was the ultimate guarantor of existence, the "crown of the edifice" of nationhood. The defence question was all the more delicate because of its central place in Canadian relations with Britain. During the 1870s and 1880s, the British government attempted to assert its authority over Canada's force of part-time militia soldiers. By this time, with the improvement in Anglo–American relations, officials in London were less concerned about protecting Canada than about using troops to reinforce Britain's overstretched army in countering crises around the world. Macdonald stoutly resisted, insisting on national control of defence except in case of a major war. In 1885 he rejected the suggestion that an official contingent be sent to help relieve besieged British troops in the Sudan. Canada, he declared, had no interests in northern Africa, and he would not have "our men and money . . . sacrificed to get [the British] out of the hole they have plunged themselves into by their own imbecility."

Macdonald had told a British royal commission on defence five years before that attempts to involve his country in such remote "brushfire" wars would only cause resentment, particularly in French Canada, damaging the imperial relationship. How much wiser to ask for assistance when Britain truly needed help. A serious threat to the empire, especially its centre, would galvanize the Canadian public and allow the government to dispense a generous response. This view was at the heart of Canada's defence and foreign policy until World War II.

The Canadian militia force was modelled on the British army, making for an easy fit into a larger imperial formation. That being said, successive governments refused either to raise defence spending or to expand Canadian military force beyond what was immediately needed within the country for such purposes as quelling the North-West Rebellion in 1885. Despite frequent urgings from Britain, no leader was prepared to commit additional tax dollars against the day when the empire might send an urgent request for troops.

Tax dollars were not readily available to develop an organization for and expertise in foreign policy either. Prime ministers had established their interest in an international personality for Canada within the context of the empire, but they had other duties and a tiny staff at their disposal. Someone had to keep track of the files and gradually build up proficiency in external affairs, particularly so after Macdonald's death in 1891 removed the one Canadian who had been in a senior political position since well before Confederation. Fortunately, Macdonald's private secretary, Joseph Pope, had been at the old chief's side for many years and he had intelligence and diligence at his command. Pope took part in an 1893 international arbitration held in London to resolve a sealing dispute between Canada and the United States, and his "zeal, ability and . . . industry" impressed all. Three years later, the outgoing Conservative government named Pope undersecretary of state, and he kept that post when Liberal Wilfrid Laurier took office as prime minister.

The undersecretary of state was a public servant. Despite his political past, Pope held himself to the strictest standards of neutrality. The job brought most of the correspondence on Canadian external affairs before him, although he was not the only official who dealt with such questions. As Canada's international role expanded, so too did Pope's. He became, in the words of the governor general, "the non-official Foreign Office of the Canadian Govt" but not in a way satisfactory to his orderly mind. The lack of either system or clear lines of authority made him think that a separate government department ought to be created, "charged with all the matters of a quasi-diplomatic character." This was eventually done thirteen years after Pope became undersecretary of state.

In the three decades after Confederation, Canada began the process of transforming itself into an internationally recognized state. The formalities directed that all relations with sovereign states be handled by and through Britain. The reality, however, reflected the determination expressed all those years ago when Macdonald had enthused about Canada's future as an ally and almost an equal of Great Britain, "a friendly nation—a subordinate but still a powerful people." Staunchly British out of loyalty and necessity, acutely conscious of the requirement to co-exist with a muscular United States, Canadians did not want full independence in foreign policy. They were nevertheless set on that path.

CHAPTER ONE

Ask Not What Your Empire Can Do for You, 1896–1914

I N 1897, QUEEN VICTORIA had been on the British throne for sixty years. Portly and placid, habitually draped in black to honour her long-dead husband, Prince Albert, she symbolized stability, solidity, longevity. She was the embodiment of "empire": the great, sprawling mass of British-controlled territory that had grown more than ten times in size during her time as monarch, so that it now covered a quarter of the earth's surface and embraced a third of the world's people. In an evocative study of Victoria's empire, James Morris comments that imperial enthusiasm was reaching its crescendo with the Diamond Jubilee of her reign. "How glorious it was, when one thought about it, to see so much of the map painted the imperial red! What giants there were about! How majestic, Britain's providential stance at the summit of the world!"

LAURIER AND THE IMPERIALISTS

Victoria was Canada's queen too; her picture hung in thousands of households. Wilfrid Laurier, whose Liberal government had been installed the year before, crossed the ocean for the first time in his life to represent the dominion at the Diamond Jubilee celebrations in London and at the 1897 Colonial Conference. Laurier was the country's first French premier, and he shared many of Quebec's traditional and understandable worries about the excesses of imperialism. For a minority group doubting that the Anglo-Saxon way was the right one and the only one, imperialism suggested some troubling directions.

Yet Laurier did not reject Britain. Fresh from having instituted a special preference for British goods in the Canadian market, the prime minister cut a popular and impressive figure in the imperial capital, and he was clearly intoxicated (as his biographer says) by "the pride of imperial might, the applause of tumultuous crowds, the hospitality of famous men and gracious women." He even found himself accepting a knighthood on Jubilee morning, although he knew nothing of the idea until his arrival in London and had to be persuaded of its merit.

"Sir Wilfrid" was not as incongruous as it appeared to many of his critics. Laurier's political and intellectual perspective was British, not French. He had a deep appreciation of British institutions and ideas, and his speeches were full of allusions to the literature and politics of Great Britain. British liberalism, he believed, had given Canadians the tools of compromise, liberty, and tolerance necessary to create a balanced and vital nation. No longer thinking that Canadians ought to rush towards independence, as he had when a young man, he frequently expressed his satisfaction with the course that British–Canadian relations were then taking. Growing dominion autonomy was combined with an essential unity of imperial aims and interests.

Laurier's great goal was to build Canada into an economically strong and politically vibrant country, in which English and French could do more than simply co-exist. "My object is to consolidate Confederation, and to bring our people long-estranged from each other, gradually to become a nation. This is the supreme issue. Everything else is subordinate to that idea." For that reason, Laurier groped towards the ground between the extremes—complete separation from the British Empire versus the sundry forms of imperial union—where he was confident that the majority of voters could be found.

The pilgrimage of Wilfrid Laurier (second from left) to the home of
the great Liberal, William Ewart Gladstone, Hawarden, England,
1897 (National Archives of Canada, C 5601)

Laurier was therefore not a part of the imperialist movement,
which sought to organize the various segments of the self-governing
empire into a powerful federation of like-minded countries with a
single structure and fully co-ordinated economic and military policies. Back in the days of Confederation, the British had shown scant
interest in their colonies, and their desire to divest themselves of
imperial responsibilities had been one of the driving forces behind
the union of the Canadian provinces in 1867. Britain's imperialism
had been on the rise ever since, however, in large measure as a result
of the threat to its economic and military supremacy from countries
such as Germany and the United States. Colonies such as Canada
were suddenly seen as potentially valuable allies, able to contribute
people and resources to the maintenance of Britain's global power.

The Imperial Federation League was founded in Britain in 1884,
and spread to Canada by the end of the decade. One-quarter of the
members of the federal Parliament were adherents, as well as a good
sprinkling of well-educated professionals and Protestant ministers.

In Canada, as in Great Britain, imperialism was a response to external challenge and perceived vulnerability. There was widespread disappointment that John A. Macdonald's National Policy of high tariffs had not generated more prosperity, severe French–English tensions existed, and many doubted that the country could survive. Imperialists were worried and infuriated by Liberal Party advocacy of all-out free trade, or "unrestricted reciprocity," with the United States. In their eyes, the policy was simply veiled treason, an admission that Canada could not go it alone and would have to submit to annexation by the Americans. The Liberals, helped by the electorate, changed their minds about unrestricted reciprocity, won power in 1896, and delighted Canadian imperialists by granting a favoured position to British imports. With Joseph Chamberlain, the heart and symbol of the empire union movement, ensconced as colonial secretary in the British government, imperialism's enthusiasts hoped that their cause was poised for victory.

Canadian imperialism combined national and imperial pride, idealism, perceived Anglo-Saxon racial superiority, Christian zeal, desire for economic gain, and anti-Americanism. Imperialists had an expansive view of Canadian possibilities in the empire and the world. "I . . . am an Imperialist because I will not be a Colonial," wrote the famous author Stephen Leacock,

> This Colonial status is a worn-out, by-gone thing. . . . It limits the ideas, and circumscribes the patriotism of our people. It impairs the mental vigor and narrows the outlook of those that are reared and educated in our midst. . . . Find for us something other than mere colonial stagnation, something sounder than independence, nobler than annexation, greater in purpose than a little Canada.

Many of the major imperialists, such as teacher G.R. Parkin and police magistrate and military officer G.T. Denison, were descendants of the United Empire Loyalists, who had fled from the United States during the American Revolution. They had nothing but disdain for an overpassionate, unstable, excessively democratic United States. Denison kept a traitors' list for the day when he would be called upon to defend his country against the infidel. Invigorated by its clean northern climate, Canada was destined to become the spiritual, economic, and political centre of the empire. If not, it was sure to be engulfed by the United States.

Laurier was a true chameleon, and he made imperialists think that he was one of them at the Diamond Jubilee and accompanying colonial meeting in 1897. He expressed his reverence for the empire in such florid and effusive language that the British newspapers concluded he was "as ardent an imperialist as Mr. Chamberlain." The prime minister asserted that growing national sentiment would some day require Canadian representation in a central organization, such as an imperial parliament. Indeed, "it would be the proudest moment of my life if I could see a Canadian of French descent affirming the principles of freedom in the parliament of Great Britain."

Nevertheless, the colonies had gone too far towards independence to submerge their interests and identities completely in the greater whole of empire federation. There was little support for federal solutions, such as Chamberlain's proposal for a "great council" in which imperial leaders would be able to bring their views to bear on the British government, in return of course for contributions "towards the expense for objects which we shall have in common." Nor was any consensus reached on Chamberlain's request for assistance to imperial naval defence. Laurier pointed out that Canada had a huge territory to develop, and claimed to have done more for imperial defence by building the Canadian Pacific Railway than could have been done by spending many millions on the military. The only economic co-operation to emerge from the conference was an agreement by colonial premiers to explore the kind of imperial trade preferences that Canada had introduced earlier in the year. As for Great Britain, it was resolutely pro-free trade and would essentially remain so, with few preferences to give any country until the 1930s.

The 1897 Colonial Conference set patterns for the future. Over his long premiership, Laurier consistently refused to take part in any imperial centralizing scheme. J.W. Dafoe, a prominent Liberal journalist, called it the policy of the "everlasting no." The meeting also proved the impracticality of empire federation; no one who took part ever pressed the idea again. The 1897 gathering was, however, the first full-fledged imperial discussion of questions of common concern, from railways and postal and telegraphic communications to the naval defence of the self-governing colonies. The delegates did also agree that they or their successors should meet periodically in the years to come. A system evolved of regular colonial, and later imperial, conferences. These were held every few years from 1902 to 1937, with top politicians and officials in attendance, and contributed to a considerable framework of military, economic, and political co-operation in the self-governing empire.

"TODAY IT IS S. AFRICA . . ."

The war that broke out in South Africa on 11 October 1899 between Great Britain and the two small Boer republics of Transvaal and the Orange Free State demonstrated both the strength and the weakness of imperialism in Canada. The British cause had much to do with the strategic importance of the region and the rich resources to be found there, and the odds against the Boers were extremely long. Even so, it was easy to think of the conflict as a legitimate response to the refusal of the Dutch-speaking Boers to grant political rights to English settlers, who had been drawn inland into Boer territory by diamonds and gold. As the Vancouver *Province* wrote,

> The fact that the Boers have been allowed to pursue their policy of injustice and oppression so long is due solely to the magnanimity of the British Governments which have shrunk from coercing a weak power. The United States went to war with Spain because Spain oppressed her own subjects in Cuba. If the United States did right to go to war as the champion of an alien people, how much more would Britain be justified in coercing the Boers, by force of arms, into granting justice to British subjects?

Righteous sentiments such as these, expressed frequently and vociferously over the course of a three-month pro-war press campaign before hostilities began, were instrumental in pushing the

Canadian government to act in support of the empire. The South African situation evoked very powerful emotions and, although some were the result of manipulation, they were none the less real for that. Affection for Mother England and pride in the empire connection ran deep in a population that was, as the 1901 census demonstrated, 57 percent British stock.

Imperialism, in short, was stronger than the rather narrowly based empire movement, with its specific goal of empire federation and sometimes excessive rhetoric. Even at this moment of imperial fervour and crisis, however, many Canadians—farmers and workers, for example—remained uninterested or, as was likely to be the case in French Canada, hostile.

Laurier, who thought right to the end that the Boers would give in, was on his way back from Chicago when the war erupted. One of his travelling companions, Toronto *Globe* editor J.S. Willison, told him that he must either provide troops or "get out of office." The Canadian House of Commons, after all, had unanimously endorsed Britain's South African stand at the end of July. Yet Willison remembered that Laurier was "reluctant, unconvinced and rebellious." The prime minister did not believe that a young country should get into the military business, with its huge expenditure, and he did not see why Canada should involve itself "in the secondary wars in which England is always engaged." He also knew something of the opposition in French and even English Canada, and hoped that it would be possible to stand aloof, as John A. Macdonald had done in 1885 when Britain was in trouble in the African Sudan. It was not to be. Even as Laurier was thinking these thoughts on the journey back to Ottawa, his minister of militia, Frederick Borden, was telling one of Willison's reporters that a Canadian contingent would be sent to South Africa "within a short time."

The Cabinet met on 12 October. Ministers had before them a telegram dated 3 October from Colonial Secretary Chamberlain expressing gratitude for the offers that had been made by individuals to serve in South Africa, and stating that the British Army would gladly accept four units of 125 Canadian men each. Quebec's Israel Tarte, the minister of public works, forcefully led the opposition to the dispatch of any government-sponsored army whatsoever, while

Borden insisted upon a contribution fully underwritten by Ottawa. A parcel of moderates argued for an official contingent, but one that would be kept small and maintained by the British. Tarte claimed that the government was being stampeded by a cadre of imperialist conspirators who did not have Canada's best interests at heart, and threatened to resign if they won the day. After six inconclusive hours, the Cabinet decided to meet again the next day.

That night the governor general, Lord Minto, wired London: "Chief opposition from Quebec; Premier personally opposed to offering troops because it would be new departure in Colonial responsibilities though he approves of Imperial action in S. Africa. All Ontario press with enthusiasm announce offer of troops as settled and public dissatisfaction [with the government's hesitancy] as very great. Discussion in Cabinet extremely heated." The governor added, "my Govt . . . are much annoyed at substance of your tel. of 3rd having appeared simultaneously in London press and here thereby increasing the enthusiasm which has nearly forced their hand."

The colonial secretary was immediately reassuring, if more than a bit disingenuous. Her Majesty's Government had not asked for Canadian troops, although they would be "highly appreciated as practical demonstration of unanimity throughout Empire as to importance & necessity of insisting on fair and equal treatment for Br. subjects and of maintaining interests of Empire in S. Africa or wherever they may be threatened." This was an unsubtle hint that imperial solidarity could be important to Canada some day. As a Colonial Office official noted in minutes at the time, Canadians easily forgot "that today it is S. Africa, but the next time it may be N. America." Chamberlain's message nevertheless may have helped to smooth feathers ruffled by his 3 October telegram, with its implication that England was telling the dominions where duty lay.

The pressure meanwhile built on Laurier to do right by the empire. Willison's influential *Globe*, close though it was to the prime minister, was wavering on its promise not to declare a position until the government did. Interventionist public meetings were being held or planned. One arranged in Montreal was particularly dangerous because it could lead to a clash with French groups that wanted no part of an imperial war and indeed might have sympathy with the Boers in South Africa. After all, French Canadians were an oppressed minority too. The Canadian Club of Toronto and other similar non-partisan organizations were calling for a commitment. Two Cabinet members who had not been at the meeting on the twelfth let their contributionist sympathies be known.

The momentum was irresistible. On 13 October, Cabinet agreed to a Canadian contribution of no more than a thousand volunteers divided up, as Chamberlain had suggested, into groups of 125. Recruitment, equipment, and transportation were to be the responsibility of the Canadian government or of the recruits themselves; Britain would pay and maintain the men and get them home after it was all over. This was, then, a less than wholehearted commitment, as was underlined by a government statement: "under no circumstances" was the decision "to be regarded as a departure from the well-known principles of constitutional practice, nor construed as a precedent for further action."

For most of the French-Canadian Liberals, including Israel Tarte, this was enough of a sop, but the brightest of them, Labelle MP Henri Bourassa, did not accept for a moment that a precedent had been avoided. This was the thin edge of the wedge, he explained, and the next time—there would be a next time—the South African War would be invoked as the reason why Canadians had to help out the imperial government. Bourassa resigned his seat in protest, left the Liberal Party, and was returned to Parliament as an Independent in a 1900 by-election. In 1903, as a direct result of the war, Bourassa and other young French-Canadian nationalists such as Armand Lavergne and Olivar Asselin formed the *Ligue nationale* to further the cause of anti-imperialism.

Lord Minto agreed with Bourassa that support for this imperial war committed Canada to future ones. As the British representative in Ottawa, and a self-proclaimed "old friend of Canada," he was pleased because he thought such an understanding would be good for the empire generally and its individual parts as well, making them all stronger and more secure in the knowledge that they could count on one another in a crisis. But Minto was upset by the extreme language and outright racism of some Ontario newspapers:

The writing of the leading opposition papers has been positively wicked—simply aiming at stirring up hatred of French Canada—so much so that Ontario farmers the other day were actually going to bed with loaded rifles and revolvers by their sides for fear of the French! It is perfectly monstrous. . . . The French papers have been more moderate than the English ones. . . . [T]he race feeling is running very high and there is much wild talk. . . . I believe that the French Canadians are very much maligned as to their disloyalty. French Canada does not wish to be mixed up in Imperial Wars and is lukewarm, but at home apparently you do not call a man disloyal if he disapproves of the war—here if he is only lukewarm and is a French Canadian he must be a rebel. . . . [T]hat is the British bulldog argument here.

Henri Bourassa (National Archives of Canada, C 4956)

More than many English Canadians, the governor general could see how unfairly the French were being treated, and how dangerous this was for national unity.

Bourassa and Tarte made much of the fact that Canada had taken on military obligations in the South African War without having any role in empire decision making. Laurier repeated that Canada was not, by virtue of the South African commitment, compelled to participate in all the wars of Great Britain; if it were, he concurred, the British would have to listen attentively to his government's views. Canada "should have the right to say to Great Britain: If you want us to help you, call us to your councils; if you want us to take part in wars let us share not only the burdens but the responsibilities and duties as well." None of these French-Canadian politicians, however, wanted any part of either burdens or responsibility.

Laurier's declaration that Britain must call Canada to its councils was a way of exposing the weakness of the imperialist cause and arguing against the entanglements of empire. A great imperial power would certainly not be prepared to listen to an insignificant, semi-autonomous "dominion." The perceptive Minto understood this very well. An invitation to Britain's inner sanctum was, he said, "the very last thing Sir Wilfrid would wish."

LESSONS IN SELF-RELIANCE

Britain won the South African War, but with difficulty. In the first months, culminating in "Black Week" in December 1899, the Boers took everything before them. The British had to deploy a huge army to reverse the tide; by the end, the empire forces totalled almost half a million to the Boers' sixty thousand. Even that great advantage was not enough. The Boers fought innovative guerrilla warfare and were finally subdued only after the British employed a scorched-earth strategy and shut women and children in concentration camps, where many thousands died. In May 1902, the Boers signed a treaty conceding victory and their territory to Great Britain.

Over six thousand more Canadian volunteers joined the original thousand in South Africa. For the most part, they served together in Canadian formations, according to their government's wishes, rather than being scattered throughout the British army. The Canadians fought with some distinction, and demonstrated particular aptitude for dealing with the Boers' unorthodox tactics, which one of the frustrated British commanders described as never standing up to a fair fight. "They are always running away on their little ponies." Four Canadians won the Victoria Cross, the empire's highest military decoration. Eighty-nine were killed, among them Harold Borden, the minister of militia's son. Although generalizations like this are always difficult, the war bred a scepticism about the British and a mood of national self-esteem in government, in the military, and in English Canada.

The war sapped British strength and confidence, much as Vietnam later did in the United States. The same internal dissension arose, the same criticism of the government's brutal war policy, and the same sense that a great power, pitted against a tiny enemy, had shown itself weaker, morally and militarily, than anyone could have imagined. European adversaries of the British Empire snickered at its plight and its incompetence. The u.s. administration, mindful of British support during the 1898 Spanish–American War, backed the anti-Boer cause, but good Anglo–American relations came at a price.

Part of that price was paid by Canada during a crisis in Venezuela in 1895, over which the United States and Great Britain took very different stands. Rumours of war between the two countries abounded, and u.s. senator Henry Cabot Lodge recommended the annexation of Canada in the event of armed conflict. The Americans claimed to be "practically sovereign" throughout the western hemisphere, and Great Britain backed down, accepting that they were. War with America was unthinkable, and quarrels that might lead to war were unacceptable.

Against this backdrop, Canada entered a dispute with the United States over the Alaska boundary. London urged Canada to settle the border on terms that would satisfy the United States, and in the process they gave away every diplomatic weapon that might have been used to further the Canadian cause.

There were simply limits to how far British power could reach. Besides, weren't the British and Americans really cousins, with similar racial characteristics, systems of government, and ambitions? As the *New York Times* had put it, "We are a part, and a great part, of the Greater Britain which seems so plainly destined to dominate the planet." Said A.J. Balfour, soon to be the British prime minister, "We welcome any increase of the great influence of the United States upon the great Western Hemisphere." "This time," the Colonial Office official had written when the South African War exploded, "it is S. Africa, but the next time it may be N. America." The fact is, however, that the British had already consigned Canada to the American sphere of influence. If next time came to pass, no one in the dominion could any longer count on Mother.

The nub of the Alaska issue was access through its long, narrow, southern "panhandle" to Canada's Yukon gold fields. If the American claim were upheld, Canada would own none of the water routes inland. The Laurier government, encouraged by prosperous times and conscious of anti-American sentiment over the Venezuelan crisis, high American tariffs, and u.s. imperialism in Cuba during the Spanish–American War, was consistently unaccommodating to various proposed compromises. The prime minister more than met his match in stubbornness after 1901 though, when Theodore Roosevelt succeeded the assassinated William McKinley as president of the United States. The new leader took a special interest in Alaska, dispatching troops to the area and telling the British that he was willing to get "ugly" if necessary.

In 1902, both Roosevelt and Laurier shifted their positions sufficiently to allow the establishment of a six-person arbitration panel, three impartial judges for each side. The u.s. president, however, then appointed partisan politicians to the tribunal: Senator Lodge, former senator George Turner of Washington, and Elihu Root, the secretary of war. Furthermore, Roosevelt instructed them to do as he said, brooking "no compromise" and threatening the British that he would "take possession of the disputed territory and hold it by all the power and force of the United States" no matter what the panel decided.

The "Canadian" component of the Alaska tribunal was made up of Lord Alverstone, who was the chief justice of England, and Canadian lawyers Sir Louis Jetté and A.B. Aylesworth. Alverstone came under considerable pressure from his own government to lean in America's direction and this he did with a vengeance. The Americans were given the bulk of their claim, all the strategically placed waterways, and—in an area where the Canadians were sure they deserved to get everything—half of the islands in the Portland Canal at the lower end of the contested territory.

The 1903 Alaska judgment was the right decision for the wrong reasons. The United States had the better case, based on use and occupation of the panhandle over many years, but Roosevelt had stacked the deck with bluster, intimidation, and coercion. Even if Canada had had the better of the legal argument, it would not have mattered. The judgment stung because Canada seemed alone in the world, bullied by the United States, abandoned by Great Britain. The Toronto *News*, an independent journal, captured it this way:

> LORD ALVERSTONE (to Canada): Is there anything more I can do for you?
> CANADA: We would like to go on drawing breath.
> LORD ALVERSTONE (to Messrs. Root, Lodge and Turner): Any objection to our young friend continuing to use the atmosphere?
> MESSRS. ROOT, LODGE AND TURNER (cheerfully): None at all just now.
> LORD ALVERSTONE (with a judicial air): My decision is that you are entitled to the temporary use of all air not required for United States purposes.

The American action was perhaps understandable. They were like that. As Laurier said in the House of Commons after the settlement, "we are living beside a great neighbour who, I believe I can say without being deemed unfriendly to them, are very grasping in their national acts, and who are determined upon every occasion to get the best in any agreement which they make." The prime minister told Lord Minto that there was an "evident American wish to acquire further territory in the North American continent." Hudson Bay, the Arctic, Newfoundland, and the islands of St Pierre and Miquelon were all possible targets of an expansionary policy that Laurier judged not an immediate threat, but "decidedly dangerous" over the longer haul.

Most of the Canadian bitterness, however, was directed at Great Britain. Some people, without meaning it, said that Canada ought to apply for admission to the United States. "We may as well go in for annexation, body and breeches, if Great Britain is going to allow us to be annexed piecemeal." Others contemplated out-and-out separation, buoyed by the prime minister's statement that "we should ask the British Parliament for more extensive power, so that if ever we have to deal with matters of a similar nature again we shall deal with them in our own way, in our own fashion, according to the best light that we have." But the "separatists" did not mean it either. All these outbursts were the mark of what the Toronto *Globe* called a "deep and settled" resentment that was strongest in proud British Canadians, "those who stand firmer than ever against annexation, and who are not disposed towards independence. Because they are 'Sons of the Blood' they resent injustice, even from Britain."

Canadians were not ready for independence. Yet Laurier seemed to suggest in his House of Commons denunciation of the Alaska settlement that Canada might begin to make its own treaties. This sounded like more separatist talk, threatening the whole concept of the empire as an integrated international unit, and the British responded with understandable concern. They need not have worried, although Laurier did receive London's permission to negotiate and sign a commercial accord with France in 1907. A British official also signed the treaty, however, thus preserving the diplomatic unity of the empire, the concept that Britain acted and spoke for the entire institution on the international stage. Critics of Alaska advised the prime minister to wreak some revenge by ending the British preferential tariff instituted in 1897, but that decision had been taken in the Canadian interest, not the empire's. In 1907 the government instituted a three-tier tariff system: imperial preference; an intermediate rate for countries that had made special arrangements with Canada; and a general rate for other countries.

The external pressures, crises, and lessons of this period pushed the government in the direction of military self-reliance. The Venezuelan incident had exposed the poverty of Canada's land defences, and put the idea of a modern national army on the agenda. The South African War had brought strong national feelings to the surface, and at the same time had emphasized the danger that involvement in imperial defence represented to Canadian unity. At the Colonial Conference of 1902, Chamberlain made another bid for assistance to the British armed services with a memorable plea: "The weary Titan staggers under the too vast orb of its fate. We have borne the burden for many years. We think it is time that our children should assist us to support it." Laurier replied in the negative, but promised to do his part for the empire by defending Canada better. A conference document read, "Canadian Ministers fully appreciate the duty of the Dominion, as it advances in population and wealth, to make more liberal outlay for those necessary preparations of self-defence which every country has to assume and bear."

Laurier, as always, proceeded slowly and cautiously, but he did act. Moves were made to uphold Canadian law and sovereignty in the North. With the Militia Act of 1904, the government took more control of the army by opening up its highest office to Canadians; until that point (and, admittedly, for a while longer), a British officer was always in command. The next year saw the assumption of full responsibility for the defence of the fortresses at Halifax, Nova Scotia, and Esquimalt, British Columbia. This meant a larger army, more defence expenditure, and a farewell to the last of the British troops stationed in Canada. After all, some newspapers pointed out, recent events showed that Great Britain would let Canada down anyway if good relations with the United States could be purchased at the dominion's expense. Laurier also took steps to create a naval reserve by building up the Fisheries Protection Service (established in the 1880s), in part by having two armed patrol vessels constructed. Even a modest Canadian naval presence was controversial, however, especially in Quebec. It took a crisis in Europe to force the naval question to the fore and keep it there.

TIN-POTS AND DREADNOUGHTS

In mid-March 1909, British prime minister H.H. Asquith told his Parliament that Germany was building sophisticated and powerful "dreadnought" battleships at a speed that threatened the empire's naval superiority. This provided ammunition for George E. Foster, a Conservative MP for a Toronto riding. He brought forward a motion in the House of Commons calling for Canada to delay no longer "in assuming her proper share of the responsibility and financial burden incident to the suitable protection of her exposed coast line and great seaports." Halifax and Esquimalt were fine, Foster said, but inevitably limited in their usefulness. As for Laurier's fleet of fisheries' protection ships, they were simply "children's toys" with no military value. The Liberals ought to fulfil the commitment they had made at the 1902 Colonial Conference that the country would be given adequate naval defence.

Though pro-British, Laurier had always regarded the "highly sentimental fads of Imperialism and militarism" with suspicion. "The military organization of Europe is simply madness and I hesitate a good deal before launching ourselves into it," he had written early in March 1909. Later on that month, in a letter to the noted historian, G.M. Wrong, he elaborated his views:

> I do not share the enthusiasm now so flamboyant in the City of Toronto. That the superiority of the British Navy should be maintained at its present strength over all nations is a proposition to which I am quite prepared to agree, but this policy should not be taken up in a panic. I wish I could share your optimistic notion that the mere announcement of Canada standing behind Great Britain would cause Germany to hesitate before moving further. I can hardly imagine that our 6 or 7 million people will strike so much terror in the German breast. . . . The whole Canadian people will stand behind England in her troubles if it comes to that, but we are very far from that.

Nevertheless, Laurier could no more resist the pressure to act—some of which came from within his own party—than at the beginning of the South African War. Rejecting the idea of some sort of emergency gift to the British Admiralty, the prime minister promised to build a small but distinctively Canadian naval service by expanding the Fisheries' Protection Service and acquiring coast defence warships. The Conservative leader, R.L. Borden, for his part supported "a Canadian naval force of our own," but he kept open the possibility of a "money contribution in time of peril."

Borden's balanced approach had its critics. The premiers of British Columbia, Manitoba, Ontario, and New Brunswick were among the prominent English-Canadian Conservatives who advocated an immediate donation to the Royal Navy. They had nothing but disdain for a Canadian navy, which was bound to be puny and inefficient: a "tin-pot navy," Premier Rodmond Roblin of Manitoba characterized it. Complicating Borden's situation further were his party's Quebec nationalists, who wanted neither a Canadian navy nor an emergency contribution to the British. F.D. Monk, a prominent Quebec Conservative, was already accusing Laurier of "imperial drunkenness," and he was also keeping a close eye on his own leader.

An imperial meeting on defence took place in London in August 1909. The British, perhaps reacting to the Australian and Canadian desire for their own navies, suggested that each dominion create its own strong fleet, centred around a dreadnought battle cruiser and capable of being slotted into the British system at a moment's notice. Somewhat surprisingly, Ottawa's representatives agreed that the Canadian navy should be a major-league affair, equipped with four 4800-ton Bristol Class cruisers and six destroyers. The battle cruiser idea was jettisoned, but so too was Laurier's commitment to a modest navy. The warships of the new navy, furthermore, would be built in Canada, and the government managed to seduce Vickers, the British armaments empire, into establishing a branch plant in Montreal for the purpose.

Parliament passed a Naval Service Act in May 1910. It created the Naval Service of Canada and the Department of the Naval Service, and made provision for a college where officers could be trained. Most important of all, the act stipulated that the new navy would be controlled entirely by Canadians, and not necessarily given over to the empire in time of war. If England was at war then so was Canada, said Laurier, but that did not necessitate an active Canadian part in all the wars of England. "That is a matter that must be determined by circumstances, upon which the Canadian parliament will have to pronounce and will have to decide in its own best judgment." The Liberal policy, Borden roared, amounted to nothing less than "empire smashing." He summoned up the vision of an enemy raider bringing down a British merchant ship while a Canadian cruiser sat idly by because Parliament had not yet authorized service at Britain's side.

Laurier's big navy never materialized. He lost his nerve after a stunning defeat in a by-election held in the Quebec constituency of Drummond-Arthabaska during November 1910. The defence issue dominated the campaign. Henri Bourassa and his growing national-ist group weighed in against the government, and it was clear that even a navy that might be imperial in some future circumstance was too much for Quebec. The Canadian navy did acquire two British cruisers for training purposes in late 1910: the 3400-ton HMCS *Rainbow*, which went to the west coast, and the 11 000-ton *Niobe* for the east coast. But naval procurement stopped right there.

Borden was meanwhile tilting towards the English-Canadian imperialist wing of his party. The emergency was now, he argued, demanding an immediate contribution to the Admiralty of the cash equivalent of two dreadnoughts. German naval supremacy could bring the empire to an end, "without war, without the firing of a shot or the striking of a blow, without invasion." The campaign for battleship superiority was on, "and the victory will be as decisive there as in actual battle." Borden did not pull back from advocating a Canadian navy, but that would take many years to develop and the empire, in its current circumstance, could not afford to wait. Any navy that Canada might construct, moreover, must necessarily be a part of the imperial navy and under central British control in time of war. It was "dangerous and revolutionary" to think or do otherwise. In fact, Canada needed closer relations with Britain, not the distance that Laurier was implicitly suggesting. In return for a Canadian con-tribution, Britain would have to find a mechanism to recognize the young country's importance and give it "some control and some voice" in making the empire's defence policy. More would be heard of this in the future.

Borden kept open the lines of communication with Monk and French Canada. The Conservatives had only eleven of their eighty-five seats in Quebec, but the naval issue offered the prospect of undermining the government's strong position there. As the Drummond-Arthabaska by-election demonstrated, opposition to

Laurier's navy was lending momentum to a developing alliance between Quebec's federal Conservatives and Bourassa's nationalists. Borden tried to do his part by denouncing Laurier's naval scheme at every turn and demanding that the prime minister submit himself to a plebiscite on the issue. Even the Conservative leader's call for a voice in imperial decision making was in part a response to a similar suggestion from Bourassa and other Quebec nationalists, although it is difficult to believe that the nationalists really wanted any such thing. Quebec Conservatives still did not approve of Borden's naval policy, and they tried unsuccessfully to dislodge him from the leadership. Yet they liked Laurier and his navy even less.

ACCOMMODATING THE AMERICANS

Laurier had other naval problems—on the Great Lakes. The United States had been consistently violating the terms of the ancient Rush-Bagot Agreement of 1817, which severely limited the number of armed vessels that the United States and Great Britain (and therefore Canada) could have on the Great Lakes and Lake Champlain. By the 1890s, the Americans were becoming a major military power and could no longer be easily held to the four small ships allowed. Under pressure from the U.S. Navy and Great Lakes shipbuilders, the government in Washington began to demand changes in the agreement and, in the meantime, to deploy large armed ships that clearly breached its terms. A way out was almost found at the Joint High Commission in 1898, giving the United States room to expand its Great Lakes fleet, but when the commission broke down over the Alaska boundary issue, that opportunity evaporated.

In the early years of the twentieth century, the Americans regularly had training warships and armed revenue boats on the Great Lakes. The Laurier administration said nothing. The United States had to use Canadian waterways, which were deeper than their American counterparts, to get their vessels onto the Great Lakes. Ottawa's politicians allowed them to do so, without always telling their own military. The alternative was worse. If thwarted, the Americans seemed certain to denounce the Rush-Bagot Agreement and to embark on a naval build-up that would make their activities to this point pale by comparison. Anti-Americanism would be stirred up in Ontario and, much more worrying, anti-Canadianism might become popular to the south. Laurier therefore acquiesced, as he put it, in "violations more or less notorious."

Another was on the way. The USS *Nashville*, by far the most powerful American trainer yet, made its way down the St Lawrence and through the Canadian canal system in May 1909. The captain dismounted the ship's four-inch guns while in Canada, re-arming only when the *Nashville* was on the American side of Lake Ontario. Even so, there was considerable outcry in the Canadian press. A correspondent of the Toronto *News* discovered the *Nashville* and five other ships later on in the summer in Lake Michigan. He told his readers that "a thousand Americans were being trained for war purposes, in warships, on the frontier which the Rush-Bagot Convention is supposed to keep clear of war-vessels, big guns and the apparatus of fighting." The editor of the *News* added, "It does not necessarily follow that these vessels, and the thousand men upon them, are specifically intended for use against Canada. . . . But if Canada and the United States should quarrel—and they are two countries, not one country, and have interests which differ and may clash—this naval militia force and these warships would be uncommonly useful to the Americans."

The controversy stiffened Laurier's resolve. He decided not to allow the United States to remount the *Nashville's* guns. This was ludicrous, because the prime minister was proposing to refuse permission for something already done months before. The United States, furthermore, had asked for authorization to re-arm the year before the *Nashville* sailed, and the Canadian government had given it. Laurier, in the event, did not make a formal protest to the Americans about the *Nashville*. The British reminded him that a Canadian rant might cause Washington to reconsider the whole Rush-Bagot arrangement. The prime minister admitted he lived "in fear and trembling all the time" that the Americans might tear up the agreement, which they had the right to do with six months notice. Laurier had communicated his unease about the drift of events to the British, however, and that had some surprising results.

Laurier's complaints led the British ambassador in Washington, Lord Bryce, to approach the president of the United States about the

Rush-Bagot Agreement. Instead of belligerence, Bryce met only a remarkable understanding from President William Howard Taft, whose exposure to Canada consisted mainly of annual treks to his summer home at Murray Bay, Quebec. Of course, Taft said, he could sympathize with Laurier's "wish that nothing should happen which would create any sentiment of disquiet or suspicion in the minds of any section of the people in Canada." But the American president went further. Rush-Bagot was an important and beneficial aspect of the relationship between the two countries; it was eminently reasonable to expect his administration to adhere more closely to the agreement. That is what Washington now did. Shortly thereafter the Great Lakes were all but disarmed, and the furor over the *Nashville* was forgotten.

Taft's goodwill towards Canada was undoubted, but it was only one part of the equation. Canadian–American relations had been undergoing a sea change since 1905, when Elihu Root became the American secretary of state and immediately fixed his eye on the long list of irritants dividing the two countries. Root had been one of the three American judges in the Alaska boundary case, but he was determined to set the past aside and clean the slate. Over the next seven years Canada and the United States systematically confronted and solved all the outstanding grievances in the relationship. Eight different treaties and agreements were concocted to cover boundary questions, including waterways and the demarcation of the border, inland fisheries, the conveyance of prisoners, wreckage and salvage operations, the North Atlantic fisheries, and the fur seal trade in the North Pacific.

The Boundary Waters Treaty of 1909 symbolized the spirit of this massive exercise in accommodation. The accord gave birth to the six-person International Joint Commission—three representatives each from Canada and the United States—as a permanent body to examine the problems flowing from the use of the shared rivers and lakes along the frontier. The IJC has been celebrated ever since as an example of the genteel way in which Canadians and Americans do business, and on an equal footing. The body has done good work in highly specialized and technical areas over many years, but its powers are a great deal more limited than publicists (and historians) often suggest, and the Americans, it is clear, take a firm hand when interests dear to them are at stake.

The period from 1905 to 1912 was crucially important in the history of Canadian diplomacy. The Laurier government did very well in negotiating a series of generally favourable bargains, and in the process some of the old Canadian inferiority complex towards Americans was erased. Lord Bryce was most helpful to Laurier, acting for Canada, not for Britain. The British indeed were concluding that Canada was nothing but an unwelcome irritant in their relations with the United States, and they began to pull back from all but the formal and ceremonial part of Canadian–American relations. Ottawa was increasingly on its own in its dealings with the United States.

In 1909, Laurier created a Department of External Affairs to organize the growing responsibilities and documentation of diplomacy. Joseph Pope, a master of the paper trail, was made the department's permanent head. Over several years he had been one of only three Canadian bureaucrats in the federal government, the governor general wrote home to Britain, who had any knowledge of foreign relations. "One drinks at times, the other has a difficulty in expressing his thoughts, and conversation with him is as difficult as it is to extract an extra tight cork, and the third is . . . Pope—a really first class official." Pope's (and indeed Laurier's) goal was efficiency, not independent diplomatic action. Canada was a long way from making or wanting to make its own separate foreign policy. For the next decade and a half the Department of External Affairs was primarily a filing and post office, and an underpopulated one at that. From 1912, however, the department was directly under the prime minister, and this at least ensured that it was close to the centre of action.

THE 1911 FREE TRADE ELECTION

The pliancy of the Taft administration in this era of good feelings may be in part explained by its fervent wish for a trade agreement to reduce tariffs substantially and reciprocally between the two countries. The American business and political community was interested in the Canadian market, in access to cheap raw materials, and in encouraging Canada to adopt the United States rather than Britain as its economic partner of the future. A reciprocity agreement was reached in early 1911, and it looked like a favourable deal for both sides. By the end of the year, however, the accord was dead and Laurier had been driven from office.

One of the central goals of nineteenth-century Canadian governments had been to resuscitate the 1854–1866 reciprocity treaty with the United States. The Americans, solidly in the grip of protectionism, resisted every overture. The Conservatives of John A. Macdonald responded with the big tariffs of the National Policy, while missing no opportunity to seek reciprocity. The Conservatives kept their overtures to the United States discreet, but the Liberals openly advocated a trade agreement, even going so far as to argue for "unrestricted reciprocity." In the election of 1891, denying that he had approached the United States with the offer of a trade deal, Macdonald was able to smear the Liberals with the charge of disloyalty. A vote for reciprocity was a vote, he shouted, for the end of the British connection and eventual annexation to the United States. "A British subject I was born, and a British subject I will die."

The Liberals were kept from power for five more years. Back in government from 1896, they showed little interest in freer trade with the United States, instead maintaining the protectionist program of the Conservatives and giving the British a break in the Canadian market. The Canadian economy, furthermore, was booming in early 1910, when the United States asked Ottawa to begin trade talks. Yet Laurier agreed to do so for reasons that are unclear. He may have been following Liberal free-trading inclinations, or searching for a policy initiative to give new life to an old government, particularly in the pro-reciprocity West. He may have been looking for a way to avoid an apparently imminent tariff war with the United States. Perhaps he wanted to keep the positive momentum in Canadian–American relations rolling. It is also possible that he miscalculated, never expecting anything of the magnitude that was achieved in January 1911.

At first Laurier's legendary good luck held. The agreement was big all right, but surely no one could object to a Canadian–American bargain in which duties on fish, livestock, and the natural products of the farm were mutually abolished and the tariff structure left intact for most Canadian manufactures. When the minister of finance, William S. Fielding, announced the news to the House of Commons, the correspondent of the *Montreal Herald* reported,

> triumph was written on the faces of the Liberals and dismay painted on the visages of the Opposition. There was not much cheering. Interest was too keen to tolerate interruption. But there were occasions when enthusiasm mastered curiosity. Free fish, free wheat, oats, barley, and buckwheat, free potatoes, free dairy products and free hay conceded by the United States brought forth a tumult of appreciation which for a moment halted the Finance Minister in his triumphal recital. And when he closed the Liberals cheered and cheered again.

The cheering did not last. Right from the start, railway interests, boards of trade, and fruit growers let it be known that reciprocity was a threat to their prosperity. The bulk of the media of Ontario, Quebec, and British Columbia demonstrated hostility. The Conservative premier of Ontario voiced his disapproval to Robert Borden,

THERE WAS A YOUNG LADY FROM NIGER
WHO WENT FOR A RIDE ON A TIGER
THEY CAME BACK FROM THE RIDE WITH THE LADY INSIDE
AND NEW STRIPES ON THE HIDE OF THE TIGER

Reciprocity equals annexation (National Archives of Canada, C 134510)

and the party began to hear happy messages from its ridings and to obstruct the Liberals in the House of Commons.

Then, less than a month after Fielding's announcement, a group of Toronto business leaders issued a powerful denunciation of reciprocity. The Toronto Eighteen, most of them Liberals, represented five banks, two railroads, three manufacturers, two life insurance companies, and other business concerns employing altogether more than a hundred thousand workers. The group argued for the status quo, believing it responsible for their current prosperity: a hard-won commercial and transportation system stretching from western to eastern Canada, the whole linked to Britain and the empire. Reciprocity, they feared, would drive Canadian trade and economic development in a more natural north–south direction, making Canadians dependent as never before on the United States. In a few years, it would only be necessary for the Americans to threaten a return to the bad old days before 1911 to make Canada capitulate to a wider deal, which this time would include a broad range of manufactured products. That in turn would weaken national and imperial ties and make it more difficult to avert political union. The Canadian experiment would be at an end.

At the end of February, the power-starved Conservatives got more good news. The West's leading Liberal, Clifford Sifton, weighed in against reciprocity, giving an eloquent speech in the House of Commons that echoed many of the arguments of the Toronto Eighteen. Canadians, Sifton declared, were just now getting to the time when they could be of use to the empire "that gave us our liberty and our traditions of citizenship." Instead they were being asked "to turn from the path that leads to the capital of the empire, and take the path that leads to Washington. I say, so far as I am concerned: Not for me." Sifton's speech, in the words of one partisan, "was the loveliest music that the Conservatives had heard for many moons."

The anti-reciprocity Canadian National League was formed in Toronto under Z.A. Lash, one of the Toronto Eighteen. The League was an informal structure, cobbled together after lunch at that bastion of Toronto business, the York Club. The aim was

to oppose the adoption of the proposed Reciprocity Agreement between Canada and the United States of America and to support such measures as will uphold Canadian Nationality and [the] British connection, will preserve our Fiscal Independence and will continue to develop our present National policy of interprovincial and external trade, under which the Dominion has achieved its present prosperity.

The League's pamphlets and articles, stuffed with statistics and high-flown rhetoric, were distributed across the country and formed part of what was becoming a major propaganda offensive. One such screed, written by Arthur Hawkes, was aimed particularly at the 250 000 very recent British immigrants to Canada: "It may rest with you and me, the British-born, more than with any other element in modern Canadianism, to decide whether that nationality has come to stay in the face of the scarcely disguised aspiration of our neighbours that their Flag and not ours shall float above our heads."

Robert Borden had not been a great success during his ten years as Conservative party leader. Dull and plodding—characteristics all the more apparent because he faced the flashy Laurier—he could also be moody and dismissive. He had been shaken by attacks on the way he conducted party affairs, and his detractors had taken a run at his leadership in 1910. He had been slow to sniff the opportunity that reciprocity offered, but he could see it now and his self-esteem was growing. The Conservative leader made a deal with Lash, Sifton, and Lloyd Harris of the Massey-Harris farm implement company for their active support. (Massey-Harris was one of the very few manufacturers directly and adversely affected under the agreement.) In return, Borden would resist American "encroachments," institute a staunchly Canadian economic policy, and maintain close British ties. His willingness to do business with the devil Liberals and to consult them over Cabinet appointments should the Conservatives win power prompted party dissidents to question yet again Borden's capacity to continue as party chief. But he now had allies, an issue, and momentum, and he was not about to be stopped.

The Conservatives ate up day after day of debate in the House of Commons, while their friends in the Canadian National League, the Canadian Manufacturers' Association, and the press did the work of educating the public on the issue. In early May, Parliament was adjourned for two months so that Laurier could attend the 1911 Imperial Conference and the coronation of George V in London. He went on the advice of the Cabinet and against his better judgment, losing, one expert witness testified, "the last vestiges of Liberal advantage so evident in January—surprise, prospective economic benefit, and entrenched power." The Liberals "had been forced on the defensive, and faced the likelihood of an appeal to the country."

The United States was meanwhile handing gifts to the Conservative strategists. The legislation necessary to implement reciprocity moved very slowly through the u.s. House of Representatives and Senate and was not finally approved until 22 July. President Taft had to sell the measure, and he did so with some unfortunate language, arguing in essence that the Americans had Canada just where they wanted it. They must act to remove the dominion entirely from the British sphere and land it firmly in the American one, where it would henceforth be a reliable hewer of wood and drawer of water for the emerging u.s. economic empire. In a letter to former president Roosevelt, Taft admitted that the agreement would turn Canada into "only an adjunct of the United States. . . . I see this argument made against Reciprocity in Canada, and I think it is a good one." The letter somehow became public. Giving the Conservatives more ammunition still, the influential Champ Clark, one of the Democratic leaders in the House of Representatives, urged support not simply for freer trade but for annexation of Canada: "I hope to see the day when the American flag will float over every square foot of the British-North American possessions clear to the North Pole." Conservative pamphleteers lovingly reproduced these statements with gory commentaries.

Parliament reconvened on 19 July. While Laurier was in London, Borden had been in western Canada, promising farmers everything but reciprocity. The Conservative premiers of Manitoba, British Columbia, and Ontario were fully behind the federal leader, each having passed anti-reciprocity resolutions in their legislatures, and the public education initiative chugged along on business dollars. The government added morning sessions in the House of Commons, hoping to damp down Conservative enthusiasm and ram the legislation through. Laurier had a huge majority and the power that went with it to get his way eventually. But the Liberals could not cut off the debate—closure was not yet in use—and their frustration was difficult to contain. Laurier dissolved the House and called an election on 29 July. He still thought he could win in the country.

He could not. The 21 September general election swept the Liberals from office. Borden won a majority of the popular vote and 134 House of Commons seats to Laurier's eighty-seven, a huge victory by any standards. The Liberal gang had been in power a long time, and it showed. There had been scandal, the party apparatus was weak, and there was no fresh blood to rejuvenate the old guard. The Borden machine, on the other hand, was powerful, particularly in Manitoba, British Columbia, and Ontario, and it was galvanized by reciprocity and the scent of power. Premier J.W. Whitney's Ontario, the home of what he liked to call "sane Imperialism," gave Borden 56.2 percent of the vote and seventy-two of eighty-six seats. Freer trade, the Liberals said, was for the farmers, and Laurier managed to take almost everything in Alberta and Saskatchewan but not in Roblin's Manitoba. Even in Quebec, the Tories cut deeply into the Liberals' strength.

Quebec's role in the election deserves some attention. French-Canadian nationalism had been increasing since the South African War, as Laurier seemed to disappoint again and again on questions of language, education, and foreign policy, and Bourassa emerged as an articulate leader of opinion and defender of French rights. In the nationalist view, Laurier was a traitor to French Canada. The Naval Service Act, Bourassa said, was "an imperialist trick to involve Canada in foreign wars," which were sure to bring the forced enlistment of young French Canadians in the armed forces. "Was it Canada's duty to share the burden Britain had imposed upon herself for her own glory and greatness?" Bourassa began to publish a newspaper, *Le Devoir*, during 1910; quickly it became a powerful vehicle of French-Canadian nationalism and opposition to the government.

The navy was the focus of attention during the 1911 election campaign in Quebec. Reciprocity, F.D. Monk claimed, was simply Laurier's attempt "to dig a big ditch to hide the nefarious policy of his Naval Bill." Monk and Bourassa entered into a marriage of convenience to elect anti-Laurier MP's. Conservative candidates in the French ridings required the seal of approval from both nationalist

leaders, and they ran on the basis of opposition to the Naval Service
Act with scarcely a reference to reciprocity. Borden co-operated by
soft-pedalling the naval issue, even in front of English audiences. A
speech given in London, Ontario, on 15 August displayed his clever
evasion: "The question of Canada's permanent co-operation in
Imperial Naval Defence involves far-reaching considerations. . . .
Responsibility for Empire defence clearly involves some voice in
Empire policy. . . . [S]uch proposals should be submitted to the people for their consideration."

Monk and Bourassa disagreed with none of these vague sentiments. They had no love for Borden, or for his naval policy of an
emergency monetary contribution to Britain, but they concentrated
on Laurier's sins. The Manchester *Guardian* newspaper commented,
"the spectacle of imperial Conservatives like Borden, and extreme
Nationalists like Bourassa, working together against Laurier is certainly remarkable. If successful, they would manifest differences so
vigorously as to prevent Borden from carrying out the chief articles
of his programme." This was perceptive, but disagreements in
Conservative ranks were for the future. Laurier won Quebec—
thirty-seven seats to the Conservatives' twenty-seven—but the
Monk–Bourassa alliance pinned him down in his home province,
where he spent fully half of his electioneering time. The Conservatives secured 50 percent of the popular vote in Quebec.

Election analysis is not an exact science. In attempting to explain
how and why the campaign of 1911 was won and lost, it is impossible
to separate the role played by reciprocity and the naval question
from that played by party organization or by those who saw their
interests jeopardized. The 1911 election, however, was one of the few
in our history in which the debate was dominated by foreign policy
issues, and comes as close as we are ever likely to get to an opinion
poll on Canada's place in the world in the early twentieth century.

Broadly speaking, three distinct nationalisms can be discerned.
Imperialists saw Canadians finally coming into their own within the
framework of the empire, and looked to the day not far off when the
country would play a positive and assertive part in its affairs. The
French-Canadian brand of nationalism concentrated on the harmful
effects of excessive contacts with the British Empire, which might

compromise Canadian "liberty and intellectual and moral progress." The third form of nationalism sought a middle way: good, friendly relations with the empire and the United States, but a minimum of external commitments so that Canadians could get on with the work of nation building.

Laurier embodied this middle ground. The other two groups despised his ideas for a navy, the first because he asked for too little and the second because he asked for too much, but the moderate majority could live with the compromise of a small, independent naval force. Reciprocity, however, posed a greater problem for the government because it could be seen as a challenge to the very idea of Canada itself. Canadian nationalists of all varieties were almost by definition suspicious of the United States. As L.E. Ellis wrote in his classic study of the 1911 free trade agreement, "pious platitudes about an undefended border had not sufficed to make all Canadians love their neighbours."

Laurier won the most seats in Quebec, and it may be assumed that his cautious policies still had considerable support there. French-Canadian nationalism was on the rise, however, with its greater emphasis on national autonomy and keeping the world at bay. "We French-Canadians belong to one country, Canada," the newspaper *La Presse* had written during the crisis over the South African War. "Canada is for us the whole world." The United States was not nearly the threat that Britain's imperialists were, for the latter had the capacity to stir up trouble in English Canada and thus to divide Canadians and divert them from the things they held in common. Reciprocity was not nearly the threat that a Canadian navy was. Yet the United States was another potentially dominant metropolitan centre, luring unsuspecting young French-Canadian immigrants southwards and arranging, in Bourassa's words, "leurs propres affaires à leur grand avantage." "No navy made in London, no reciprocity made in Washington," was the nationalist's war cry in 1911.

In English Canada, pride in association with the British Empire loomed large, and the British connection was commonly seen as a bulwark against American values and influences. The purple-prose makers worked overtime during the 1911 campaign, dredging up hatred of the United States and probing for instinctive imperial responses. Just days before the election, Sir Hugh Graham's *Montreal*

Daily Star printed an editorial jammed between a huge British Union Jack on one side and an equally imposing Stars and Stripes on the other. The newspaper asked readers to choose which flag they wanted to live under. Beginning calmly enough, the piece professed admiration for America, but the shrillest of chauvinism quickly took control, degenerating into an awful verse of patriotic doggerel: "A Southerner shall never place his heel/ On the men of the Northern zone." The editorialist went on to claim that although many Canadians had deserted the country for the United States in the difficult economic conditions of the last century, those who stayed behind had fought for Canada and won the battle. "We have filled our cities; we have banded our half-Continent with railways, we have laughed at leagues of wilderness and leaped over mountains; and we have drawn . . . the sturdiest army of farmers in the world." No one doubted the future of Canada. Even the defectors were returning and the country was going to become the keystone of the British Empire, perhaps the most powerful state in the world. But reciprocity had brought it to a crossroads:

> We will either continue to march on the highway toward national greatness with the flag of Canada floating in our clear northern air over our heads; or, we will turn aside toward absorption in the "great and glorious Republic," to the south of us, surrendering to a calculating smile what we have long defended from hostility in every form—armed invasion, tariff persecutions, bullying over boundaries, even insolent disregard of treaty obligations.

Such rhetoric was common, and there is no question that it had an impact. Anti-Americanism was a constant and important factor in Canadian life, but it should not be overemphasized. Canadians and Americans agreed on much and they shared much. Even as reciprocity was being rejected, commercial and cultural ties were strengthening. The United States was the source of 60 percent of Canada's imports and a market for more than 40 percent of Canadian exports. These figures were growing, as were the levels of American investment in the Canadian economy. Unlike most British investors, u.s.

businesses liked to set up branch plants and to control resource companies; there were 451 American-owned concerns in Canada by 1913. Canadians had always migrated to the United States in large numbers, and in the first decade of the twentieth century Americans returned the favour, coming to the prosperous prairies in droves. Canadians played American baseball, read American magazines, and took up American fashions. Citizens from the two countries prepared to mark a "century of peace" along a border unfortified since the end of the War of 1812, and revelled in the moral and spiritual differences between the Old World and the New. North America was a shining, peaceful haven, Europe a cauldron of tension and historic conflict.

The emotion of the reciprocity debate could therefore be put aside. The new prime minister, Robert Borden, and his chief strategist, Clifford Sifton, did not make careers out of their election rhetoric. Borden rapidly let it be known that he harboured "no spirit of unfriendliness or hostility to the United States," and he sent emissaries to reassure u.s. investors that Canada was as interested in them as ever. Sifton, for his part, was open to the idea of another reciprocity negotiation because he thought that the next time the Americans would be easier to deal with "after so pronounced an indication that the Canadians intended to protect their integrity."

Sifton's personal experience perhaps reflected the catharsis of the election for all Canadians, the release of pent-up emotions that had been building since at least the Alaska boundary disagreement. He had been directly involved in drawing up and presenting the Canadian case to the tribunal for that dispute, and he had displayed strong anti-Americanism before and during the free trade election. But he apparently seldom displayed that attitude thereafter.

THE NAVAL EMERGENCY

Borden moved rapidly to reassure the Americans, but not so those in English Canada and Great Britain who had great hopes for an invigorated imperial dynamism and a more assertive plan for naval co-operation: for an end, in short, to Laurier's narrow nationalism.

Borden simply said that he would repeal the hated Naval Service Act, and he halted the development, such as it was, of the Liberal navy. That was all for the short run. It was "infinitely better to be right than in a hurry," the new prime minister told the House of Commons.

The Hamilton *Spectator* had greeted Borden's election with satisfaction. "Mr. Borden has been returned to power with a majority sufficient to permit him to be independent of Quebec, or rather that portion of it which is hostile to Canada's participation in Imperial naval warfare. He is in an ideal position and he should take full advantage of it." The Conservative leader, however, clearly gave his highest priority to party unity. He brought Monk and two other Quebec nationalists into the Cabinet, B. Nantel and Louis-Philippe Pelletier, and did not include the naval problem in his first throne speech. A worried governor general, Lord Grey, wondered aloud to Borden whether he could satisfy Parliament "that the presence of Mr. Monk as one of your colleagues on the Treasury Bench does not mean a weak or retrogressive naval policy."

Grey was undoubtedly disappointed. For the first several months of his premiership, Borden busied himself with other concerns, while vaguely outlining a naval strategy for the future that had something for everyone. First of all, "a permanent policy" providing for a Canadian navy would have to be devised, and it "ought to be threshed out and debated before the people, and they should be given an opportunity of pronouncing upon it." This promise of consultation was designed to placate Monk and his nationalists, as was Borden's vow that his navy would not be nearly as big or ambitious as Laurier's original conception.

For the consumption of the imperialists, for the governor general and the provincial premiers, and for the big new contingent of English-Canadian members of Parliament, the prime minister committed himself to much closer co-ordination with the British on naval matters. Borden rejected utterly the notion that Parliament should decide what the navy would do and where it would go in the event of war. It had to speed to Britain's side, Borden stipulated, and immediately become a part of the Royal Navy for the duration. As to the question of an emergency gift, the government "shall take pains to ascertain . . . what are the conditions that confront the empire, and honourable gentleman on this side of the House without exception, will be prepared to do their duty as representatives of the people of this Dominion, and as citizens of this great empire." Borden completed the package with a declaration that any contribution to London would have to be accompanied by a "greater voice in the councils of the Empire."

Borden travelled to London in the summer of 1912, and what he heard there made any further procrastination on the naval issue impossible. The prime minister asked for and got advice about his plans for the Canadian navy, but the British emphasized that they badly needed a cash contribution to *their* navy. Winston Churchill, the first lord of the Admiralty, described a serious expansion in Germany's naval strength and that of its allies, Italy and Austria. The future of the United Kingdom and all the components of the British Empire was threatened. The Germans were already the second-ranking naval power in the world and even at their present pace of development would outstrip the present Royal Navy by 1920. "There are practically no limits to the ambitions which might be indulged by Germany, or to the brilliant prospects open to her in every quarter of the globe, if the British Navy were out of the way." Churchill asked Borden specifically and pointedly for an emergency transfusion of $35 000 000 to build three dreadnought-class battleships.

Borden was willing enough. He made it clear, however, that the British must find some way of giving Canada a say in the making of their policies. "I conceive that those who accept a share in a responsibility for the defence and security of this vast Empire are no longer to be considered as wards by self-constituted guardians." The British offered representation on their Committee of Imperial Defence when matters of interest to Canada were being discussed. It was not much, but it allowed Borden to claim that he was making good on his pledge to get something tangible in exchange for Canadian participation in building up the Royal Navy. In fact, the prime minister was soon boasting to Parliament that no important step in imperial foreign policy would henceforth be taken without consulting Canada. This was not true, and Whitehall's mandarins were quick to correct Borden, although they did so privately. Borden never retracted his words.

The Liberals claimed that Borden was reacting not to an imperial crisis but to a Conservative Party one. A cartoonist from the *Canadian Liberal Monthly* depicted a heavily perspiring Conservative leader trying desperately to ride two horses, each pulling in a different direction. The $35 000 000 would obviously please the imperialist beast, but Borden still had hopes of holding on to the Quebec reins too. He thought that the French nationalists would stand by him if he could prove that the empire faced real crisis, that London was prepared to give up some of its power, and that a very modest national navy remained the long-term goal. They did not. Monk resigned after Borden announced his decision to give a cash contribution to the British and not to put a plebiscite on the question to the country, as Monk demanded. The prime minister made a special appeal to the other French-speaking Conservatives, reiterating his promise of a permanent policy down the road and holding out the possibility of Quebec-based shipbuilding to go with it. The majority stayed with the government on the issue, but far from all.

The Naval Aid Bill was introduced in December 1912 and made provision for a gift of $35 000 000 to the British Admiralty. (Total government expenditure for that year was $144 000 000.) It never

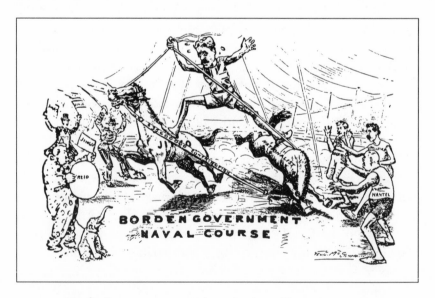

Borden's emergency (*Canadian Liberal Monthly*, Ottawa, 1911)

became law. Having had a lesson in obstructionism from the Conservatives the year before over reciprocity, the Liberals returned the compliment with interest. Week after week of bitter debate passed before Borden used closure, which was invented for the occasion, to cut off the Liberal filibuster and get the measure through the House of Commons in May 1913. But the bill died in the Senate, stacked with Liberals appointed during Laurier's fifteen years in power.

The Naval Service of Canada was an orphan with few resources to draw upon. Its budget had been drastically cut, and by the summer of 1913 it had only 350 personnel and two warships, the lonely *Niobe* and *Rainbow*, to put them in. All the officers were drawn from the Royal Navy, and a German naval officer concluded after three weeks in Halifax that they were second rate and the *Niobe* next to worthless:

> All the English sea officers aboard the *Niobe* are in some respect inferior—either physically or in regard to their professional competence. . . . The docks present a melancholy aspect. Fresh water cannot be brought the ships as there is no barge. . . . The *Niobe*, with the breeches of all guns removed, is tied up alongside the dock as there are no maintenance personnel. . . . [A] voyage aboard her [is judged] as risky.

Yet the Canadian armed forces were not completely unprepared for war. Spending on the militia, as the army was called at the time, was up substantially despite the end of an economic boom, and Borden authorized a naval reserve in 1914 over the objections of his French-speaking MPs. The port of Halifax was adequately defended, and good planning was underway to protect the rest of the country.

Borden had been convinced that an emergency existed in the empire and that it necessitated an immediate contribution to the Royal Navy. "Undoubtedly the conditions confronting the Empire are very grave," he told former Conservative prime minister Sir Charles Tupper after returning from London in 1912. At the turn of the century "our flag was dominant on every sea and in every ocean; today in the North Sea only." The Royal Navy's supremacy was crucial. Without it the empire could be manoeuvred out of existence in the flickering of an eye. Canada had come to a point in its history when it had the size and capacity to alter the balance, to make a difference. That was only right, because the country owed Britain everything. When George Foster set fire to the naval debate in Canada by placing his resolution before the House of Commons in 1909, he drew a flowery but heartfelt picture: "The old mother empire . . . who . . . has mothered nation after nation, people after people, continent after continent, brought them out of darkness and slavery and set them upon the path of a better civilization." Canada was well down that "civilizing" path and possessed not only "great and varied resources" but also "that spirit of self-help and self-respect which alone befits a strong and growing people." The key elements of Borden's external policy, the acceptance of national responsibilities in the empire and the demand for a voice in British decision making, flowed directly from such reasoning.

Borden and Foster were members of a breed of imperialist-nationalists. They put the country and its status and welfare first, but also wanted to see what Canada could do in and for the empire. It was about time, the British might think. The old mother empire needed her family more than ever before.

CHAPTER TWO

A Nation That Is Not a Nation, 1914–1921

I N THE SUMMER OF 1914, the Archduke Francis Ferdinand, heir to Emperor Francis Joseph I of Austria, was murdered by Serbian nationalists in Sarajevo. The Austrians seized the opportunity to precipitate a diplomatic crisis. After making demands of Serbia that were sure to be rejected, they declared war on 28 July. Alliances and international agreements of long standing clicked into gear, and the situation rapidly escalated out of control. Russia mobilized its armies against Austria-Hungary, which reciprocated, and Germany declared war on Russia and France. This took German armies into Belgium on their way to France. The British, although under no precise obligation to defend Belgium, ordered the Germans to withdraw. When they did not, Britain was at war.

CANADA'S WAR—OR BRITAIN'S?

The governor general of Canada received a telegram from London at 8:55 p.m. on 4 August 1914 announcing the outbreak of hostilities with Germany. When one part of the British Empire was at war, all were. There was no need for a Cabinet meeting, no need for Parliament to deliberate about whether to jump in or stand aloof.

Canadians had the right and the responsibility to decide the scope of their involvement, but on that score there was never any official doubt or hesitation. Sir Robert Borden, as he now was, had already promised the British on 1 August "that if unhappily war should ensue the Canadian people will be united in a common resolve to put forward effort and make every sacrifice necessary to ensure the integrity and maintain the honour of our Empire." The leader of the opposition, Sir Wilfrid Laurier, was unequivocal in his support for Borden and in his appeal for an end to partisan wran-

DON'T BE SCARED: I'M HERE!

(Welland *Telegraph*, 1914)

gling. Britain was threatened, and a call for assistance had come. The answer, Laurier declared, "goes at once, and it goes in the classical language of the British answer to the call to duty: 'Ready, aye, ready.'" At the beginning of October, a force of 31 200 Canadian soldiers, the largest military contingent ever to cross the Atlantic, set sail from Quebec.

The conflict was not yet a world war—the United States, notably, remained neutral—and most knowledgeable folk predicted that the troubles, awful though they promised to be, would be over by Christmas. But hundreds of thousands more Canadians joined the fray over the next four years, and 61 000 never returned home. They were the victims of industrialized warfare: machine guns that could cut down five hundred soldiers in the space of two minutes; high-power, long-range artillery whose shells burst into thousands of killing fragments; poison gas; impassable, razor-sharp barbed wire. Each of these horrors was multiplied by modern mass production, and poured into the battle with deadly efficiency by railway and road systems. The Canadian Expeditionary Force first experienced the full fury of the nightmare in August 1915, when the part of the allied line it was defending at Ypres, Belgium, became the target of a massive German offensive. The Canadians held, when many around them did not, but in four days of fighting they lost over six thousand men—killed, wounded, or captured—some two-thirds of the total number that had been in the front line. Lengthy casualty lists became a staple item in newspapers across Canada.

In the beginning, though, there was a great deal of good cheer and high spirits. Canadians believed that they had a chance to do great things, but this sentiment was ambiguous. Was the war for nation or for empire? Some, many even, made no distinction between the two. The Toronto *Globe*, which advertised itself then as now as "Canada's National Newspaper," editorialized the day before war was declared, "Of one thing let there be no cavil or question: If it means war for Britain it means war also for Canada. If it means war for Canada it means also the union of all Canadians for the defence of Canada, for the maintenance of the Empire's integrity, and for the preservation in the world of Britain's ideals of democratic government and life."

In English Canada, phrases such as "standing shoulder to shoulder with the Motherland" came easily and naturally, particularly for the many very recent immigrants from Britain. This group contributed 65 percent of the first wave of volunteer soldiers; half of all those who freely enlisted in the Canadian forces during World War I were British born. Yet it is striking that French Canada also enthused about a war that offered the prospect of fighting for France and Britain abroad and of reconciling the two peoples at home. Henri Bourassa and his nationalist newspaper, *Le Devoir*, were carried along by the wave. The government had promised, after all, that there would be no conscription, no forced enlistment of young men.

Some, but only a few, saw the war as a glorious opportunity to forge closer imperial ties and thus to achieve a more powerful Canada. One of these imperialists found himself close to the prime minister. Born in Amherst, N.S., and trained in law at Harvard, equipped with a wonderful mind and a restless idealism, Loring C. Christie had joined the Department of External Affairs as its legal adviser in 1913 at the princely salary of $3000 a year. There was not much law to do, and Christie rapidly became the prime minister's key foreign policy counsellor, a source of facts, rationales, and energy directed at gaining a potent role for Canada in the empire and globally.

Christie had little competition in the fight for Borden's ear. There was always the governor general, but the elegant and informed Lord Grey had been replaced in 1911 by the Duke of Connaught, Queen Victoria's third and favourite son. Connaught was nothing but trouble for Borden, particularly after the outbreak of war, when the governor general assumed that command of the armed forces was part of his job description. The Department of External Affairs had only fourteen employees in 1914, and it busied itself with minor policy. The number two in command of the tiny bureaucracy was E.A. Walker; his work centred around passports, treaties, and financial and administrative questions. Sir Joseph Pope, the department's head and founder, had a limited view of its responsibilities and of the country's possibilities. As he wrote, "Canada by herself is not a nation, and I hope I may never live to see her one."

Christie agreed that a life for Canada "by herself" was unsatisfactory, but he had an expansive vision of the future. Canadians were coming into their own and must soon take control of their foreign policy. The question was how. One method, undoubtedly too radical for the time, was to separate Canadian from British policy and control external relationships entirely from Ottawa. Christie preferred the equally revolutionary option of creating a truly imperial foreign policy, in which Canadian voters, officials, and politicians would have a tangible say. Christie was a member of the Round Table, a group of intellectuals from Britain and the dominions who hoped to create a new, integrated British Empire in order to counteract the declining power at the imperial centre and meet the demand of rising nationalism in the dominions.

The Round Table failed in its mission. The tide of history flowed in another direction, and as World War I raged on Canadian Round Tablers such as the aristocrat Vincent Massey, historian George Wrong, and newspaper editor John Willison found it impossible to accept the various proposals for a very centralized form of empire federation proposed by the movement's guru, the Englishman Lionel Curtis.

Christie did not relinquish hope for his own brand of the empire dream until the events of the 1920s extinguished imperialism once and for all. He saw World War I as "the greatest opportunity ever held out to a young nation," "a chance at last to save our [*sic*] soul of Canada." The members of the British family must "come more closely together and deliberately join their destinies," or the dominions would grow in strength, local preoccupations would dominate more than ever, and common aims would fall by the wayside. The war, a clash of European nationalisms, showed how important it was to contain the parochial and accentuate broader international goals and interests.

Although a British Empire patriot and a believer in co-operative policies, Borden never envisaged this close a relationship among the parts of the empire. Right from the beginning the prime minister went out of his way to justify the war effort in distinctively national terms. This was Canada's war, "a struggle in which we have taken part of our own free will . . . because we realize the world-compelling consideration which its issues involve." The "future destiny of civilization and humanity" and the "cause of freedom" were at stake, and the Canadian commitment to see a just war right through to the end was absolute. Borden held to this view consistently throughout the war. As he put it in 1918, "Probably no part of the Britannic Commonwealth was more disinterested in reaching a decision as to its duty. We are ready to fight to the last for the cause as we understand it, for every reasonable safeguard against German aggression and for the peace of the world."

Borden's conception of the war as a righteous crusade requiring total involvement—and the complete defeat of the Germans—ensured that his compatriots would be asked to give and give again and that Canada would ask Britain for something in return for sacrifice. By the end of 1914, the Canadian prime minister had offered another contingent of troops and announced that fifty thousand additional men would be kept continuously in training. To press reports of an expeditionary force to Europe that might reach a hundred thousand, Borden responded, "I prefer to name no figure. If the preservation of our Empire demands twice or thrice that number we shall ask for them." The prime minister had begun, however, to allude to a price for Canada's contribution. Decisions about the great issues of war and peace were made in "the councils of Empire" by the British alone. That had to change, so that "the men of Canada, Australia, South Africa and the other dominions will have the same just voice in these questions as those who live within the British Isles. Any man who doubts that will come, doubts that the Empire will hold together."

1915–1916: "TOY AUTOMATA"

The British showed a marked disposition to treat Canada as a colony. Orders for war supplies went to the United States but seldom to Canada. Canadian-owned ships were requisitioned, without consultation, for British use, an irritation that was not smoothed over until 1917. Borden and Sir George Perley, who doubled as a Cabinet minister and acting high commissioner in London, made various efforts to squeeze simple war intelligence out of the British government and bureaucracy, but to little avail. In July–August 1915, Borden visited England and had to threaten that Canadian co-operation might not be forthcoming in the future just to get the government of H.H. Asquith to give him some basic facts. He returned home without any agreed method of including the Canadian prime minister in war planning, or even of keeping him up to date on what was happening to Canadian soldiers in the field.

Borden continued to give nevertheless. On 30 October 1915, the government authorized an increase in the Canadian contribution to 250 000 troops. The same day, Borden asked Perley to tell the British that although he quite understood the necessity for central control of empire armies, "Governments of Overseas Dominions have large responsibilities to their people for conduct of war and we deem ourselves entitled to fuller information and to consultation respecting general policy in war operations." The British colonial secretary, Andrew Bonar Law, responded that he fully recognized "the right of the Canadian Government to have some share of the control in a war in which Canada is playing so big a part." Nevertheless, he was "not able to see any way in which this could be practically done." One idea was to place a dominion prime minister on Britain's War Council, but that seemed likely to satisfy only the part of the empire whose leader was chosen.

Borden was getting nowhere in his quest for a role in the higher direction of the war. Yet he again raised the number of recruits to be trained for combat, this time to five hundred thousand—from a population barely over eight million. The announcement was part of his 1916 New Year address to the nation, and was made without telling his Cabinet.

It does not seem to have occurred to Borden to demand reform of the British system *before* he made any further promises. Perhaps he was too personally committed to the war effort, perhaps he did not have a solution, or perhaps he hoped that the growing moral pressure on the London government would eventually force consultation. The fact is that the problem was not being confronted. As the prime minister complained in a telegram to Perley written three days after his New Year's message,

> During the past four months since my return from Great Britain, the Canadian Government (except for an occasional

telegram . . .) have had just what information could be gleaned from the daily press and no more. As to consultation, plans of campaign have been made and unmade, measures adopted and apparently abandoned and generally speaking steps of the most important and even vital character have been taken, postponed or rejected without the slightest consultation with the authorities of this Dominion.

It can hardly be expected that we shall put 400,000 or 500,000 men in the field and willingly accept the position of having no more voice and receiving no more consideration than if we were toy automata. Any person cherishing such an expectation harbours an unfortunate and even dangerous delusion. Is this war being waged by the United Kingdom alone or is it a war waged by the whole Empire? If I am correct in supposing that the second hypothesis must be accepted, then why do the statesmen of the British Isles arrogate to themselves solely the methods by which it shall be carried out in the various spheres of warlike activity and the steps which shall be taken to assure victory and a lasting peace?

Borden subsequently told Perley not to do anything further with this message, which nevertheless conveyed precisely his state of mind and level of frustration. Over the next several months his anger can only have increased. All he received from the British were some compliments and a single pile of British secret documents.

1917: "NOT *FOR* US, BUT *WITH* US"

Change came quite suddenly. David Lloyd George, a member of the British government whom Borden had liked during his visit to England, replaced Asquith as prime minister in December 1916. When Borden heard the news, his mind inevitably went back to their meeting of the year before, when Lloyd George had been critical of the British war effort and sympathetic to the Canadian's complaints.

Perhaps Lloyd George also remembered the encounter. Almost his first action as prime minister was to send out a summons to his dominion counterparts to join him in London, where they would form an Imperial War Cabinet. Shortly after taking control of the government, Lloyd George wrote to a colleague that Canada and the other dominions had made enormous sacrifices but felt left out. "As we must receive even more substantial support from them before we can hope to pull through, it is important that they should feel that they have a share in our councils as well as in our burdens. We want more men from them. We can hardly ask them to make another great recruiting effort unless it is accompanied by an invitation to come over to discuss the situation with us." One of the British prime minister's aides summed up the new mood: the dominions "were fighting not *for* us but *with* us." The war was dragging on, and Britain needed the dominions. It simply made good political sense for Lloyd George to involve them, or to make them think that they were involved, in decision making at the highest echelon. Borden understood that only too well.

The two leaders presented an interesting study in contrasts. Although both were short, stocky, grey-haired, and sported mustaches, they did not look the least bit alike. There was something wild about Lloyd George, while Borden was always well manicured and perfectly groomed. The difference went beyond appearance. As Borden's biographer explains, the Canadian was careful, self-contained, unable to show the deep emotion and commitment to people that he felt. Consequently, he was much criticized for lacking "the arts which most appeal to the popular imagination." Lloyd George, much more charismatic, had flair and daring. He was a creative force, quick to innovate, willing to use and take advantage of new ideas. His commitment to dominion autonomy was imperfect but he had a quality of openness, a capacity to treat the former colonies as adults rather than children. Together, the plodding Canadian and the Welsh wizard made an impressive team, and they helped to usher in a new way of looking at the British Empire.

Borden left Canada for England in mid-February 1917. The Imperial War Cabinet did not forgather until almost a month after Borden arrived in London, but he used the time to sop up all the documentation that he had been denied over the previous two and a half years. "Range and area of subjects enormous," he wrote, "touching

Sir Robert Borden (National Archives of Canada, C 694)

every conceivable question and extending to almost every country in the world." The Imperial Cabinet met first on 20 March. Czar Nicholas had been overthrown just days before and the Russian Revolution had begun. Although Borden and his colleagues did not know it quite yet, Russia, their ally, was about to leave the war, with all the implications that had for the allies' Eastern Front.

Lloyd George's opening salvo at the first meeting was predictable: "We must get more men." With this came, in meeting after meeting, the intelligence and expertise of the British war machine. Some things were undoubtedly held back, but there was no need to stint the bad news that reinforced the case for further troop commitments. The actual decisions taken by the Imperial Cabinet did not touch on high policy. Those were reserved for the British War Cabinet, a small, tightly focussed body also invented by Lloyd George.

The Imperial War Cabinet considered the terms of a peace that must then have seemed a long way off. Canada had a long list of territories that it wanted to cart away at the end of the war: something in the Alaska panhandle to give Yukoners access to the sea; Greenland; the Gulf of St Lawrence islands of St Pierre and Miquelon; and the West Indies. None of these desirable commodities, unfortunately, belonged to Canada's enemies, an undoubtedly fatal error in tactics and judgment. The British themselves, for example, were expected to give up the West Indies, and they were understandably livid when suddenly informed of the Canadian plan. This exercise in ambition stands in stark contrast to Borden's rhetoric about Canada as the most generous of the allies, interested only in doing its duty to God, humanity, and civilization.

Borden drew enormous satisfaction from the Imperial War Cabinet experiment, even though it talked more than it acted. It was composed of ministers—prime ministers, where possible—who represented their parliaments and peoples and acted on their behalf. They were informed about a broad spectrum of imperial and military affairs and were given an opportunity to express their views openly. Borden welcomed Lloyd George's suggestion that the Imperial War Cabinet ought to convene annually, as "an accepted convention of the British constitution." The momentum towards the kind of co-operative, consultative empire that Borden had been advocating seemed unstoppable. A fast-expanding Canadian autonomy would be demonstrated, preserved, and given its ultimate expression, he fervently hoped, in an association of nations whose members determined policies together.

Resolution IX of the Imperial War Conference, a meeting held concurrently with sessions of the Imperial War Cabinet, put all this idealism and optimism into concrete form. Readjustment of the constitutional relations of the empire was necessary, the resolution stated, but also too important and intricate for wartime. A special imperial conference would be summoned as soon as possible after the cessation of hostilities to discuss a new form of empire founded upon three principles: full recognition of the dominions as autonomous states of an "imperial commonwealth"; their right to an adequate voice in imperial foreign policy; and continuous consultation, backed up where necessary with concerted action "in all important matters of common Imperial concern." Borden took the lead in drafting and promoting this resolution. One of his allies was the highly respected General J.C. Smuts, the South African minister of defence.

"We must get more men," Lloyd George had said and Borden had agreed. Saddened by his many visits to Canadian troops in hospitals and in the trenches, unwavering in his belief that total victory over the Germans was the only victory worth having, the Canadian prime minister returned home convinced that he would have to introduce compulsory military service. This he did decisively, the Military Service Act becoming law on 29 August 1917. Borden had asked Laurier to come into a coalition government for the purpose of making conscription a national and bipartisan policy. Laurier refused, as did almost every French Canadian whom Borden approached, but the prime minister was able to find many English-Canadian Liberals who would join him. At the end of 1917, Borden submitted his new Union Government to an election, the first since 1911. He won everywhere except Quebec, which gave sixty-three of its sixty-five seats to the Laurier Liberals.

Enthusiasm for the war had waned in every part of the country but nowhere more than in Quebec. The links to the empire were least powerful there, and Ontario's restriction of French-language education made many Québécois think that they had as much of an enemy next door as overseas. Nor would French Canada quickly forget that conscription had been forced on them, or that a Conservative leader had been the one to do it.

The view has often been expressed that Canada became a nation on the battlefield, Easter Monday, 9 April 1917, when the Canadian Corps broke the German stranglehold on Vimy Ridge. The British and French had been unable to do so for more than two years. Corporal F.F. Worthington, who fought at Vimy, later reflected that

Slacker (National Archives of Canada, PA 5076)

before the conflict, "we were content to be Colonials . . . but Vimy Ridge was the first battle in which Canadian divisions fought as a whole, and it was purely a Canadian effort. . . . [A] National spirit was born . . . ; we were Canadians." This great triumph, however, has to be placed beside the federal government's ruthless imposition of conscription, which severely divided French from English Canadians and suggested to francophones and other non-British Canadians that something outside the country mattered more to

English Canada than the country itself. Military historian Desmond Morton has perhaps captured it best: Canadians did great things in the war, but they did not always do them together.

THE UNITED STATES AND US

The United States declared war on Germany, 6 April 1917. Even then, America stood apart as a reluctant ally with quite different aims from those of Britain or France. In fact, President Woodrow Wilson stipulated that the United States was an "associated power," not an ally at all. "We fight without rancor and without selfish object," he said, in words that had a familiar North American ring to them. Borden also made claims to disinterestedness, although there was nothing tentative about the way that Canada entered or fought the war.

Canadian newspapers greeted the news of American entry into the war with mixed emotions. The editorial page of the *Manitoba Free Press* displayed a huge American flag "unfurled in the cause of civilization." The Toronto *Daily Star* paid tribute to Wilson's high-mindedness, and Montreal's *La Presse* denounced his detractors as "disgracieux et antipatriotique." But the Toronto *Globe* and Montreal *Gazette* were both more restrained, noting that the other democracies had been waiting a long time for the United States to do the right thing. The *Gazette's* editorial of 7 April cautioned, "It is well . . . to remember that the United States comes in at the eleventh hour. Britain and her allies have borne the heat and burden of the day for more than 2½ years, years of suffering and sacrifice beyond all precedent. Nevertheless, it would be ungracious to reproach our American friends for their dilatoriousness in entering upon the war."

The *Gazette's* sentiments seem to have reflected broadly held views. In the glow of optimism in 1914, Canadians could briefly forgive American neutrality, seeing themselves as the representatives of North American principles in the European conflict. As the war went on and went badly, however, considerable resentment arose that the United States could remain aloof when so much was at stake. If we can judge from films, which were then in their infancy, this irritation generated a surge of Canadian nationalism expressed through the production of distinctive dramas and documentaries.

American involvement in the war only intensified the mood, because U.S. war films soon appeared with the message that Uncle Sam was doing it all single-handedly. Cinema historian Peter Morris has demonstrated that by 1918, "almost every Canadian newspaper had printed editorials condemning the quality and quantity of American war films" and urging "the production and distribution of more British and Canadian films." It is no coincidence that these were very active years in the creation of Canadian cinema.

American entry into the war did little to simplify the problems of defending Canada. During the last weeks of American neutrality, the prime minister had been so worried about a desperate strike into Canada by German agents and sympathizers in the United States that he had wanted to increase dramatically the number of home troops already available. Forty thousand had generally been maintained since August 1914 for border defence. The army chief, Major-General Willoughby Gwatkin, believed that Borden was over-reacting. Since the beginning of the war, when the nervous prime minister had first insisted that substantial garrisons be maintained to guard against invasion from the south, Gwatkin had placed his faith in the close watch maintained in American border towns by agents of the Dominion Police. No last-minute attack materialized before the United States declared war, but even though events proved Gwatkin right he was reluctant to reduce the home guard too much because of the possibility of domestic unrest—what he called the "danger of popular turbulence"—as impatience with the seemingly interminable war spread and pro-enemy American agitators did their work.

In maritime affairs, Canada was all but excluded from the network of co-operation built between Great Britain and the newly belligerent United States. This was particularly galling because of Canada's vital importance in the protection and delivery of North American resources across the Atlantic to Britain. American entry into the war coincided with the Royal Navy's adoption of convoy—the sailing of merchant ships in groups escorted by warships—as a last-ditch bid to staunch losses to the German submarines, known as U-boats. Canadian east coast ports played a major part in assembling convoys, not least because their position well along the short "great circle" route to Europe made them the most economical gathering places for a good deal of shipping from the United States. This vast activity made the Canadian coast a tempting target for German submarines, and intelligence proliferated about the dangers of attack.

Nevertheless, the Canadian navy soon learned that there was no hope of assistance for its inadequate escort-and-patrol flotilla of converted yachts and other civilian vessels. Without informing the dominion government, the British Admiralty arranged for the limited anti-submarine fleet of the United States Navy (USN) to be deployed to European waters. The British and Americans also made arbitrary decisions about the convoys and their routes, transferring one important convoy from Halifax to New York in early 1918. The government in Ottawa became "very sore" because this had an important impact on the shipment of goods and the overall economy. Several first-class merchant ships vital to the movement of high-value goods from the St Lawrence, for example, were removed from the Canadian trade.

In the first months of 1918, a Canadian naval officer visiting London made an unpleasant discovery. The British and Americans had excluded Ottawa from top quality intelligence confirming that German submarines would cross the Atlantic within a few months. The government's bitter complaints finally led to an arrangement for co-operation with the USN. Six USN "submarine chasers," small vessels not much better than Canada's own, and three less effective American ships operated under Canadian command from Halifax and Sydney during the summer and fall of 1918. In addition, the Americans assumed responsibility for the defence of the mouth of the Bay of Fundy, and sent two squadrons of anti-submarine seaplanes to begin operating in Nova Scotia in September 1918. In the meantime, the USN assisted the Canadian navy in organizing its own anti-submarine seaplane service.

Helpful as these measures were, they were too small and too late to help much with coastal defence when three u-boats hunted off Nova Scotia in August and September 1918. The Canadian navy did contribute significantly, along with overstretched American and British forces, to an effective, albeit shoestring, defence of the main convoys, but at a cost. Shipping schedules were dislocated, and fishing fleets that had to be all but abandoned to their fate suffered heavy losses.

The real requirement was for fast, powerful destroyers. After promising to provide these vessels from either British or u.s. sources, the Admiralty then joined the Americans in denouncing Canada's increasingly urgent requests. Nevertheless, within the constraints imposed by British demands and the urgent situation in European waters, the Americans had been generous, and Canadian and American sailors had worked well together in this first instance of defence co-operation. It was, however, a false start. Defence co-operation would not be re-initiated or mature for another generation. Partly as a result of the legacy of World War I, the dominion government took careful measures to ensure that Canadian maritime security and interests were not again left to the mercy of distracted friends and allies.

1918: IMPERIAL CABINETRY AND INTERVENTION IN RUSSIA

The Imperial War Cabinet next met in June 1918. The war was going disastrously, with Russia out, the United States not yet fully in, and the Germans, freed from their burdens on the Eastern Front, on the march. Borden had been critical all along of the British Army High Command, but he now had detailed inside information from Lieutenant-General Sir Arthur Currie, who had taken over the Canadian Corps after Vimy Ridge.

Currie, the first Canadian to hold the post, had been a crucial part of the British Flanders offensive in the fall of 1917. Ordered to complete what the British, Australians, and New Zealanders had begun at Passchendaele, near Ypres, Currie had done the job. It cost 15 654 dead and wounded, exactly the kind of heavy toll that he had predicted. The Canadian general railed at the British lack of preparation, organization, foresight, and intelligence, and he remembered "Pash" until the end of his days. It seemed to him the best advertisement imaginable for never going to war again.

Supplied with ammunition from Currie, Borden went on the attack. His voice shaking with emotion, he informed Lloyd George, "Mr. Prime Minister, I want to tell you that, if ever there is a repetition of the battle of Passchendaele, not a Canadian soldier will leave the shores of Canada as long as the Canadian people entrust the government of their country to my hands." William Morris Hughes, the fiery prime minister of Australia, made similar arguments, as did the usually uncomplaining New Zealanders. Lloyd George in fact wanted to bring his generals under greater civilian control, and so welcomed assistance to do so. He suggested that a committee of prime ministers be struck to consider and report upon recent military failures and the High Command's conduct of the war.

The new committee brought the dominions to the point of their highest prestige during World War I. Here, in a small and select group, the overseas premiers discussed war policy with all the documents and Britain's top military and civilian leadership at their disposal. The status inherent in such an arrangement is self-evident. Influence, however, is more difficult to define and assess. Historians commonly say that Borden and his dominion colleagues had a lot of it in the fall of 1918, but there is no precise evidence for this assertion. Lloyd George's main interest was to buttress his case against the generals and perhaps to divert eyes away from his own role in the military debacle of the previous months. It is well to note that between the meetings of the Imperial War Cabinets of 1917 and 1918 he reverted to the old ways of the Asquith government, never involving Canada in the formulation of military policy or the uses being made of Canadian soldiers. The decision to make General Currie head of the Canadian Corps was taken in England, and simply confirmed in Canada.

Even in the prime ministers' committee of 1918, the dominions never penetrated through to the centre of British foreign policy or strategic decision making. What is more, the events of the war were to make the work of the committee irrelevant. While the political chiefs decried the errors of the past and planned for a future that seemed to them likely to stretch into 1920, the allies smashed through enemy lines at Amiens, France, in August, launching a hundred-day campaign that routed the Germans and brought the war to a sudden end on 11 November 1918. Currie's well-trained, battle-hardened Canadian Corps, now recognized as an élite force, was consistently at the front of the final thrust.

In its other business, the 1918 Imperial War Cabinet continued the broader constitutional talks that had led to Resolution IX the

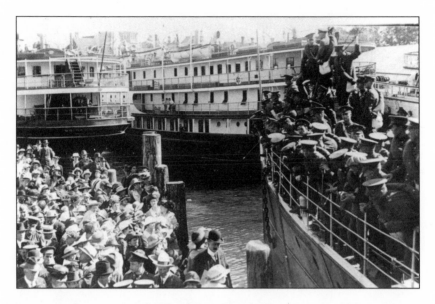

Canadian regiment leaving for war, 1918 (British Columbia Provincial Archives, 18896)

year before. Borden reiterated his desire—his demand—to have a piece of major imperial decisions from now on: "Canada was a nation of 8 000 000, twice as large as the United States when they became independent, and they must have a voice in foreign affairs. Unless she could have that voice in the foreign relations of the Empire as a whole, she would before long have an independent voice in her own foreign affairs outside the Empire."

The dominion leaders, anxious to have easy access to Lloyd George when the Imperial War Cabinet was not meeting, were able to win the right of direct communication with the prime minister of the United Kingdom. Lloyd George was also willing to establish a committee to get started on other reforms, but there was some suspicion (though not from Borden) that he was out to make the empire more unified at the expense of dominion prerogatives. Further changes in the system would have to wait until the postwar constitutional conference promised by Resolution IX.

Participation in rarefied interchanges about big issues carried responsibilities that might not have come Canada's way otherwise.

The Imperial War Cabinet had wanted the Eastern Front reconstituted in order to prevent the Germans from concentrating their attention in the West, and the prime ministers' committee recommended an allied intervention in Russia to assist those who were fighting against the Revolution. Because Borden had been a prominent exponent of the idea, he was an obvious target for a British request to help do the deed. In the spring of 1918, a few Canadian soldiers accompanied British forces to Murmansk, and some five hundred others went to the Archangel region. In 1919, a larger Canadian contingent was dispatched to Siberia, along with a mission under Department of Trade and Commerce official Dana Wilgress, who had great hopes for a huge Russian market after the Revolution was defeated.

June 1919 saw the last of the Canadian military in Russia, but bitter memories lingered in the newly emerged Soviet Union. Political leaders, commentators, and academics frequently harked back to the way in which the British, Americans, Japanese—and Canadians—tried to take their revolution away. Canada's "ruling classes," it was claimed, had been driven by "class hatred." Canadians for their part saw the Soviet Union as beyond redemption, in the clutches of a godless communism that turned people into slaves. The Cold War of the future had its distant origins here.

1919: PEACE AT PARIS

Borden had been promised participation in the peace process as early as 1915, long before he had been promised participation in the higher direction of the war. Perhaps, that far back, it had been to put his more immediate demands off. By the time of the armistice, Canada's appetite had been whetted by the successes of the Imperial War Cabinet and its prime ministerial subcommittee. Borden was going to insist on more than token representation at the peace conference. Indeed, as the prime minister travelled back to London in November 1918, his mind was running in a revolutionary direction: "I am beginning to feel more and more that in the end, and perhaps sooner than later, Canada must assume full sovereignty."

It was unclear at the beginning what form representation would take. Lloyd George had invited the premiers to London, but he thought that it would suffice if he simply talked to them before getting down to the real business of international negotiation. Consultation, in fact, seemed likely to be a sometime thing. Without telling Borden and his dominion partners, the British leader and other top allies went ahead with a decision to put the German Kaiser on trial. The Canadian was outraged by both the idea and the process, complaining about the "irregular procedure and oversight." He had not come all the way from Canada "to take part in light comedy."

This incident can only have hardened attitudes that Borden already held very firmly. He assured the British that Canadian politicians, press, and the people alike took it for granted that their country's contribution to the war would be recognized by a place at the peace table. In the Imperial War Cabinet at the end of December 1918, Lloyd George resisted separate representation for the dominions, suggesting instead one slot on the British delegation covering them all and an additional role, also on the British delegation, when an issue particularly concerning them was under consideration. Canada and Australia demanded more. As Borden and Hughes said, their dominions ought to have at least as much of a presence as the smaller allied nations like Belgium and Portugal, whose military contribution to the war was hardly comparable. Lloyd George backed down and agreed to give the dominions their own delegations *and* membership on the British team.

The affair was not over yet. Lloyd George had to take the brief for separate representation to Paris, where the peace conference would be held and where preliminary interallied consultations were taking place. This time it was u.s. president Woodrow Wilson and his secretary of state, Robert Lansing, who resisted. Lansing asked why Canadians should be concerned about Europe. Lloyd George, in high dudgeon, retorted that Canada and the other dominions cared because they had left hundreds of thousands of their sons on the old continent during the war. They "had died for the vindication of the public right in Europe." Canada and Australia had both lost more men than the United States. Wilson pointed out that the dominions had Britain, one of the most powerful members of the alliance, to make their arguments for them, an advantage Belgium did not have. What more was needed? The American president eventually agreed, however, that the dominions' claims were great and therefore put his reservations to one side.

Belgium did edge a bit ahead in the status game. It was given the right to send three representatives to plenary sessions of the conference. Canada and Australia got only two each, New Zealand one, and Newfoundland received no distinct rights at all despite a substantial and distinguished war record. Hughes, Borden, and the New Zealanders were irked by these fine distinctions, but in the final analysis the numbers mattered less than the fact of international recognition, particularly when it quickly became clear that none of the small countries had any clout whatsoever in Paris. As Clemenceau, the French prime minister, bluntly informed Borden, the major allies called the conference, invited the participants, and would make the decisions at meetings they alone would attend. "I make no mystery of it," Clemenceau declared, "there is a conference of the Great Powers going on in the next room."

When Borden or other dominion leaders made it into "the next room," it was in their other capacity, as members of the British Empire Delegation (BED). In this way, as Loring Christie put it, the Canadians were "at the heart of the machine and had access to all papers regarding the proceedings of the Conference." The BED was the name given to the Imperial War Cabinet, which had transferred its activities from London to Paris. Christie was himself an assistant secretary of the delegation, and Borden on occasion chaired its meetings. The prime minister was also the vice-president of the Commission on the Greek Question, one of the principal bodies of the conference. As well, he took part in the major deliberations about what would be done with Germany's colonies, and he attended a number of high-level meetings as the British Empire representative. Other Canadian delegates served in prominent appointments on, for example, the Inter-Allied Economic Commission.

Impressive though all of this sounded, it did not amount to much real power. The British Empire Delegation mattered less and less as a busy and preoccupied Lloyd George and his American, French, and Italian friends rushed headlong towards exclusive deci-

sions. There could be a gap of up to three weeks between disposi-
tions by the big powers and BED discussions of the same issues.
Borden began to think that his time would be better spent at home.
Lloyd George tried to convince him to stay. Finally, with the
Canadian Cabinet clamouring for his return and his critics hectoring
that there was more important business to do in Ottawa, Borden
could wait no longer. He went back to Canada in May 1919, before
the peace conference ended.

Borden had not been out for a harsh peace. He and his Canadian
colleagues in Paris worried that Germany was being squeezed too
hard, and that it could never pay the enormous reparations the allies
were demanding. The prime minister rejected his Cabinet's suggestion
that the bill for the 1917 Halifax explosion—the tragic result of a har-
bour collision between a French munitions ship and a Belgian relief
vessel—be presented to the Germans. That would just make other
nations more greedy and demanding. Borden supported Woodrow
Wilson in opposing the annexation of German colonies by parts of the
British Empire. Canada did not go into the war in order to add territory to the empire, he said grandly and not for the first time.

Before Borden left for Canada, he arranged for dominion signa-
tures of the peace treaties. This was entirely his initiative although
Lloyd George was in full support, just as he had eventually been over
the issue of separate representation at the Paris conference. Accordingly, although Borden was not there on 28 June 1919 to sign the
Treaty of Versailles formally ending the war with Germany, two
members of his government attended in his stead. They signed "for
the Dominion of Canada," as the South Africans, Australians, and
New Zealanders did for their countries. The five British delegates,
however, endorsed the treaty not for the United Kingdom alone, but
for the entire British Empire. Technically, the Canadian signature
was superfluous. The treaty had already been signed by the British
on Canada's behalf.

Nevertheless, this first Canadian signature of a major multilateral
treaty was another step towards international recognition of Canada's
status in the empire and in the world. It was all the more striking
because the Canadian prime minister insisted on approving the
treaty in Parliament before allowing the British to say that the

empire had agreed to its terms. No one could deny that Canada was more a nation and less a colony because of what Borden had done since 1914. Slowly, the country was developing a global presence. Or, in Loring Christie's precise lawyer's language, Canada was "in some degree an international person" after Paris. This was constitutional evolution the way Canadians liked it: gradual, partial, arising from necessity, neither premeditated nor driven by theory.

THE LEAGUE AND UNLIMITED
LIABILITY

More confirmation of its new status came with Canada's own seat at the League of Nations, the organization arranged for in the peace treaties to ensure that the insanity of World War I never happened again. It did happen again, of course, but in his memoirs of the next great war Winston Churchill rightly called the League "an instrument which will for ever constitute a milestone in the hard march of man."

Canadians were important supporters of League endeavours in areas such as protection of minorities and child welfare, and chapters of a good-sized League of Nations Society sprouted up across the country. Even so, Ottawa governments consistently undermined the collective security provisions of the League Covenant, all the while brandishing their moral superiority, claiming that if only Europeans could live as peacefully as North Americans did, all would be well. As the prime minister told the League Assembly at Geneva in 1928, Canada was "a land of reconciliation in which two races who had fought on the Plains of Abraham, were now living together in perfect harmony with each other and with their neighbour to the south."

The right of Canada to individual representation at the League of Nations was not seriously questioned at Paris, but its present and future degree of autonomy continued to be ambiguous. The British seat at the League actually belonged to the British Empire, and for years thereafter London claimed that it spoke for the dominions as well as for Great Britain and its colonies. American delegates at the peace conference used the rationale that public opinion in their country resented a bonanza of extra British places of influence to contest Canada's position. They also contended that Canadian membership in the International Labour Organization, which came into being at the same time as the League, did not encompass eligibility for election to the ILO governing body.

Prime Minister Borden retorted that he was "confident that the people of Canada will not tamely submit to a dictum which declares that Liberia or Cuba, Panama or Hedjaz, Haiti or Ecuador must have a higher place in the international labour organization than can be accorded to their country which is probably the seventh industrial nation of the world, if Germany is excluded from consideration." He added that Canada would withdraw from both the ILO and the League if simple justice were not done. Lloyd George put Borden's arguments to the French and to President Wilson, and it was agreed that the dominions could stand for election to the ILO governing body as well as to a non-permanent seat on the Council, the League's executive.

When the issue of American membership in the League of Nations came before the United States Senate in 1920, the debate was rife with criticisms about the many extra votes available to the British Empire. This helped to seal the fate of the League in the United States. The country whose president had been the greatest advocate for the world body never joined it.

The substance of the League, its core concept, was that nations ought if necessary to be forcibly prevented from aggression against their neighbours. Article X of the League of Nations Covenant pledged that signatories undertook "to respect and preserve as against external aggression the territorial integrity and existing political independence of all States members of the League." The Canadians at the Paris Conference in 1919 made clear their opposition to Article X, which dictated that France's wars, Italy's wars, and perhaps even Germany's wars were going to be Canada's wars "wherever and whenever such a war is initiated by territorial aggression." C.J. Doherty, Borden's minister of justice, argued that Canada was very unlikely to be invaded by anyone, and therefore ought not to be asked to defend anyone. Nor was it fair to require the same amount of international commitment from young, underdeveloped countries as from long-established and wealthy states. Article X, moreover, restricted autonomy just when Canada was getting its share of it. Before the war, there had been opposition to the doctrine that when Britain was at war, Canada was at war. Now Canada was asked under the Covenant to accept even greater obligations.

Future Canadian governments agreed that Article X made the League into "a mutual guarantee society of unlimited liability." Their goal throughout the early 1920s was to subvert the article, or even to remove it entirely. In 1923, Canada failed by only one vote to get an interpretive resolution through the League Assembly stipulating that the Council was bound to take into account "the geographical situation and special . . . conditions of each State" and that it was up to each member country to decide the nature and extent of its obligation to employ military resources to enforce Article X. In Canadian senator Raoul Dandurand's memorable phrase, the country was "a fire-proof house, far from inflammable materials," and it was not Canada's responsibility to solve the world's quarrels.

THE DEATH OF AN ALLIANCE

Sir Robert Borden left the premiership in July 1920. His successor was Arthur Meighen, who had been a principal architect of conscription and other divisive wartime policies. Meighen's greatest asset was his oratory, a powerful, acerbic, no-nonsense speaking style perhaps unequalled in eloquence by any prime minister before or since. His biographer, Roger Graham, described one of his early speeches as leader, given at a picnic in Stirling, Ontario. The citizens must have been struck by Meighen's face, Graham imagines, with its almost alarming gauntness and expression "of brooding intensity, of care-worn fatigue, as though even more than the weight of governing a country rested on the slight shoulders of the man. . . . The conventional opening remarks were disposed of quickly, as though he wanted to waste no time in coming to the real point of what he had to say, and then he spoke for an hour, earnestly, sparing of gesture, his words forming a faultless, felicitous prose."

Yet Meighen's brilliant speaking on the stump and in the House of Commons could be a liability. He said what he meant, which can be fatal in a politician. In the election of 1921 one of the prime issues would be the tariff. Meighen evoked the memory of John A. Macdonald and the National Policy as a means to a highly desirable end, a Canada separate and distinct from the United States. Everywhere he went he promised stiff tariffs, even though he realized that they had no political appeal on the prairies. Meighen brooked no subtlety. His election opponent, Mackenzie King, on the other hand, promised less protection if necessary but not necessarily less protection. King won the election (though not on the tariff alone) and was seldom out of office for the next three decades. His unheroic posture fit the weary postwar era, a large, diverse country, and, some said, the bland Canadian personality.

During his brief stint as prime minister in 1920–1921, Meighen had domestic matters more on his mind than foreign policy. Nevertheless, he was a prominent advocate of accommodation between the United States and Great Britain. These wartime allies had returned to being peacetime rivals: one the new great power on the rise; the other an aging giant in relative decline. In Paris, Robert Borden had made much of the need to reconcile British and American interests and indeed had gone further, underlining that for Canadians the world did not begin and end with the British Empire. If the empire co-operated with another country against the United States, no one should expect Canadian approval or support.

Meighen made exactly the same point, which is hardly surprising. No expert in external affairs, he relied heavily on Loring Christie, Borden's chief foreign policy adviser. One of the great goals of Christie's distinguished career in the public service was to bring the Americans and the British together. When he visited Washington in 1920 he was therefore dismayed to discover a "most unlovely" mood of sullen anglophobia, caused in part by armed conflict between Britain and Ireland, the British colony that was the homeland of so many Americans. Christie was "damn glad to get out of the town."

Christie feared that the upcoming renewal of the Anglo–Japanese Alliance, a mutual assistance treaty against unprovoked aggression, might irreparably damage an already fragile Anglo–American relationship. For Christie, alliances were not only "objectionable in themselves" but unnecessary in the modern era. The League would take care of any trouble in the Pacific or elsewhere. His real objection, however, was because the United States vigorously opposed an alliance that presented the possibility of two of the greatest naval powers in the world combining against it. Christie noted that the greatest danger of a continued alliance was the impact it would have on "English-speaking concord," "the cardinal feature of our policy." He proposed a conference of Pacific powers to examine problems in the region and to help extract Britain from the alliance without embarrassing Japan.

Christie adhered to the common view that Canadians were bred to interpret the United States to Great Britain. He thought that a Canadian representative should travel to Washington as a go-between to help mediate the dispute, but the idea was rejected by British prime minister Lloyd George. Meighen's adviser ratcheted up his rhetoric. Should the Anglo–American relationship turn sour, he claimed, Canada would be the battleground, the Belgium of a future war. The British must recognize "that in matters of high policy respecting North America the voice of Canada should be predominant as far as the British Empire is concerned."

Christie and Meighen were soon off to the Imperial Conference of 1921, where the Anglo–Japanese Alliance promised to be high on the agenda. The British were themselves very concerned to have American friendship, and by no means set themselves against the idea of a Pacific conference. Nonetheless, the balance of political and official opinion in London was in favour of keeping the alliance. Said Lloyd George about his World War I ally, "We must not insult Japan . . . when this gallant little people in the East backed us through thick and thin. . . . I think the British Empire must behave like a gentleman." Hughes of Australia was also adamant that the alliance must be maintained. His country, "with a coastline of 13,000 miles, with a great continent to defend, within three weeks of a thousand million of Asiatics," needed an assurance of safety. If asked whether his fledgling democracy favoured the United States or Japan as a friend, the answer would be obvious, historically and culturally. The United States, however, had not offered to defend Australia. Japan, through its alliance with Britain, had.

Meighen, a lonely but effective voice, made the arguments that had been put his way by Christie. The British wanted to find a form of alliance that would not displease the Americans, but Meighen was positive that any alliance at all was going to be unsatisfactory to the United States. If, on the other hand, the purpose of renewing the alliance was "to create a combination against an American menace," there was no chance that Canada would ever agree. "We ourselves have got along with the United States for 100 years and have overcome many difficulties, and we meet there a spirit which convinces us that we can still get along." Canada had expert qualifications and knowledge on the subject of the United States, and therefore also had "a special right to be heard."

The British scurried around looking for a way out of the difficulty. They had a horror that the British Empire might appear disunited. Having come through the war with difficulty, they had learned that the empire was a source of potential strength and that the dominions could be deployed for military or diplomatic gain. The empire was bigger than ever as a result of the war, but also, as its strategists knew only too well, weaker than ever: "disjointed, disconnected and highly vulnerable," in the words of a leading British military adviser. Thus the former colonies needed to be kept sweet and content. Canada was neither, and something had to be done to prevent the most important dominion—the oldest, biggest, wealthiest dominion—from making a public fuss, from ostentatiously opting out of an important foreign policy decision. It helped, of course, that the British wanted to reassure the Americans as well.

The answer, as is often the case in diplomacy, was discovered in a lawyer's briefcase. In the deep workings of London's bureaucracy in Whitehall, a legal opinion was concocted to explain that there was no hurry to renew the alliance. It could remain in force while the interested parties concentrated their attention on finding an instrument amenable to all. At the Washington Conference later in 1921, the Anglo–Japanese Alliance was quietly put to sleep, and two vaguer international agreements and a naval disarmament treaty were put in its place. Canada attended as part of a British Empire delegation. A four-power accord signed by Britain, the United States, France, and Japan promised to respect one another's rights in the Pacific and to consult each other in the event of aggression by another power.

No real substitute for the Anglo–Japanese Alliance was found, and its abandonment was a major strategic error for both Great

Britain and Canada. Britain no longer had a guarantee of Japanese support in the Pacific, and that area now had to be added to the many others safeguarded by an overextended Royal Navy. Canada had to depend more heavily on the United States in view of potential instability in the Pacific. The Americans might insist on protecting any Canadian territory that could be used as a springboard for an attack on their own country. Unless Britain could assist Canada, or unless Canadians were willing to spend much more on defence, the country would find itself (in the words of a future chief of the naval staff), "entirely in the hands of the friendly neighbour."

The 1921 Imperial Conference also marked the end of another alliance: the empire partnership that Borden had sought to build during World War I. An association cannot survive on ultimatums, and that is what Meighen had given the conference. His priorities and ambitions and viewpoints must be met completely, and those of Australia relegated to the dustbin, or Canada would not co-operate. In short, Meighen implicitly rejected the notion of consensual empire policies reached in the interests of the whole.

Borden's co-operative, consultative empire was doomed to failure anyway. To make the imperial alliance work, the dominion prime ministers had to be present in London. Wartime experience had demonstrated that the premiers would not delegate that responsibility and that the British would not pay any attention to lesser lights from the colonies. It was a long voyage to London, however, especially from Australia and New Zealand, and a prime minister constantly away from home paid a huge political price, as Borden had discovered. The urgency, moreover, had gone with the war's end. The British had been willing to share some of their power in 1917–1918, when their situation was desperate, but they had no overwhelming desire to continue the experiment. Meighen showed in 1921 how irksome and inconvenient collective decision making could be. The constitutional meeting provided for in Resolution IX of the 1917 Imperial War Cabinet, with the aim of closer imperial co-operation, was never held.

Something else was happening too. Meighen's contention that Canadian advice on American questions must be followed by the whole empire was the logical outgrowth of a World War I Canadian nationalism, which was increasingly incompatible with a unified empire. More and more Canadians believed ever more strongly that they were going to have to control their own future. Even the devotedly pro-empire Borden became unhappy with the country's peculiar constitutional condition. The prime minister had written to his wife from the Paris Peace Conference that Canada was in "an anomalous position; a nation that is not a nation." That had to change.

CHAPTER THREE

Doing Good by Stealth, 1921–1930

W ILLIAM LYON MACKENZIE KING was by nature the most careful and circumspect of people. He was capable of decisive movement, but creative inaction and compromise were the prominent features of the King political style. He always felt safest and most at ease in the middle, searching for consensus, avoiding what he thought was poor public policy. As one of his severest critics, F.R. Scott, summarized the philosophy,

> Let us raise up a temple
> To the cult of mediocrity,
> Do nothing by halves
> Which can be done by quarters.

Unimpressive in appearance, uninspiring, even a bit timid, King understood that he had no personal magnetism or flair. All he could do was to make the best of his considerable intellect and qualities of judgment. If he was not memorable, that might just be an advantage—so little was expected of him. Yousuf Karsh, the famous photographer, recalled that King was anxious above all else "to discourage the slightest animation or brightness in his personality," because it might conflict with the grey, colourless image that he cultivated. "He might be laughing heartily at some anecdote . . . [but] at the threat of the shutter, he would struggle to retain his look of composure, his public stage act, protesting, 'Karsh, you must *not* take a picture now!'"

The Liberal election victory in 1921 did not bring King an assured majority in Parliament. He had just short of half of the 235 seats. The Progressives, a Western protest party that had prevailed in a stunning sixty-five constituencies, could not be lured into the Cabinet. They would have to be constantly watched and wooed. Nor was King completely secure within his own party. Members of the protectionist wing of the Liberal Party had challenged his leadership in the past and might do so again, especially as he seemed likely to try to satisfy the Progressives with lower tariffs. The prime minister was a relatively inexperienced politician, as he privately acknowledged. He had been a member of parliament for scarcely five years, and had only limited ministerial experience. On the day that he gave his first House of Commons speech as the country's leader, King wrote in his diary, "Members & the public forget that in actual parliamentary experience & practice tho' Prime Minister I am really a novice of but two or three years' experience. I can hope to grow with practice."

Caution extended to foreign policy. King's watchword was unity, as Laurier's had been, keeping the disparate parts of a young and developing country together and focussed on the national task ahead, attempting to reconcile the different points of view about Canada's global future. Quebec had given all its seats to the Liberals in large measure because they had opposed conscription during World War I, and they displayed scepticism towards British Empire commitments. The Progressives were no less suspicious of external entanglements. Arthur Meighen's Conservatives, on the other hand, took enormous pride in Sir Robert Borden's wartime vision of national greatness within a greater imperial whole. National salvation lay in the strongest possible tie to Britain, Tories believed, and Canadians would always be ready to fly to its side if and when some unspecified need arose.

King was an amalgam of all views: nationalist, isolationist, imperialist, internationalist. He had no difficulty in sympathizing with Quebecers and Progressives who saw the dangers of imperial association. Indeed, he liked to reflect on the legacy of his grandfather, William Lyon Mackenzie, who had led a rebellion against the British in 1837. Like his namesake, King had serious reservations about the direction in which English politicians might want to take Canada and the empire. Yet the prime minister cherished and admired Great Britain and the imperial tradition for giving Canada its freedoms, for imparting a sane and responsible political culture, and for keeping Canada out of the American orbit.

HINTS AND HALIBUTS

If there were to be true national unity, if Canada were to be more than a British satellite, King's government would have to demonstrate to Canadians that they and they alone could make decisions about their external life. That meant disengaging Canadian foreign policy from that of the British Empire, and necessitated some very firm and bold foreign policy steps in King's early years as prime minister. This was the paradox: a careful man who set out on a radical course, so that Canadians could control their own future in as cautious or as radical a manner as they chose.

Such a policy was appropriate for the time. The 1920s were a decade of nationalism, when organizations such as the Canadian Institute of International Affairs, the League of Nations Society, and the Canadian Radio League sprouted up with the aim of creating an educated public and a separate national identity.

King's first major foreign policy act was to visit Washington in July 1922. He loved to indulge in personal statesmanship and in the exchange of warm, woolly, and high-minded international rhetoric, the bulk of which he genuinely believed. He was very much at home in the United States, having spent postgraduate years at Harvard and the University of Chicago and World War I as an industrial consultant to the great Rockefeller and Carnegie business empires. Little wonder that many Tories called him "the American."

While in Washington, King did not follow up on Borden's initiative to establish Canadian diplomatic representation there. Instead he pushed for a modernization of the Rush-Bagot Agreement, the accord that had regulated naval armaments on the Great Lakes since 1817. The agreement had sometimes been bent out of shape by American or British military ambitions, but it had survived to become one of those potent symbols of friendship between Canada and the United States. The two countries had had no need to fortify their borders for well over a century, the mythology ran. Their leaders talked over their problems and reached solutions amicably. King had himself been one of the leaders of a pre-war movement to celebrate a century of North American peacefulness. How better to send a message to the bloodthirsty Europeans about the proper conduct of international business?

A draft Rush-Bagot Treaty was duly produced and sent to the British for examination. The important point to note is the Canadian government's commitment—made clear in its communication to London—to a separate signature of any accord resulting from the Canadian–American negotiation. Although this might have sounded mundane, it was actually highly significant. The British counted among their imperial prerogatives the signature of all treaties entered into by any of their "self-governing dominions." The theory was that the empire had and must continue to have a diplomatic unity; Britain spoke for Canada and the other dominions on all the great issues of foreign policy. Ottawa had in fact been negotiating its own commercial agreements for many years, and signing them as well, but there was always a British countersignature.

No further progress was made on the Rush-Bagot front, and the idea was dropped, but King had hinted strongly that he was going to demand greater autonomy in the formulation and conduct of Canadian external policy. Thus the British should not have been surprised when King soon made the same argument over another proposed Canadian–American treaty, this time for the protection of the Pacific halibut fishery. Surprised the British may not have been. Upset and indignant they certainly were, but King let it be known in no uncertain terms that he would immediately appoint a full-fledged diplomatic representative to Washington if he were denied the right to a separate signature on a purely North American instrument. Faced with the greater threat of an independent Canadian legation in a pivotal foreign capital, the British crumbled. On 2 March 1923, the Halibut Treaty was concluded, with a Canadian minister signing alone on behalf of his country for the first time.

THE LION AND HER CUBS

Even before the Halibut Treaty, Mackenzie King had demonstrated his determination to distinguish between British and Canadian diplomacy. In the fall of 1922 the Chanak Affair erupted, so called after a beleaguered British garrison town on the Dardanelles Straits in Asia Minor. The garrison was threatened by Turkish nationalist troops, hell-bent on driving out occupying armies left over from World War I. The British government decided to fight to maintain its position at Chanak and at nearby Constantinople.

Out went the telegrams from Colonial Secretary Winston Churchill requesting the assistance of the empire in this time of crisis. The Toronto *Globe* headlined, "British Lion Calls Cubs to Face the Beast of Asia." Veterans of the last war volunteered in the king's service. Later into the crisis, Arthur Meighen trumpeted that, when the lion roared, there could be no other answer but "Ready, aye ready; we stand by you." The prime minister, however, did not share in the enthusiasm.

Churchill's bad manners and bad tactics had not helped to bring Canada on side. On the Friday evening of 15 September, the colonial secretary sent his message asking the dominions if they wished "to associate themselves with the action we are taking and whether they would desire to be represented by a contingent," diplomatic parlance for a request. Only a few hours later, as the telegram was being decoded, Churchill issued a manifesto to British newspapers repeating the entreaty made to the dominions. In a clear breach of imperial etiquette, a private appeal had been made public, and this before the original message had reached the prime minister. The telegram took a long time to make its way through the weekend bureaucracy, and King at any event was away from Ottawa in his constituency. A Toronto *Star* reporter informed him on Saturday afternoon of the British invitation.

Surprised and miffed, King was noncommittal. There would be a Cabinet meeting on Monday, he told the reporter, where the matter could be considered. King saw immediately that the issue was a serious one. Privately, he wrote that it would "arouse jingoism & with jingo-ism passion, which combined with the prejudice against me on account of conscription & and war feeling still lingering, will mean a heavy & difficult role for me. It might mean anything, attempts at my life etc. I shall be firm . . . I am convinced that it is not right to take this country into another European war, & I shall resist to the utter-most." Parliament would have to make any such weighty decision, and King did not think that it would favour a Canadian contingent. He was certain that the people were with him.

Churchill soon returned with another telegram moderating the British stance. The real targets of the original request were Australia and New Zealand, he said, but sending a Canadian contingent would be an immense contribution to empire solidarity. An announcement of Canada's willingness to associate itself in the enter-prise and to send forces if necessary would be "quite sufficient." Cabinet members had been annoyed during the Monday meeting, but they now seriously considered lending moral support to the imperial cause. Nevertheless, King's reluctance won out. A further request on 19 September from British prime minister Lloyd George was met simply with a terse rebuff; Canada did not need to take lessons in imperial loyalty from anyone.

Conflict did not come at Chanak. In mid-October an armistice with the Turks was agreed to and the crisis was over. While he had felt his way carefully from step to step—mindful, among other things, of his minority government—King had known his own mind from the outset. Another war was simply unacceptable so soon after the last one and in so remote a location, particularly when Churchill had admitted in his second telegram that the situation was in all probability not that serious. King nevertheless cleverly deflected responsibility by arguing that the matter was for Parliament and not the government alone to decide. The strategy served him well, but it was essentially dishonest. King and the Cabinet had no intention of summoning Parliament unless they, as the country's executive author-ity, were going to recommend intervention, and they were not pre-pared to do so. "Parliament will decide" was a hollow promise.

For Canadian nationalists, Chanak was a decisive event. King had beaten off the imperial centralizers. O.D. Skelton, a Queen's

University professor and authority on Canadian foreign and economic policy, exulted in a letter to the prime minister: "Never again will a Canadian Government be stampeded against its better judgement into giving blank cheques to British diplomacy, now that your Government has set this example of firm and self-respecting deliberation." Skelton had made a powerful plea for a separate Canadian external policy in an address at the Ottawa Branch of the Canadian Club earlier in the year. King was in the audience, and was mightily impressed.

But the Chanak crisis was not so much a British attempt to achieve a centralized imperial policy as it was a bid by Lloyd George and Churchill to use the dominions for their own ends. Their diplomacy was certainly not in the tradition of the common foreign policy championed by Sir Robert Borden (and by Lloyd George himself) during World War I. No information or consultation came Mackenzie King's way in the weeks and months leading up to mid-September 1922, and Canada had no opportunity to play a role in the development of British thinking. British politicians and officials were growing increasingly tired of the various efforts to bring partners into the foreign policy enterprise of their great empire. In that sense, Britain and Canada were much more in agreement than they realized. Both wanted their freedom.

Chanak was not a grand precedent. Canadian prime 'ministers since Macdonald had been chary of involvement in faraway imperial skirmishes, and England had in no way been threatened during the crisis. If it had been, Canadians would have demonstrated their allegiance. As Mackenzie King vowed to the Imperial Conference of 1923—admittedly behind closed doors—the population of Canada would respond to a "great and clear call of duty" when it came, just as in 1914. Such was the continuing power of imperial feeling in Canada.

Arthur Meighen dealt a major blow to his own political career with his "Ready, aye ready" speech, surely calculated to echo Laurier's words at the outbreak of World War I. King had cannily responded neither positively nor negatively, but Meighen committed himself in such a way as to reinforce his reputation as an outrageous imperialist out of touch with moderate public sentiment. Three years later, Meighen declared that Parliament ought to be summoned and its decision ratified by a general election before troops were ever again sent "beyond our shores." This reversal of position was clearly aimed at Conservative Party fortunes in Quebec, and he later jettisoned it when it yielded no electoral bonus.

In another postscript to Chanak, the 1923 Treaty of Lausanne brought peace between Turkey and the British Empire. King wanted none of it. Much to his relief, Canada was not invited to the peace conference, and the prime minister refused to have a Canadian representative sign the treaty. The British foreign secretary took the view that his signature bound the entire empire, Canada included. King did not dispute this interpretation, simply arguing that it would be for the Canadian Parliament to decide—"should the occasion arise, in the light of all the circumstances, and in light of the manner in which this Treaty was negotiated"—the extent of any obligations the country might have. The diplomatic unity of the empire lived on, in other words, but its meaning was being redefined and its scope limited by King's strictures. It is worth noting, however, that all this hairsplitting would undoubtedly have been lost on an American or an Argentinian at this stage. To most foreigners, Canada was a British dominion, and that meant subordination, pure and simple.

TOTAL VICTORY

The Imperial Conference of 1923 was Mackenzie King's first, and the prospect exhilarated and frightened him. Great Britain was his emotional touchstone. He wished he could emulate the scope and style of British leaders. He was in awe of the monarchy. He revelled in London society: the ritualistic exchange of calling cards, dressing up for cocktail parties and grand dinners, rubbing shoulders with the wealthy, famous, and titled. Fifty invitations awaited him when he arrived at his London hotel in late September.

King worried that he was not up to the physical and mental demands that would be put on him over a gruelling five weeks. "I am filled with terror," he wrote. "It is much worse than a general election." Although he greatly admired the British and sought their company, he did not fully trust them. He would remember the Chanak incident until the end of his days, knowing that the imperialists were always set to spring another trap. It was quite clear, the prime minister recorded in his diary, that the "whole purpose of the Conference is a centralizing imperial policy, first re foreign policy to be made in London & next for control of Navy and distribution of cost of upkeep among outlying dominions."

King fortified himself against the wiles and temptations of London by bringing in O.D. Skelton as an adviser. Over the summer, Skelton single-handedly created a briefing book for the conference. In fluent, clear-minded, persuasive prose, his memoranda argued that decisions about foreign policy had to be taken in Canada, for Canada, by Canadians. That had been the trend over a great many decades, supported by and large by both political parties. Ottawa in fact already occupied most of the external affairs ground. Canadian officials and politicians made tariffs and trading arrangements; they controlled immigration and emigration; they handled most local defence matters; and they managed the complex day-to-day relationship with the United States. But under the recent influence of Borden and Meighen, Skelton stated, generations of healthy development were being compromised. If this dangerous movement towards a united imperial foreign policy were to take permanent hold, a common policy exercised through the British Foreign Office with as little consultation as possible would impose the maximum of responsibility and the minimum of control.

Historians such as C.P. Stacey and Philip Wigley have argued that Skelton was at best misrepresenting the state of affairs in Anglo–dominion relations and at worst out-and-out lying about them. His most conspicuous sin was to suggest that the British were making a unilateral grab for power and attempting to reverse the course of Canadian history. Instead it was King who was going back on arrangements worked out freely by the two governments since Borden's election in 1911. Moreover, Wigley suggests that it is fanciful to think a common imperial policy robbed Canada of all the parliamentary and executive authority it had established in the area of

O.D. Skelton (National Archives of Canada, C 2126)

foreign policy down the years. He admits, however, that the Chanak incident did lend a certain plausibility to Skelton's notion of an evolving system in which the British controlled the machinery and Canadians were expected to do as they were told.

Skelton was now an important participant in Canadian foreign policy. He was frequently called anti-British, and there is no doubt that he could display a hard edge when he spoke or wrote about Great Britain. He clearly did not have King's emotional and political stake in the British connection. What he did have was a deep sympathy for the French fact in Canada and a strong regard for the inheritance of Sir Wilfrid Laurier, his friend and the subject of one of his biographies. This led him to worry that imperialist emotions tempted Canadians away from tolerance for differences in language, religion, and outlook. How much better to develop as true Canadians and not as tiny reproductions of the English. How much better the decency of North America than the internecine rivalries of Europe.

J.W. Dafoe, the powerful editor of the *Manitoba Free Press*, the leading foreign policy newspaper in the country, also accompanied King to the conference. Like Skelton, Dafoe was a fervent Liberal and nationalist. Unlike Skelton, Dafoe was also a fervent anglophile. He sought full Canadian autonomy but wished to retain the closest possible ties with Great Britain. The prime minister included Dafoe in the delegation because he could be counted on to send home favourable reviews of the Canadian performance at the conference. Otherwise, it seemed all too likely to King that Canadian newspapers would be full of dispatches from "Tory Imperialist sources."

Dafoe was no fan of King: "I am afraid his conceit in his ability to take care of himself is equalled only by his ignorance." Nonetheless, Dafoe generally approved of the prime minister's stands on Chanak and the Halibut Treaty, and he was anxious to be of use and to put forward his views. Dafoe and his boss, Sir Clifford Sifton, advocated a definition "in black and white [of] the actual constitutional status of Canadian equality with Great Britain under the Crown." Without such an understanding, weak leaders might at some point accept commitments that circumscribed or even destroyed Canada's growing autonomy.

King rejected Dafoe's idea of a formal declaration out of hand, but he was more than happy to fire Skelton's bullets at the proponents of unified empire policies. The British foreign secretary, Lord Curzon, began his conference description of foreign affairs with the comment that the Foreign Office was carrying on "the foreign policy which is not that of these islands alone, but that of the Empire." King noted the remark and, following his academic adviser's reasoning closely, responded that the habit of self-government was the very stuff of the British Empire. The dominions had that right just as did

Great Britain itself, and it was inevitable that they would all seek to control the foreign relationships that primarily concerned themselves. That was not isolationism or separatism. Where the arc of Canadian interests intersected that of British interests, or where issues arose common to all parts of the empire, the King government would be glad to confer at an imperial conference or through some other means. But Ottawa must ultimately decide its own actions.

We have seen that the Foreign Office personnel also wished to be free of the notion of a common policy commonly arrived at. They continued to believe that they were administering the foreign policy of an empire, but they did not want to share that authority. Why should they? The dominions were very small powers, and their leaders narrow provincial folk apt to want status for themselves and their countries without the will to take on wider responsibilities. Besides, international diplomacy moved too fast to allow consultation and consensus. Someone had to be in charge of the foreign policy of the huge, scattered British Empire. If not the British foreign secretary, then who?

When the conference resolutions on foreign policy were drafted by Curzon's staff, therefore, the continuing existence of an imperial foreign policy was assumed. King exploded that he could approve nothing without the knowledge and sanction of his own Parliament. Curzon appeared to give way after what the prime minister described as "a most difficult and unpleasant hour or two," but the foreign secretary returned to the attack the next day. King countered with a paragraph of his own, "putting in so many words that we could not permit an obligation in matters of foreign policy beyond those things which we regarded as of immediate and direct interest." Prime Minister Jan Smuts of South Africa arrived on the scene as a mediator, chuckling, "Mackenzie King, you are a very terrible person; you are giving us an awful lot of trouble." Curzon was not as good natured, telling his wife with some justification that King was "obstinate, tiresome and stupid . . . nervously afraid of being turned out of his own Parliament when he gets back."

Despite all his personal insecurities and desire to be liked, King was willing to make enemies. He warned his imperial colleagues that if he did not get his modifications the Canadian government would have to consider whether it could accept an invitation to future conferences. When Curzon persisted in opposing King's paragraph, the prime minister threatened to produce his own public statement repudiating the conference conclusions. Curzon gave way and the final report carried King's sting, devastatingly so from the imperial point of view. "This Conference," the document read, "is a conference of representatives of the several Governments of the Empire; its views and conclusions on Foreign Policy . . . are necessarily subject to the actions of the Governments and Parliaments of the various portions of the Empire, and it trusts that the results of its deliberations will meet with their approval." Smuts told King, "You ought to be satisfied. Canada has had her way in everything."

"Everything" included a notable advance in the treaty-making power of the dominions. Much to King's surprise and pleasure, the victory came without much of a fight. Realizing that the dominions had been "encouraged by the events of the last few years to regard themselves as members of a community of free nations," the British decided to regard the Halibut Treaty not as an aberration but as a precedent. Each dominion therefore received exclusive full powers to negotiate and sign its own bilateral treaties. The path was open to a conference declaration along these lines.

DEFENCE AGAINST WHOM?

Canada took the same autonomist line on defence questions. The first lord of the Admiralty, Leopold Amery, assured King before the conference that the conception of a navy run from London and subscribed to by the dominions was completely dead. Amery's department nevertheless issued a pre-conference plan calling for the development of dominion navies capable of co-operating with Britain in dominion and empire defence. For Skelton this was an attempt to achieve an old aim by a circuitous route. As he interpreted the Admiralty documents, "Each Dominion is to have its own Naval Force, but the Admiralty is to be a central controlling authority, outlining policy and fitting the various local units into a mosaic." Particularly worrying was the British proposal to make the Admiralty manifesto public by issuing it to the press. More shades of Chanak?

In the period since the end of World War I, no Canadian government had shown much interest in defence—not the Borden or Meighen administrations and certainly not that of Mackenzie King. As a device for cost-cutting and efficiency, King consolidated the three services in a single department under a minister of national defence from 1922. His first defence budget reduced expenditure to a little over $12 million, down from $15 million. At $1.46 per capita, this was a trifling amount by any standard. When the prime minister was done with his handiwork, the navy was left with a $1.5 million share. Naval authorities thought it best to use such a small sum primarily for a reserve force, which might form the core of something substantial in the future.

Why did Canada need more? "Defence against whom?" as King had asked when opposition leader in 1920. The Canadian army did have Defence Scheme No. 1, which envisaged an attack to the south designed to buy time in the event of a British Empire conflict against the United States, but it was surely folly to plan for a war that could never be won, and one against a powerful friend to boot. From the rest of the world, there seemed little need for protection. The country was not sponging on the British for defence, Skelton advised King. "Canada is not contributing in any appreciable measure to the sum of risks in which the British Empire may be involved; she is practically immune, or may easily be made so from any permanent and crippling attack by an overseas power."

Almost as soon as he arrived in England, the prime minister let Amery know that his dominion was neither going to spend any money on the navy nor allow the Admiralty to release its memorandum urging empire-wide action. The latter was a transparent attempt to go over the head of the government directly to the Canadian people, and King resented it. Not daunted, Amery took King and the other prime ministers aboard a warship to inspect the magnificent sight of the British fleet arrayed at Spithead. The British cabinet minister could not refrain from telling his Canadian guest that the Royal Navy "is why you are Prime Minister of Canada and not, at best, one of the Senators for the American State of Ontario." This was tactless but partly true, as King would have readily admitted. The prime minister, however, was too seasick to say anything.

King refused absolutely to embark on even a reduced version of the naval program Amery wanted. According to Dafoe's diary, the Canadian leader, again echoing Skelton, informed the conference that

> Canada had not given and would not give Empire any problems of defence or obligations; her policies would not involve Empire in trouble. She had made immense contributions, men, money for defence of Great Britain when attacked. Naval policy for Canada must take cognizance of geographical considerations; this was equally true of Great Britain and Australia. If Canada were similarly situated, Canadian feelings would be different. Among Canada's many problems, one of the most serious was to compete with the u.s. in attracting and holding money and people. Difficulties would be accentuated if impression was created that people of Canada were much more likely than people of u.s. to be involved in war.

The discussion on air defence followed the same pattern as the naval talks. The British had by now jettisoned a post-armistice call for an imperial air force, but they had not lost their interest in standardization, co-ordination, and extensive co-operation. The Air Ministry pointed out that airpower had made London, "the Capital of the Empire," vulnerable for the first time in many centuries. The Royal Air Force was therefore concerned about the form of organization that would best promote mutual assistance should the necessity arise. The secretary of state for air conceded that it was up to the dominions to develop their own air forces, but "the greater the development . . . the better it will be for us and the easier it will be to solve our problems." British officials pointed out that in the event of war both sides could expect to have their aircrew wiped out in short order. Success or failure would turn on "how rapidly others could be drafted to take their places." The first brunt of the air attack would obviously fall upon the British, but "subsequent reinforcements of the British Air Forces by Dominion pilots would come in a most invaluable form and at a most critical moment."

The British agreed that Canada needed only a modest air force. King was unwilling, however, to make any commitments beyond "a willingness to have our organization uniform . . . and a readiness to accept suggestions." Nevertheless, he told the conference "that in considering defence, having regard to the necessity of going to Parliament to ask for appropriations, it may be possible for us to do more at one particular time with one branch than with another. Just at the present time, the matter of Air Defence is one to which we have been giving a good deal of attention and we expect to give it a good deal more." Development of the air force was the most promising area of defence expenditure at this time, the prime minister believed, because "the machines could be used for civilian purposes—surveying, anti-smuggling etc.—and the matter [of military expense] could be therefore to some extent disguised." Despite his reputation for pusillanimity, King was one of the very few Canadian politicians to argue in the 1920s that the development of an air force was "wholly essential."

A draft British resolution on air force questions provoked further disagreement at the Imperial Conference of 1923. A relatively innocuous-sounding document, it recommended the maximum possible co-operation in organization, training, doctrine, and equipment, so that the air forces of the empire could work together in peace or war. This was in line with long-established principles of imperial defence, and the draft made clear that nothing would impair "the complete control" of the various governments and parliaments. Yet King retaliated with several drafts of his own, ultimately leaving the British effort in tatters. Even a reference to the regular exchange of air force officers between member countries of the empire was sacrificed. King explained that this had been done in order to avoid any possible misunderstanding. The New Zealand leader asked, "Do I understand you to say, Mr. Mackenzie King, that there is no objection to the interchange of personnel?" The Canadian chief replied that he had no difficulty whatsoever. "It is being done at the present time." It was left to the South African premier to end the discussion. "It is," said Smuts of King's method, "what they call doing good by stealth!"

This was as accurate and subtle a description as has ever been offered. Nothing was more calculated than the imperial issue to bring out the inherent divisions in the Canadian psyche, a challenge that King answered with evasion, indirection, and sometimes with downright deceit, always certain that he was doing what was necessary and best. He told his hosts in 1923 that he was acting in their interests and in those of a healthy and vibrant Anglo–Canadian relationship. Imperial defence commitments would play into the hands of Canadian enemies of the British Empire, those who wished to fight "against me in my desire to see the Empire maintained and developed." There was more than a hint of the self-serving in this argument, but also a genuine concern for the future of the empire.

"GONE FAT"

Three years later King went to his next imperial conference largely satisfied with the state of Anglo–Canadian relations. By 1926 Canada had most of the freedoms it needed. The distinction between what

The imperial conference of 1926: British prime minister Baldwin and Mackenzie King flank King George V (National Archives of Canada, PA 1877700)

was national and what was imperial might cause further problems, "but with good will and some experimenting I have no doubt that the line of demarcation will eventually be drawn with reasonable clearness." The tie with Britain remained strong, as King believed it should and must. Canada would continue to grow to liberty under "one king, one flag and one ideal."

Circumstances contributed to King's sense of well-being. Europe, so often threatening to pull Canada into its difficulties, had been stabilized by the 1925 Locarno Treaty. This guaranteed the common frontiers of Belgium, France, and Germany, brought the latter back into the world community, and won the Nobel Peace Prize for British foreign secretary Austin Chamberlain. The accord had a clause exempting the dominions from its terms unless their governments explicitly chose otherwise. After the 1926 election, King finally had a comfortable margin in the House of Commons, and he was relieved of looking over his shoulder at rivals in his own and other parties. He also had a trusted confidante and counsellor in foreign policy. O.D. Skelton had been brought into the Department of External Affairs on a permanent basis. Loring Christie, with whom the prime minister was never comfortable, had been squeezed out of the department, and Skelton became for King what Christie had been for Borden. The right advice was available hour by hour, and a start could be made on a department that really meant something.

The radicals in the British Empire were no longer the Canadians but the Irish and the South Africans, who were pressing hard for decentralization on a grand scale. Australia and New Zealand, the other members of the self-governing part of the empire, were committed by both loyalty and strategic necessity to stand by Great Britain, almost no matter what. King was in the middle, where he preferred to be. An Irish Cabinet minister, disappointed by the Mackenzie King who turned up at the Imperial Conference of 1926, wrote home that the Canadian prime minister had "disimproved" since 1923, "gone fat and American and self-complacent."

The main preoccupation of the conference was to find a means of accommodating J.B.M. Hertzog, General Smuts's successor as prime minister of South Africa. Hertzog had been elected on a tough nationalist platform, and he served notice that a form of words must be manufactured to announce dominion independence to the world. This was very much the kind of thing that we have seen Dafoe and Sifton whispering about to King; Skelton took the same tack in the advice he gave the prime minister prior to the conference. King, as before, would have preferred no formalized declaration whatever, public or otherwise, but he and the other delegates had to take notice of Hertzog, who was threatening dire consequences if he did not get what he was after.

King was suffering from a bad cold. He was none too vocal at the meetings of the Committee on Inter-Imperial Relations, chaired by former British prime minister Lord Balfour. The committee considered various draft definitions of dominion status. Quietly, however, the Canadian kept the protagonists talking, moved them towards consensus, and softened extreme language. He took a particular stand against any hint of "independence." A declaration of independence had been the method employed to break the American colonies away from Britain a hundred and fifty years before, and King told his conference colleagues that it would be politically disastrous for him to return home with a separatist tract. Hertzog dropped the reference to independence and in return received King's help in salvaging much of the South African message. Slowly the sentences emerged to satisfy most tastes. The dominions were described as "autonomous Communities within the British Empire, equal in status, in no way subordinate one to another in any aspect of their domestic or external affairs, though united by a common allegiance to the Crown, and freely associated as members of the British Commonwealth of Nations."

The Hertzog definition was not a complete nationalist rout. The report of the Balfour committee, in which the new formula was embedded, underlined the responsibilities, interests, and goals that held Britain and the dominions together. There might be such a thing as equality of status, but there remained a distinct inequality of stature. Britain was the ringleader of the empire and would continue to speak and act on behalf of the entire group in the big questions of diplomacy and defence. Hertzog, so recently a rebel but now appeased, accepted this interpretation. As the other delegates did, he went home full of goodwill and faith in a future together. "No common cause will, in our opinion, be . . . imperilled," the Balfour Report confidently asserted.

Yet there was clearly a different order of things, symbolized by the unaccustomed prominence given to the term "the British Commonwealth of Nations." The equality of British and dominion status was recognized as "the root principle governing our Inter-Imperial Relations." As old Balfour put it, drafting his report as he sat up in bed, "Every self-governing member of the Empire is now the master of its destiny. In fact, if not always in form, it is subject to no compulsion whatever." The British Empire had changed forever. Attention would inevitably now be focussed on all the cases in which form did not meet the fact of equality.

The one Canadian demand at the imperial conference was a good deal more modest than Hertzog's. King was intent on clarifying the role of the governor general, who not only represented the Crown but also served as agent of the British government and official channel of communication between Ottawa and London. King and many others around the empire had long considered the political character of the office a holdover from colonial days. The prime minister, it is true, was at first greatly impressed by Lord Byng. Byng had heroically commanded Canadian troops in the great battle at Vimy Ridge in 1917, and had been governor general of Canada since 1921. Prime minister and governor general were on extremely friendly terms, and as late as April 1926 King could write that Byng had "succeeded in banishing from the public mind and from the mind of his Ministers any suspicion that he regards himself as the representative of the Government of Great Britain or of any of its Departments rather than as the representative of His Majesty." But that was before the King–Byng Crisis.

The crisis had unfolded after King called an election in October 1925. The Liberals won fewer seats than the Conservatives but enough to carry on in power with the help of the Progressives. The King government soon embroiled itself in a customs scandal, however, much to the disgust of the Progressives, and was about to be censured in the House of Commons late in June 1926 when King went to the governor general to request the dissolution of the House and an election. Byng, who thought that King should have stepped aside after the election, opted to give the leader of the opposition a chance to govern. Conservative leader Arthur Meighen accepted, but his administration collapsed in a matter of days. Byng then handed Meighen the dissolution that he had denied to King. Using the cry that the constitution had been violated and Canadian autonomy compromised, King glided to an impressive win in the general election of September 1926. Although other questions also moved the electorate, the constitutional issue carried conviction and votes.

Byng had not actually acted improperly, but it was easy for King to believe that he had. A British governor general had refused to take his Canadian prime minister's advice, and must have done so, King thought, because of English Tory bias. Responsible government meant nothing. In fact, the governor general had the power and the duty to prevent King from having an election when an alternative government was available. Byng never consulted the British government, despite King's extraordinary suggestion that he do so, or in any way acted as an agent of Downing Street. The governor general behaved throughout in a completely upright, honest, and decent manner, but he was soon on his way home beaten and disillusioned. King proved the better politician and tactician, if not the better person.

King came to the imperial conference right after the election campaign, with the Byng issue and perhaps a bit of revenge on his agenda. The prime minister gave the impression that reform in this area was crucial to his full co-operation in future imperial affairs, but his pugnacious stance encountered no dissent. The conference report stated that the governor general was no more and no less than a stand-in for the Crown, holding in all essentials the same position in the administration of the dominion government as the monarch did in Great Britain. The report said nothing about either what Lord Byng had done in Canada or what the powers of the governor general were as a representative of the monarchy. Although difficult to define precisely and always potentially controversial, those powers remained unimpaired.

A position was needed to replace the governor general as the British government representative in Ottawa. King plumped for a high commissioner with "diplomatic and consular powers." The idea found favour in Whitehall, not least with Leo Amery. Amery had been appointed in 1925 to fill the new post of dominions secretary, created to reflect the changed status of the self-governing colonies. Amery was one of a number of British politicians and officials who sought to create a new imperial unity through an integrated policy of preferential tariffs and capital investment in and emigration to the dominions. The appointment in 1928 of a British high commissioner to Canada with economic expertise was an explicit victory for the Amery vision. Along with his diplomatic duties—he was in effect the British ambassador in Canada—Sir William Clark was specifically charged with the task of stimulating trade and investment and, in the British prime minister's words, helping Canadians "to repurchase in time, the control of Canadian industries now in American hands."

Clark was able to do little along these lines. Neither the British nor the Canadian government in the 1920s was willing to take the hard steps to reinvent the empire economically. Few changes were made in the tariff policies of the two countries. The Americans surpassed the British as the premier non-resident investor in Canada. Five hundred thousand British immigrants came to Canada in these years, but a relatively small number—perhaps 20 percent—came under the provisions of various empire or British government settlement plans.

THE "DOCTRINE OF SEPARATION"

King was well aware that Canada's emerging international status required a machinery for diplomacy. The key to everything was Skelton, who had been persuaded to take a leave of absence from Queen's University in 1924 and the next year had become the undersecretary of state at the Department of External Affairs, replacing the aged Sir Joseph Pope. Skelton's goal from the beginning was an independent foreign policy and an external affairs ministry of scope, depth, and quality to go with it. There was a long way to go. Skelton took over a department that had 101 employees but only three officers who could be expected to carry out high-level administrative or policy tasks. The undersecretary was one of the three. Skelton had a big appetite for work, but as he reported to King after nine months in the job, "It is absolutely impossible, even with 7-day weeks and 16-hour days to secure the independent and exact knowledge of external affairs which has now become desirable."

Skelton sought out well-qualified personnel, patterning External Affairs after the British Foreign Office, with the all-round, adaptable foreign service officer at the core of the system. First came Jean Désy, a bilingual university professor and the department's first senior francophone. He was followed by a group of younger men in their late twenties and early thirties, all with work experience, extensive academic training, and—because Skelton insisted—a commitment to Canadian autonomy. A believer in the merit principle, Skelton brought in the majority of his recruits by competitive examination. Some of the major figures of later years, including L.B. Pearson, Norman Robertson, Hugh Keenleyside, and Hume Wrong, entered the Department of External Affairs during the period from 1927 to 1929. Wrong did not have to write an exam. As the grandson of a nineteenth-century Liberal leader, Edward Blake, and the son of historian George Wrong, he did not have to suffer that indignity.

Canada had had a high commissioner in London since 1880, and immigration and trade offices abroad from the nineteenth century, as well as a government representative in Paris from 1882 and at the League of Nations from 1925. Yet none of these had any diplomatic standing. In the late 1920s, Canada sent its first diplomats to foreign countries. Vincent Massey, a Cabinet minister who had been ousted at the polls, became Canadian minister (a junior form of ambassador) to the United States in 1927. The government had its eye next on Japan, which offered a window on the Pacific but was also, more importantly, the source of a sticky immigration problem. Bigotry raised the spectre of "yellow hordes" on the Canadian west coast, and there were demands for the exclusion of all Japanese immigrants. King instead wanted to use a Canadian legation in Japan to screen and limit applicants rigorously. Before Tokyo, however, France should be recognized more fully. King decided to upgrade the office of the commissioner general in Paris to a legation as a tribute to the importance of French Canada. In 1928 Phillippe Roy, commissioner general since 1911, was given the post. The Japanese turn

The grand style—Canadian diplomats in Japan: Herbert Marler is
seated with his wife (National Archives of Canada, PA 120413)

came in 1929. Herbert Marler, like Massey a very rich and expend-
able ex-Cabinet member, was the choice.

Both Marler and Massey were inclined to take themselves very
seriously. Their love of ceremony and diplomatic uniforms did not
sit well with their Skeltonian junior officers, who had been schooled
to hate ostentation, but wealth was an enormous asset for the first
Canadian envoys. It allowed them to live as they were accustomed to
do, and to make generous gestures to their government. Marler personally bought the land and building for the first legation in Tokyo.
Canada's exquisite embassy in Japan, built in the early 1990s, sits on
that site.

No more appointments were made until 1939. Despite the help of
rich diplomats, representation abroad ate up scarce resources. Rich
diplomats, indeed, were likely to have expensive tastes, even when
they were using other people's money. Massey found a lavish combination of home and office for himself on prestigious Massachusetts

Avenue in Washington; it cost the Canadian taxpayer $500 000. Nor did the idea of diplomatic representation find universal support. Many Anglo–Canadian partisans thought it disloyal to the empire to dispatch envoys as independent countries did. R.B. Bennett, who replaced Meighen as Conservative Party chief in 1927, boomed that the decision to send an envoy to Washington represented the "doctrine of separation." It was "but the evidence in many minds of the end of our connection with the Empire. For that is what it means. It is nothing else ultimately, because if we are a sovereign state we cannot belong to the British Empire."

TOWARDS A STATUTE OF WESTMINSTER

Bennett was proud and unrepentant in his imperial-mindedness, but the decisions of the Imperial Conference of 1926 were driving the empire-commonwealth in quite another direction. Lord Balfour's Committee on Inter-Imperial Relations had recommended a meeting of experts to study the many ways in which the dominions remained legally subordinate to Great Britain. Clearly more change, more equality, was on the horizon.

A uniform system of laws was part of the glue that bound the British Empire. The Parliament at Westminster was imperial in name and authority, and a complex legal nexus made the whole more than, and superior to, the parts. The parliaments of the dominions owed their origin to acts of the imperial parliament, which in turn defined dominion legislative powers. These enactments, such as the British North America Act in Canada, conferred the right to legislate for "peace, order and good government." Dominion legislation, however, was subject to Westminster's over-riding power to disallow or to reserve—that is, to withhold—assent to a dominion law. In most cases the scope of a dominion's legislation did not extend beyond its territorial limits. Moreover, the Colonial Laws Validity Act of 1865 stipulated that any dominion act that conflicted with imperial legislation was, to the extent of the conflict, null and void.

The powers of reservation and disallowance were by the 1920s mostly theoretical, not having been used for a very long time. Canadians, however, had felt the punch of the Colonial Laws Act very recently and tangibly. The Judicial Committee of the Privy Council in London was the final court of appeal for the entire British Empire. In a major court case, *Nadan v. the King*, the British had allowed a man convicted of liquor smuggling in Alberta to appeal to the JCPC on the grounds that Canadian legislation abolishing appeals to that body in criminal cases went against British laws allowing those appeals. The Nadan decision came down just before the Imperial Conference of 1926, and Canadian law journals and newspapers alike were full of complaint and outrage.

The meeting of legal specialists called for in the Balfour Report convened in 1929 as the Conference on the Operation of Dominion Legislation and Merchant Shipping. British officials planned extensively for the affair and were willing to make concessions. They suggested that a balanced deal be struck, a formal agreement written, and the whole arrangement given legal force as an act of the British Parliament. The act, concluded a key British functionary, "will rank as one of the landmarks of British constitutional history, and, as such, might properly be given some distinguishing title. The 'Constitutions of Westminster' or the 'Statute of Westminster,' with the addition of the year in which it becomes law, have been suggested as appropriate and are not without historical precedent." The Labour government of Ramsay MacDonald, however, was adamant that it could not go anywhere near as far, demanding instead that its bureaucrats move slowly and attack reforms one at a time.

The politicians could demand all they liked, but Britain was not in control of the process. The Balfour Report had made promises and established a momentum. The South African and Irish representatives at the conference were intent on radical surgery, as was the Canadian delegation. The delegation was led by Minister of Justice Ernest Lapointe of Quebec, a strong autonomist, and O.D. Skelton, who had set out his aim the year before as the removal of imperial legislative supremacy. A British delegate wrote that before the conference his colleagues had supposed the Balfour Report left "ample room for discussing the details of . . . an agreement, but the supposition has proved illusory. There is no argument which the Dominions have urged which cannot be justified from some part or another of the Report." The British were defeated on every single issue. The conference reached a consensus fairly quickly that the best solution was a Statute of Westminster giving the dominions their full legal freedom except in cases where they chose to remain subordinate.

The British government seriously considered refusing to sign the final report. Lapointe intervened decisively at this stage, putting "the fear of the Lord" into the London delegation, Skelton recalled. The report would have to go to cabinets and parliaments around the commonwealth, and to an imperial conference as well, but all sides agreed that their recommendations would almost certainly have to be implemented. There was no alternative, given the nationalist governments that held sway in South Africa, the Irish Free State, and Canada.

When all seemed lost for the British, and on the eve of the Imperial Conference of 1930, Whitehall received good news from Canada. Mackenzie King had gone to the people in a summer election, and this time he did not prevail. After almost a decade of Liberal rule interrupted only by a few weeks during the King–Byng crisis, the Conservatives were back in power. The British hoped that a sympathetic new Prime Minister R.B. Bennett would help them to revisit the Conference on the Operation of Dominion Legislation. A Statute of Westminster was perhaps not going to be necessary after all.

CHAPTER FOUR

Alberta, Not Abyssinia, 1930–1939

I N THE EAST BLOCK of the Parliament Buildings, O.D. Skelton sat at his desk thinking that he had badly miscalculated. Not long before the election of 1930, Queen's University had offered to make him principal, its highest office. If only he had known that the Liberals were going to lose, Skelton mused, he could have returned to the university to which he had devoted so much of his adult life. Now the Department of External Affairs and its chief officer were in the sights of a prime minister outspokenly opposed to the whole idea of a separate Canadian diplomacy. Conservative MPs were suggesting that the money spent on missions abroad would be better used for old-age pensions. Rumours swirled around Ottawa that External Affairs might be reduced in size, drastically revamped, or abolished altogether.

"BY A STATUTE, NOT BY CHOICE"

Whether the department was really headed for the guillotine is unknown and probably never will be known, but Skelton was certainly not in Prime Minister R.B. Bennett's plans. The undersecretary of state for external affairs was one of the country's leading Liberals and a prominent symbol of Mackenzie King nationalism, regarded by many of Bennett's generation and ideology as having undermined the imperial ties that had sustained the Canadian experience. Bennett recalled that he had every intention of "disposing" of Skelton at once. "He was close to Mr. King and his views were so far removed from any I had . . . but I made a great mistake. I didn't do it within the first 48 hours, and then I began to find that I couldn't get along without him. He knew everything. I kept saying, I'll fire him next week."

Skelton survived, and so did External Affairs. Bennett knew what Skelton represented, but hesitation and suspicion were slowly displaced by confidence and respect. Some years later, Bennett said that he could not imagine a better public servant than Skelton. Even though Bennett governed during the worst years of a catastrophic economic depression, Skelton's department was allowed to grow modestly, bringing in recruits such as Charles Ritchie and Léon Mayrand. Bennett was a confrontationalist, and some uncomfortable disagreements erupted with Skelton, but the plain fact is that the prime minister usually had little time for or interest in foreign policy. "I am Minister of External Affairs by a statute, not by choice," he freely and publicly admitted. Skelton consequently had more freedom to manoeuvre, more influence, than he had ever had under King, who had watched every aspect of foreign policy closely and made all the major decisions himself.

Bennett made two highly personal, and some said idiosyncratic, additions of his own to the Department of External Affairs. He first fired Vincent Massey, who had been moved by Mackenzie King from the mission in Washington to London just before the election. In Massey's place the prime minister appointed the premier of Ontario, Howard Ferguson. Before he had even left Canada for London, the new high commissioner proclaimed that his beloved empire was in trouble. British pride and patriotism were disintegrating, and someone was needed to revive the old self-respect. Ferguson, apparently, was that someone. As the historian-commentator Frank Underhill joked at the time, "The English nation, it appears, is decadent; and he is setting out on a crusade to make it more like Toronto." Ferguson was completely uninformed about the nuances of diplomacy and foreign policy. When he represented Canada at the League of Nations in 1935, an American diplomat wrote, it gave Ferguson "an awful pain . . . to hear some little fellow representing some little nation, and speaking some language other than English get up and talk for an hour or so, and to know that the little fellow had the same right as he did to cast a vote."

Bennett's second diplomatic choice was William D. Herridge to be minister to the United States. Herridge was Bennett's friend, political adviser, and speechwriter. He married the prime minister's sister in April 1931, the month after being named to the Washington post, and thus consolidated his unique position of access to the centre of government. The restless Herridge was full of ideas and schemes, one of them being a North American free trade zone. He liked to think of himself and his mission as an independent diplomatic force and was perturbed by the thought that there was anything, even a prime minister, between him and the achievement of his goals.

Herridge's arrogance could be stifling. Once he telephoned Bennett's office to ask about the fate of one of his projects. When told that the prime minister was thinking the matter over, Herridge replied, "Oh, God pity us. We'll never get anywhere as long as that stupid, stubborn bastard is the head of the government." Bennett was listening in on the call and was apparently amused, but he was a good deal less so on other occasions. The relationship between brothers-in-law was by all accounts frequently strained. For all this, and despite being somewhat anti-social, Herridge worked hard to represent Canadian views in the American capital and to get to know the people who counted. He became someone to be reckoned with in the Washington of President Franklin Delano Roosevelt and his New Deal. Some of the spirit and vision of that period in the United States was transmitted through Herridge to Bennett; Canada also had its version of the New Deal in 1935.

Herridge often supported Skelton in pressing for the closest possible relations between Canada and the United States, and for the closest possible identity of Canadian and American policies in international affairs. Bennett, however, looked to Great Britain for inspiration and leadership. The United States had let the world down, turning its back on Europe after World War I and reinforcing a tradition of isolationism and irresponsibility that went back as far as the presidency of George Washington. The British, by contrast, had consistently been a force for international peace and stability.

"A PASSIONATE DEVOTION
TO ENGLAND"

As a young man, Bennett's imagination had been fired by Joseph Chamberlain's vision of a principled union of British nations in which burdens, liberties, and benefits would be shared equally. He was certain that Canada would in due course become the most important member in this reconstituted British Empire, "when we may be able as the dominant partner to protect the destinies of the race and breed to which we belong." Where the British flag had gone, "there has followed order, justice, freedom, equality under the law." Later, when the Conservative leader had become prime minister, the private secretary to the governor general observed that Bennett had a "passionate devotion to England & things English; to the King, as King & as a man; to the English language (though he is an incurable splitter of infinitives!)." Bennett's own private secretary recalled that at the core of his credo was a commitment to stand by "the Crown and the whole British community through thick and thin."

Shortly after he became prime minister, Bennett's "passionate devotion to England" was put to the test at the Imperial Conference of 1930. On the agenda was the report of the Conference on the Operation of Dominion Legislation (ODL), which recommended that the British dominions be given their full legal freedom subject only to voluntary restrictions. As we saw at the end of the last chapter, the British hoped—admittedly it was a faint hope—that the new regime in Canada might help them by refusing to approve the ODL findings.

Alas for London, it did not happen. When the ODL report had come before Parliament prior to the election of 1930, Bennett and his Conservatives had expressed regret that the empire would cease to be a powerful international political unit, becoming instead merely a free association of autonomous states of no particular distinction. Nonetheless, they did not force a vote on the issue, and Bennett announced when he arrived at the imperial conference that he considered himself bound by the House of Commons resolution approving the content and direction of the ODL final document. The prime minister might regret the disappearance of what he called the "old political Empire," but he knew that there was little support even in his own party for the kind of measures necessary to turn the clock back.

With Bennett's agreement and that of the other imperial conference delegates, the British Parliament passed the Statute of Westminster on 11 December 1931, giving effect to the ODL recommendations. The Australians and New Zealanders were reluctant signatories and did not implement the statute until the 1940s. By contrast, South Africa and the Irish Free State moved decisively to consolidate their new liberties. Canada was in the middle, happy to have the theory of independence without necessarily all of its substance.

Historian A.R.M. Lower wrote in the 1940s that 11 December ought to be recognized as Canada's Independence Day, "for on that day she became a sovereign state." He was wrong. With the Statute of Westminster, full independence was there to be grasped if Canadians wanted it, but it is clear that they did not. Certainly very few politicians did. Thus the British Foreign Office continued to act for Canada in most of the countries of the world; Canada had diplomatic representatives in only three foreign capitals throughout almost all of the 1930s. Canadians also remained British citizens; a Canadian citizenship act was not passed until 1946. In 1932, the Bennett government abolished appeals to the Judicial Committee of the Privy Council for criminal cases, but it was the late 1930s before a firm move was made to wipe out other appeals to London and 1949 before the Canadian Supreme Court in fact became the final court of appeal in all matters. Furthermore, as stipulated in the Statute of Westminster, the power to alter the British North America Act stayed with the British Parliament while the federal government and the provinces tried to work out an amendment formula. It took them fifty-one years to do so. Lower was closer to the truth when he said that the Statute of Westminster brought Canada as close to independence "as was practicable without revolutionary scissors."

Perhaps the empire could be stitched back together with economic co-operation. So Bennett hoped, or said he hoped. At the

Imperial Conference of 1930, he offered the British a deal. If they would give Canadian producers a break by imposing tariffs on foreign, that is non-imperial, food—a policy resisted by Great Britain since early in the century—in return Bennett would increase the Canadian tariff wall against everyone outside the empire. He had sent tariffs soaring in a special session of Parliament earlier in the fall and had no intention of lowering rates for the empire. Rather, he was promising to raise foreign tariffs still higher. The British, under a pro-free trade administration, said that the suggestion was hum-

R.B. Bennett, off to the 1930 imperial conference (*Winnipeg Free Press*, 23 Sept. 1930)

bug, which it was. Nevertheless, they agreed to meet in Ottawa for a special economic conference in a year's time.

The year became two, and by the time that the Imperial Economic Conference met in the hot Ottawa summer of 1932, Britain's government and situation had changed. Protectionism was now in the saddle there too, and London was ready to bargain. The resulting Ottawa Agreements introduced an empire-wide system of preferences and discrimination against foreign trade. This fell far short, however, of economic integration, and the negotiations seemed anything but co-operative. Bennett was ill-prepared, surly, uncongenial, and thoroughly nationalist when it came down to hard cases. Britain's secretary of state for dominion affairs was quite sure that the Canadian had tapped his team's telephones. The head of the British delegation told a friend that "Bennett had a brainstorm every day which wiped out what he had agreed to the day before," while Chancellor of the Exchequer Neville Chamberlain remarked that Bennett lied like a trooper, alternately bullying, crying, and obstructing.

Bennett did not miss an occasion to say how much he loved the empire. Chamberlain, son of the great imperialist and one of a number of British political figures animated by the vision of imperial economic co-ordination, could only shake his head in wonder and repeat the quip of a Canadian politician: Bennett had the temperament of a Hollywood actor and the manners of a Chicago police officer. As the conference lurched to a conclusion, Chamberlain wrote to his sister that he counted "the days till Saturday when I sail, and I never want to see Canada again." Undeterred, Bennett went to Quebec to see Chamberlain's ship off, saying, "Don't bear malice against me. Love to Annie. God bless you."

THE LEAGUE IN CRISIS

The depression had an enormous impact on international affairs. World trade was worth 40 percent less in 1933 than in 1929, and its volume declined by one-quarter in the same period. Unemployment in individual countries skyrocketed, reaching at least 27 percent in Canada during 1933. Nations turned in on themselves, pursuing the policies of nationalism and protectionism. Bennett had done so immediately after coming to power in 1930, and shortly before that the Americans had imposed the cruelly high tariffs of the Hawley-Smoot Act. The empire did it with its Ottawa Agreements, thoroughly annoying many foreigners and none more so than the Americans. Economic catastrophe undermined democracies and assisted in the rise of militarism in Japan and Adolf Hitler's National Socialism in Germany. These forces saw border expansion as the answer to their economic problems, and the depression made Western countries such as Britain, France, the United States, and Canada all the more cautious in confronting the new dangers, fearing further disruption of their economies.

The League of Nations had been put in place to deal with problems of nationalism, armaments, and aggression, but it was only as strong as its members would make it. The first real test came in September 1931. Overzealous Japanese military officers in Manchuria, the resource-rich northern province of China, moved against the capital city, Mukden. Over the next five months they brought the entire territory under their control and established the Japanese puppet state of Manchukuo. China appealed to the League, which set up a commission of inquiry under the Englishman, Lord Lytton.

For Hugh Keenleyside, second in command at the Canadian legation in Tokyo, the Japanese action against Manchuria was aggression, pure and simple. Japan did have long-standing treaty rights in Manchuria, and these had been repeatedly and intentionally violated by the Chinese. It was also true that Japanese citizens there had been badly treated. The use of force to redress these wrongs, however, was unacceptable.

Keenleyside's boss, Herbert Marler, a former businessman with an eye on Canadian and British interests in the Far East, put a different cast on the same events. "The animus of Japan was not the gain of territory, nor is she seeking to gain something she does not already own." A loose association of principalities under a weak central government, China could not really be called a nation like others in the international community. Besides, Marler added prophetically, none of the great powers would in the end do anything except make speeches recording the pious desire that their wishes for peace should be respected.

In Ottawa, Skelton read the dispatches from Marler and Keenleyside with interest and concern. He concluded that Japan had real grievances and vital interests in Manchuria but was "as definitely the aggressor as any country could be." "The fact that other Imperial powers have taken similar action in the past does not justify a breach of the higher code of international conduct which the world has been endeavouring to build up since the Great War." A higher code could not, however, include the economic boycott or military intervention outlined in the League Covenant. European nations would never act together to put real teeth into the League, and they would certainly not dream of coming to the aid of any non-European country in time of need. Bennett's adviser thought that the League was a fine thing as long as it was in the business of mediatory diplomacy and marshalling public opinion. It had no future as an instrument of punishment.

Prime Minister Bennett apparently took the League more seriously than Skelton did. He believed that it represented a noble opportunity to develop a "law of international life" to counter the negative forces of aggression and violence. Furthermore, in joining the League Canada had solemnly undertaken an international commitment as part of the arrangements that put an end to World War I. "Did we sign or did we not?" he would ask. "If we did, what obligations did we assume? . . . [I]n the name of common sense, let Canada carry out its obligations as undertaken." The League cost very little—"perhaps two days' expenditure in the Great War"—and had made progress in creating an international will "that I am not without hope . . . will control the attitude of European governments."

In practice, however, Bennett was prepared to go little further than Skelton in turning the League Assembly in Geneva into more than an elegantly decorated talking room. Bennett believed that Japan's actions in Manchuria amounted to "a clear-cut fundamental . . . intrinsic violation of the very raison d'être of the League," but he did not think that sanctions ought to be applied. The central mandate of the League was to find methods of conciliating international disputes and to devise methods of international co-operation. Although he demanded that Canada "carry out its obligations as undertaken," Bennett also wondered, "What can a man do who represents only ten and a half millions of people?" Canada was in his view too insignificant to matter, and the United States was not even part of the League. It made all the more sense to follow the British lead in the world, because they had the experience ("where I have none") and because the empire was "the greatest influence for peace in the world."

The Lytton Commission reported in September 1932, dispensing wisdom for both sides of the question. It identified Japan as an aggressor and made clear that the establishment of Manchukuo had been illegitimate. China was also found to be at fault, however, and no sanctions were recommended. Japan ought to return Manchuria to China, but Japanese rights there must be safeguarded. The British, endeavouring to balance the scales and also to keep Japan in the League, interpreted the even-handedness of the report as vindication of their conciliatory policy. American Secretary of State Henry Stimson wanted tougher action, or at least tougher rhetoric: a condemnation of Japanese aggression and no recognition of Manchukuo, adding up to a lesson that crime did not pay.

The triumvirate of Skelton, Herridge, and W.A. Riddell, the Canadian advisory officer at the League, favoured the American approach. For all his reservations about the League, Skelton distrusted the British more. He liked the idea of a stance that might not only deter Japan but also have the happy by-product of bringing Canadian and American policies into closer alignment. Riddell had been at the League since 1924, and he was a believer in collective security. Concluding that Japan was guilty of a sin against the community of nations, he told an American official in Geneva that Canada was completely in accord with the United States in wishing to censure Japan. Herridge was even more blatant in his search for solidarity with the United States against what he called the "little yellow bullies" of Japan. He went so far as to tell Stimson that Canada was marching in lock step with him, saying that Bennett greatly admired the secretary of state's "policy regarding the Manchurian matter, and he wanted to have Canada conform exactly to it." This was imaginative at best and mendacious at worst.

We know, and Skelton knew, that Bennett was likely to have quite different views. When Cabinet minister C.H. Cahan was named to represent Canada at the League Assembly in Geneva in the fall of 1932, the government instructed him to exhaust all the possibilities of a conciliatory settlement and to eschew any discussion of sanctions. But as Riddell later recalled, Cahan had his own negative ideas "regarding countries with weak or unstable Governments. . . . China was one of those countries and therefore he had a great deal of personal sympathy with Japan." He also thought that the Lytton Report was propelling Britain (and therefore Canada) towards war with Japan, while France, Holland, and the United States, all with interests in the Far East, would stand aloof.

When a group of smaller League states called for condemnation of Japan, Cahan therefore co-operated with the British in trying to damp down the enthusiasm. He spoke to the Assembly on 8 December 1932 and emphasized that the conciliatory process had not been pursued to its logical conclusion and that there was blame enough to spread around, but that was not what made his address memorable. Cahan poured scorn on the Chinese, implied that Japan might not be responsible for establishing Manchukuo, and gave a short history of Canadian opposition to collective security arrangements. He then went on to confuse the issue thoroughly by reading almost verbatim the text sent to him by his government, which included the statement that "further delay without any clear evidence of readiness to co-operate on the part of Japan might prove most unfortunate." One observer commented at the time that Canada had managed to plead eloquently on both sides of the question.

Dr. Skelton was not prepared to be that charitable. As he wrote to Riddell, the various reports of the speech in the Canadian and international press gave the impression that Cahan "had gone out of his way to offend Chinese susceptibilities and buttress the Japanese position." Canadian representatives at the League must realize "that the views they express will inevitably be ascribed to their Government, and should, therefore, be confined to the presentation of the policies which have commended themselves to the Government." The undersecretary was embarrassed to receive the protests of the Chinese consul general and the warm congratulations of the Japanese minister, which he "did not refuse to accept, . . . thinking we had better keep at least one friend for the time being." Skelton also kept his sense of humour about what Washington must be thinking after having been told that Canada was with them in wanting to hold Japan accountable. Had the Americans not known "that we Canadians are simple folk, unversed in the ways of diplomatic intrigue, they would have thought we had double-crossed them."

The system, such as it was, for management of international crises was in chaos. The prime minister, in his capacity as secretary of state for external affairs, was well-intentioned but ignorant of foreign problems and unwilling or too busy to remedy the fault. His interventions were impulsive and seemed to be based solely on a deep attachment to the British Empire and a vague desire to fulfil international "obligations." Bennett paid no attention to detail, did not make decisions consistently, and did not follow through to ensure policy implementation. Sensing their leader's weakness, his subordinates made their own policy: Skelton in Ottawa, Herridge in Washington, and now Cahan in Geneva.

It was Skelton's responsibility as undersecretary to lead the Department of External Affairs if Bennett would not, but the deputy does not seem to have exceeded his authority. Cahan and Herridge, on the other hand, acted unprofessionally. Although Cahan's speech could be construed as an attempt to keep the lines of communication with Japan open, he specifically violated his instructions to remain impartial and not to discuss sanctions. Herridge's behaviour was also directed at a laudable goal: better Canadian–American and British–American relations. His methods, however, were thoroughly reprehensible. Lying about government policy to another government can never be acceptable.

Cahan had given his address while Bennett was in mid-Atlantic. Immediately upon landing, the prime minister summoned his colleague to London. Away from Skelton and closely in touch with British officials, Bennett told Cahan that he was "quite pleased" with the address and asked him to return to the fray in Geneva at the side of Britain. Upon Bennett's return to Canada, an insider told Riddell, "Dr. Skelton had . . . the most serious discussion he had ever had with the Prime Minister, and . . . convinced him of the seriousness of the situation." Bennett now changed his mind yet again; Cahan was shortly on his way home.

Canadian representatives in Geneva supported last-ditch conciliation proposals and watched helplessly as attempt after attempt to win Japanese co-operation failed. Riddell was one of the delegates who spoke forcefully on 24 February 1933 in favour of the report of the Committee of Nineteen, a subcommittee of the Assembly, which accepted Lytton's judgments, declared that Manchukuo should not be recognized, and in effect condemned Japanese aggression in China. The report was adopted the same day, and Japan immediately gave notice of its intention to withdraw from the League, comparing its plight to Christ on the cross.

As Christopher Thorne points out in his fine book on the diplomacy of the Far Eastern crisis, "the aggressor . . . had defiantly retained his prize, and had departed from Geneva with little more than verbal censure as the price of his deed. . . . In France and Germany as well as Britain and the United States, there was disillusionment and dismay." And yet, Thorne adds, none of these big powers had the will, capacity, or desire to bell the Japanese cat, "especially since it was strongly suspected that their fellows might then privately seek to improve their own place in that dangerous animal's affections." Even Stimson's policy was all bluff and moral exhortation, and did not have widespread support in the United States. The American secretary of state realized that he had only "spears of straw and swords of ice" to fight the Japanese.

The departure from the League of Nations of Japan in March 1933 was a serious blow to the cause of international peace and security. The country had been one of the principal allied powers in 1919 and a pillar of the far-from-global League. Later the same year Germany defected under its new leader Hitler, and the Geneva Disarmament Conference collapsed. When Italy, another great power, wartime ally, and founding League member attacked Ethiopia in October 1935, many supporters of the organization believed that it was now or never. If the League did not act to deter Italian aggression, its reputation would in future be merely derisory.

Bennett's attitude towards Italian preparations for war against Ethiopia was complicated by the general election campaign of the late summer and early fall of 1935. Plagued by political failure and economic misfortune, with Bennett tired and recently ill, the Conservative Party faced almost certain defeat. From Washington, Herridge suggested that Ethiopia (or Abyssinia, as it was also known) was potentially more than a bothersome intrusion into domestic politics. It could be turned into an electoral advantage, *the* campaign issue, a promise that Canadians would not be forced to fight abroad, made in terms so compelling that the voters would forget everything else.

Bennett refused, seldom mentioning the question in public. In the first of his election radio broadcasts, however, he did state that it was "the solemn duty of government, by all just and honourable means, to see that Canada is kept out of trouble. We have bought and paid for security and for peace, and we mean to have them. . . . We will not be embroiled in any foreign quarrel where the rights of Canadians are not involved." At a late August Cabinet meeting, he repeated that he wanted to do nothing that might bring war to Canadians. Nevertheless, he was clearly not yet done with the League, adding that he was "inclined to favour personally" a policy of economic sanctions against Italy should it attack Ethiopia.

For Skelton, even economic sanctions were too much. The undersecretary produced an unbalanced listing of the pros and cons of Canadian participation in any League program of sanctions, the cons easily winning the day: Canadian governments had always backed the conciliation features of the League Covenant but never the punitive aspects; the United States was overwhelmingly isolationist, making any action by Canada doubly complicated; and the Canadian people were "immensely more interested in Alberta than in Abyssinia." Economic sanctions amounted to "war or next door to war." "Passions rise," Skelton wrote in his wonderful staccato prose, "incidents multiply out of embargoes and blockades of this stringent character, and recourse to arms is difficult to avoid."

The Canadian delegation at the League was led by the high commissioner to London, Howard Ferguson, assisted by W.A. Riddell. They took their lead from the British delegation, and in particular from the British foreign secretary, Sir Samuel Hoare. On 11 September, Hoare thrilled the Assembly with the declaration that "in conformity with its precise and explicit obligations, the League

stands, and my country stands with it, for the collective maintenance of the Covenant in its entirety, and particularly for steady and
collective resistance to all acts of unprovoked aggression." He also
emphasized that if there were to be risks, they must be run by all
League nations, but this caveat seems to have gone largely unnoticed. Hoare intended the address as a revivalist enterprise, which, he
recalled in his memoirs, "might start a new chapter of League recovery," or at least "deter Mussolini by a display of League fervour." One
observer noted, "No one present in the Assembly, and who shared the
dramatic change of mood from the bored attention to such perfor-
mances, to one of excitement and elation, could fail to see the speech
as the event which galvanized the League into action against Italy."

The Canadian delegation was intoxicated by the foreign secretary's address to the Assembly. The Canadians supported sanctions
strongly at meetings of delegates from Commonwealth countries.
Acting without instructions—in fact deceiving Ottawa about their
intentions—they then used this platform to push successfully a
Canadian claim to membership on the Committee of Eighteen, an
Assembly body set up to consider penalties. In the committee meetings, the Canadian delegates were immediately in the vanguard of
those advocating quick and effective sanctions, such as a complete
embargo on arms shipments to Italy.

In Ottawa, by contrast, Bennett vacillated, perhaps leading his
people in Geneva to think that they could do as they wished. On 13
September, following the advice of the Department of External
Affairs, the Cabinet decided to refrain from comment on the Hoare
speech. Later that same day, Bennett called Skelton and other advisers in to say that he had decided—alone—that Canada would not
"welsh," that "if he never did anything else in his life he would stand
by . . . Hoare." Ferguson was instructed to tell the Assembly that his
government "cannot agree that any member is warranted in resorting
to war to enforce its claims. . . . We hope that an honourable and
peaceful solution . . . will yet be reached. If . . . not, . . . Canada will
join with the other members of the League in considering how by
unanimous action peace may be maintained."

In early October, after Mussolini began his invasion and with
only days remaining until the election, Bennett again seemed to shift

gears. The Canadians at Geneva were told to abstain from voting on the question of Italian aggression because it was impossible to anticipate the action of a new parliament. Ferguson was sure that he would become a laughingstock if he deserted his Commonwealth colleagues and appeared to side with Italy and her few friends in the League. He told members of his delegation to come to his office with their golf clubs, and he then put in an urgent telephone call to Ottawa asking Bennett to contact Geneva. The high commissioner waited. If he could not convince Bennett to change his mind, the delegation would go golfing rather than be humiliated in the League Assembly. Bennett called back in time and Ferguson received permission to do as he saw fit. Canada thus voted with the majority on the resolution to condemn Italy. Skelton was outraged, thinking that Ferguson's actions involved a commitment to apply sanctions. The prime minister disagreed, but said "that if it did require such commitment, [we] cannot evade that. No doubt we signed Covenant; no doubt of Italy's guilt; we must take the consequences."

THE AMERICAN ROAD

The Ethiopian crisis was far from over, but the election of 14 October 1935 removed the mercurial Bennett and his henchman Ferguson from the equation. The Liberals won 178 of 245 seats, the greatest victory in a federal election to that point. Bennett's party was reduced to forty seats, and the remainder of the House was made up of a sprinkling of members from smaller parties. Mackenzie King had a big majority for the first time in his political career.

Two foreign policy issues played a part in a campaign that was inevitably dominated by the government's record in dealing with the economic crisis. First of all, the Liberals matched Bennett's promise that Canadians would not participate in any war over Ethiopia. That quarrel was not worth the life of a single Canadian citizen, said King's Quebec lieutenant, Ernest Lapointe. Second, Bennett had opened a trade negotiation with the United States just before he called the election and had great hopes that a mid-campaign agreement would demonstrate a continued capacity for developing fresh ideas and getting things done. He was unable to get anything like the deal he wanted. The Americans were in no hurry, suspecting the motives of someone so identified with economic nationalism and knowing that a Liberal administration more sympathetic to the United States was very likely to be elected. Once it became clear that there would be no quick deal, Bennett asked the electorate instead for a mandate to complete the talks. King was relieved that the Conservatives had been denied success in Washington, and he promised a trade agreement of his own. By the end of the campaign he had made a commitment—just about his only specific one of the election—that he would achieve his goal before the year was out.

Mackenzie King returned to power in 1935 aiming to minimize international commitments and to maximize external trade. The first of these goals was consistent with his long-standing desire to do nothing that would alienate or divide the broad mass of public opinion. A League of Nations crisis over Ethiopia loomed, but Catholic Quebec was unlikely to approve of strong measures to discipline Catholic Italy. The new Cabinet was deeply divided. Ministers from English Canada who wanted to assist the League were pitted against Lapointe, who wanted anything but, and threatened to resign "if the Government [were] to decide for military sanctions."

King reluctantly supported the application of economic sanctions against Italy while ruling out military action. The first post-Bennett official public statement on the crisis demonstrated that the government gave lip service to League ideals, as did President Roosevelt in Washington. Like the Americans, however, King emphasized that geographical distance and domestic fissures made a forceful Canadian stand on military intervention impossible. The central purpose of the League was not and never had been to guarantee the territorial status quo or to rely upon force to maintain peace. Said the prime minister, "Our own domestic situation must be considered first, and what will serve to keep Canada united."

King's second goal in foreign policy centred on his belief that Canadians could only escape the economic depression by trading their way out of it. The crisis had been caused by economic nationalism and the absence of trade; tariff and other barriers had to be broken down through patient international negotiation. In the view of King and of some other leading international figures of the time, including the u.s. secretary of state, Cordell Hull, lower tariffs were weapons to fight instability and war. Prosperous nations, nations whose goods flowed easily across the world's frontiers, had no need or desire to argue. The new Liberal government moved vigorously to negotiate commercial agreements with the United States, Great Britain, and Germany and to end trade wars with Japan and the Soviet Union. All of this work was successfully completed within six-teen months. King captured the aims of his policy when he wrote in his diary about lifting the Bennett government's embargo against Soviet exports in September 1936: "I feel the national friendliness essential, & . . . we need the trade."

America came first. On Thanksgiving Day, 24 October 1935, just a few hours after he assumed power, King walked alone to the home of Norman Armour, the American representative in Ottawa. The visit was reciprocated the next day. The prime minister claimed that he wanted—if the United States "made it possible for him to do so"—to travel the "American road," the road of closer political and economic relations, and for that reason he wanted an understanding on trade. Time was of the essence, King insisted. An agreement must be negoti-ated forthwith in order that it could be signed on 11 November, when the anniversary of the end of World War I was annually marked by remembrance ceremonies. In that way, King expounded in his diary,

> we, in the New World, would be setting an example of what could be accomplished in the arts of peace. If the countries of Europe see that the New World is breaking down these nation-alistic barriers, and developing their trade, it will serve more than anything else to bring the European nations to their senses, and may even be the most important of all the factors in termi-nating the present war, and certainly of preventing its extension.

Fanciful though it was, King believed that a North American trade agreement, not a firm stand by the League of Nations, was the way to stop the war in Ethiopia.

King dispatched his trade negotiators to Washington, and fol-lowed them personally on 7 November. He was greeted warmly by

President Roosevelt, who recalled airily that they had been friends almost since boyhood. They had in fact met only once before, but that was the Roosevelt style: cheery, optimistic, not preoccupied by the details. The president emphasized co-operation in the western hemisphere as an antidote to what was happening in Europe, and it seemed right that he and the new Canadian leader ought to get along as good neighbours did. The White House guest was told by Roosevelt that "it was great just to be able to pick up the telephone and talk to each other in just a few minutes. We must do that whenever occasion arises. I will always be glad to hear from you."

Over the next ten years the two leaders met eighteen times, sharing crises and political confidences and forging a remarkable partnership. Roosevelt had a genuine, if quite selfish, interest in Canada, and he and his advisers judged that King was much more flexible and malleable than Bennett. The Canadian was in awe of the slick and popular president—his gushing diary entries make for some embarrassing reading—but he never took his eye off the national good. King remained wary of the Americans; he certainly never wanted to travel the "American road" to the exclusion of traditional and vital British ties. He knew, however, as more and more Canadians knew, that the country's future lay increasingly in close relations with the United States.

With King and Roosevelt both anxious for a trade deal that they considered to be as much about politics as economics, a meeting of minds was rapidly reached. The American president announced the accord on 11 November at the Arlington Cemetery Armistice Day ceremonies, just as King had wished and only three weeks after he had assumed power. The agreement was signed with silk top hats in evidence and great fanfare at the White House on the 15th. Under the 1935 Canada–United States trade agreement, Canada cut its tariff on eighty-eight U.S. exports and bestowed most favoured nation (MFN) status on all American products, giving them the rate accorded to Canada's best foreign trading partners. In return, the Americans guaranteed MFN treatment to Canadian exports and gave specific concessions on lumber and timber, certain minerals, some agricultural and fisheries products, and a few manufactures. The United States, intent as in 1911 on wooing Canada away from Britain through tighter trading arrangements, concluded that it had won a huge victory. Many Canadians concurred, but King was more desirous of *an* agreement than the perfect agreement because it would lend weight to his campaign for global freer trade and send a signal of "international good-will, as vs. international hate," to the Europeans. Mussolini showed no signs of noticing.

"THE BIGGEST EXPERIMENT
YET TRIED"

The Italians did take note, however, of what King's officials were doing at the League. On 1 November 1935, Walter Riddell, who had replaced Ferguson at the helm of the Canadian delegation, told his colleagues on the Committee of Eighteen that they were participating in "the biggest experiment yet tried among the nations." Together "they were building up a structure of sanctions through the concerted action of the nations and should be wary of anything that threatened that structure." Although "a long way from the seat of trouble," Canada was prepared to play its part. Were others? Riddell's speech was widely praised at the League, and the next day he was again in the lead, proposing sanctions against the export of oil, coal, iron, and steel products to Italy. Petroleum, he reasoned, was the crucial commodity. If Mussolini's oil supplies could be dried up through a world boycott, his attack must fail.

Shortly after the Canadian election results were known, the new government had told Riddell to remain quiet pending instructions. Ottawa supported economic sanctions, and was even willing to go along with any decision of the Committee of Eighteen, but Riddell had gone too far. He had made policy on his own and catapulted Canada to the forefront of countries demanding an end to aggression in Ethiopia. In his capacity as secretary of state for external affairs, King sent a firm private reprimand to Riddell in Geneva. "[The] position which you took was not in my judgment in conformity with important factors in [the] Canadian situation and not within the scope of your authority. As I have already indicated no position on any question of importance should be taken without positive and definite instructions." King had in mind two "important factors": the potentially explosive impact that leadership in world affairs might have on an always fragile Canadian unity; and the government's desire not to assume a stance obviously different from that of the United States.

If King had a rule in foreign policy, it was to avoid the spotlight. Riddell had made that impossible. As the days and weeks of November passed, the oil sanction, the symbol of getting really tough with Italy, became indelibly identified with Canada. Headlines around the world in newspapers such as *Le Temps* in Paris, the *New York Times*, and the *Times* of London gave prominence to the "Canadian proposal." At home, newspaper opinion on sanctions was lukewarm in English Canada and in Quebec downright chilly. Italy threatened that a petroleum embargo would provoke a firm response from its government. From his vacation retreat in Sea Island, Georgia, where he had gone with the faithful Skelton after signing the Canadian–American trade agreement, Mackenzie King grew more and more uneasy. On 2 December, under orders from the prime minister, Ernest Lapointe as acting secretary of state for external affairs issued a public repudiation of Riddell. The Canadian delegate in Geneva had been acting entirely on his own. "The Canadian Government has not and does not propose to take the initiative."

The irony is that sanctions, and in particular oil sanctions, were going nowhere. The idea stirred passionate enthusiasm in Geneva; Riddell was not alone in his eagerness for bringing Mussolini to heel. Yet the British and French governments had agreed as early as mid-September to go slowly on sanctions and to do everything possible to keep the Italians "on the Allied side." In early December the foreign secretaries of those two countries produced their infamous Hoare-Laval Pact, conceding a large chunk of Ethiopia to Italy. The outcry was such that both London and Paris backed away from this shameless surrender of another country's rights, but the thrust of big-power thinking was clear enough. No one had the stomach for confronting Italy, and Britain and France regretted having annoyed a once and future ally. Nor was the United States, the chief non-League oil producer, willing to go along with sanctions, particularly on oil.

All dressed up and nowhere to go (*The Spectator*)

Without friends, Ethiopia collapsed by May 1936. In September of that year, Mackenzie King went to Geneva with the intention of burying League issues that had proved divisive in Canadian politics. The League was a fine and necessary forum for mediation, conciliation, and acts of conscience, he reiterated, but not for coercion or punishment. An international war office headquartered in the Swiss capital was not practical politics because it ran counter to "a general unwillingness of peoples to incur obligations which they realize they may not be able in time of crisis to fulfil, obligations to use force and to use it at any place, any time, in circumstances unforeseen, and in disputes over whose origin or whose development they have had little or no control." As King had told the House of Commons in a major address of 18 June 1936, collective bluffing could not bring collective security.

"I SHOULD DESERVE TO BE SHOT..."

League commitments might be evaded, but others could not be. The prime minister recognized an obligation "to our country to protect it in a mad world." The Canadian military had been laid low by the depression, and something had to be done to prepare for the unthinkable, another world war. "I should deserve to be shot did I not press for immediate action & should a war come on with nothing accomplished meanwhile." From the summer of 1936, King led an almost single-handed effort to give Canada a respectable defence policy, an effort for which he has received almost no credit.

A general European war seemed on the horizon. As Mussolini invaded Ethiopia, Germany was re-arming and in the process trampling on the Treaty of Versailles. Italy finished its African handiwork off, and Hitler's troops entered the Rhineland, which had been demilitarized and taken away from Germany at the end of World War I. This was another violation of Versailles. Many in the democracies nodded approvingly at the German occupation as a simple reclamation project, taking back lost property, but King saw a case for concerted Anglo–French resistance to Hitler: "Germany has treated her treaties as 'scraps of paper.'" Within a few months, in July 1936, a civil war began in Spain between Republican government forces and Fascist rebels under the leadership of General Francisco Franco. Germany and Italy backed Franco. The Communist state of the Soviet Union supported the Republic, as did leftward-leaning people the world over, including a number of Canadians. Some thirteen hundred volunteers from Canada, the so-called Mackenzie-Papineau Battalion, would serve in the International Brigades that fought

Franco, despite the 1937 Foreign Enlistment Act outlawing unofficial service in foreign wars.

The prime minister saw a pattern of disintegration everywhere around him: "Fascism vs. Communism, Capital vs. Labour—class warfare in all the European countries, & who will say not also in America. The world is in a terrible state." The British, even so, might perhaps be able to keep out of a European war, and if they could, Canada could. Certainly the dominion was fortunate that it had Britain and the United States as close allies and that other, less friendly countries were too far away to do much direct damage. As the prime minister had said in Geneva, Canada rejoiced "in our neighbours, and in our lack of neighbours." Only Minister of Agriculture J.G. Gardiner and, understandably enough, Minister of National Defence Ian Mackenzie supported their leader in asking for a substantial jump in the military budget.

Still, King remained determined to take an initiative on defence, and his trip to Europe in the fall of 1936 reinforced his resolve. He had a wider perspective on international affairs than did his colleagues, realizing that defence questions had broad implications for Canadian self-respect and self-preservation. It would be a humiliation "to accept protection from Britain without sharing in the costs, or to rely on the United States without being willing to at least protect our neutrality." If Canada were independent, it "would have an enormous cost to meet in the way of defence and . . . unless we were ready to do something, we might get the support neither of Britain nor of the United States except at a price which we might deeply regret." President Roosevelt had already hinted at the price. In a private Quebec City meeting in 1936, he warned King that leading Washington politicians were saying the United States would have to "go in and help" if British Columbia were attacked by Japan. At Chautauqua, New York, during the same summer he publicly declared that the Americans would "defend ourselves and defend our neighborhood." Roosevelt was threatening, not for the last time, that Canada had better act on its own behalf or the United States might feel compelled to take over the military responsibility for an unprepared Canada.

King remembered his Liberal predecessor, Laurier, who had also struggled to reconcile the conflicting views of Canadians about their place and responsibility in the world before 1914. "I am now where Sir Wilfrid was, in a more dangerous time in the world's history—but still between the devil & deep blue sea in having to steer between Imperialism & Nationalism in extreme forms." In the House of Commons, the Conservatives would want a great deal more assistance to Britain than King felt able to give, while the Co-operative Commonwealth Federation (CCF), the new party of democratic socialism under J.S. Woodsworth, was committed to Canadian neutrality in any future war, no matter what the cause or who the enemy. Anti-war feelings were running high in both Canada and the United States. Arms dealers were excoriated in best-selling books, which argued that these "merchants of death" were the only ones who really profited from war. On the other side, some Canadians agreed with British politician Winston Churchill that ugly forces had been unleashed in the world and that not nearly enough was being done to contain them.

As always, King's strategy was to discover the moderate way. With an hour-long speech, he won over his caucus of Liberals by promising not to spend too much and to spend it only on national defence, and by pointing out that Canada already had enough divisions without adding to them:

> When we look around, what do we find: Strange disruptive influences at work in almost all the Provinces. Take Alberta—with sinister forces defying the rest of Canada, preaching economic isolation; and that may lead to political estrangement. Take the Province of Quebec, where there is open advocacy of the establishment of a Republic on the St. Lawrence; where the old veneration for the Confederation has disappeared and where agitation for separation is rampant. Take New Brunswick where . . . again the work of Confederation is threatened. You will find similar tendencies in practically all the Provinces. But what is to be the result? What is our duty—our duty is clear, to

be united in regard to policy and to recognize that the unity of Canada comes first and foremost, and we must preserve this unity at all cost.

Canada sometimes seemed as unruly as the world outside. The Liberal Party was in government, and the duty of its members of parliament was to support sane, rational compromise in all national endeavours.

In the same speech, King made an appeal on behalf of the Commonwealth. Just weeks before, that institution had been tested by the demand of King Edward VIII that he be allowed to marry Wallis Warfield Simpson. She was an American and a commoner, which was bad enough, but she was also once divorced and about to be so again. Divorce was unacceptable in those days, particularly so as Edward was the titular head of the Church of England. The dashing king had been on the throne for less than a year and was extremely popular throughout the British Empire, where he had travelled extensively as Prince of Wales. Every government in the Commonwealth, however, refused to agree to the king's wish that Mrs. Simpson become his wife with or without the title of queen. Edward abdicated on 10 December 1936, rather than give up his love, ensuring himself immortality as one of the century's most romantic (or most foolish) public figures.

As a fervent monarchist himself, and aware of the attachment that many Canadians had to the monarchy as a link to Mother England, Mackenzie King took his responsibilities in the affair very seriously, monitoring every development and scrap of paper carefully. In the final analysis, he took heart from the crisis because, as he told the caucus, it had "proved to us that not only can the Commonwealth stand united, but that in an emergency the democracies of the world can stand united as well. If the conflict is between democracy and autocracy, then the forces of democracy shall stand fast."

The military budget came before Parliament in February 1937. Spending was set at a ceiling of $35 million for 1937–1938, much less than the chiefs of staff had requested but up from $20 million the previous year. Total government expenditure for the year was some $500 million. The minister of national defence spoke exclusively about "the protection of Canadian shores, the protection of Canadian homes, the protection of Canadian shipping terminals and harbours," and to that end he made much of the air force and the navy, both of which could be justified as purely domestic defence forces. The army, on the other hand, was associated in the public and therefore the political mind with expeditionary forces to Europe, the horrific losses of World War I, and the possibility of another bout of conscription.

King had a particularly soft spot for the air force, and by the fiscal year 1938–1939 it was receiving almost 50 percent of the defence budget. Airpower had the advantage of being highly mobile and adaptable and could therefore be used not only at home but also at short notice abroad. If a war requiring an overseas commitment should break out, how much better to contribute an air force, with its relatively small personnel requirements, than a huge army with all the potential for casualties on a big scale.

The 1937 military estimates debate must have been sobering for any Canadian concerned about either defence or the empire. Not a single Conservative participated, making it look as if the government alone wanted a heavier emphasis on defence. Speaker after speaker from the CCF and the Social Credit Party paraded suspicions about imperial wars to come and scepticism that Canada needed any more defending. Many Liberals expressed concerns as well; some Western MPs had raised objections in the caucus, and sixteen French-speaking Quebec Liberals spoke up in the debate to underline that they could support only national projects. Some, in fact, said that they could not vote for any increases at all. Echoing the words that King had uttered while leader of the opposition in 1920, Maxime Raymond, the Liberal member for Beauharnois-Laprairie, asked, "Defence of Canada! against whom and against what? Where lies this sudden threat which requires such a considerable expenditure for defence purposes?"

Not a single prominent politician was willing to stand up for the empire—except the prime minister. King employed all the requisite arguments about the importance of national defence, but he made no pretence that the country had to fear a major attack. "Relatively," he admitted, "our danger is small." It was true "that what we are doing we are doing for Canada," but he hoped that the substantial jump in defence spending would also be seen as "making some contribution towards the defence of the British Commonwealth of Nations as a whole" and "towards the defence of all those countries that may someday necessarily associate themselves together for the purpose of preserving their liberties and freedom against an aggressor, come from wherever he may."

THE PEACEMAKER

For King it was not enough to prepare for a war that could destroy Canadian unity and ultimately the country itself. World peace must be actively encouraged because, as he told President Roosevelt, if that cause were lost, "nothing else will matter very much." King had been a highly successful strike settler in the United States during the last war, and was the author of a heavy-handed volume, *Industry and Humanity* (1918), preaching how to achieve industrial harmony. He believed that problems between nations were susceptible to the same persuasion, negotiation, and arbitration as problems between labour and capital. King saw his own special mission as helping in the search for international peace and had faith in his own special gifts for doing so.

The same message was coming to the prime minister from the Beyond. A deeply repressed and lonely man, King took great comfort and reassurance from his contacts with the spirit world, with his long-dead mother and the departed figures of the British and Canadian Liberal Party. On the night before the election of 1935, the ghost of Lord Grey, who had been the British foreign secretary before World War I, appeared at one of King's séances. Grey told the Canadian leader what he wanted to hear:

> Long ago I saw what was before you in this world.
> Long ago I saw that you would be a peacemaker.
> Long ago I answered a call to the same thing.
> Long ago I tried to end war.
> Long ago I failed to achieve that end. You will succeed.

God has chosen you for that purpose.

God loves those who love their fellow-men.

Mother spoke in the same vein: "Long ago I knew that God had chosen you to be his instrument to make peace among Men and Nations."

In March of 1937, the prime minister visited the American president again, hatching a vague and impractical scheme for a permanent conference to examine and solve the great social and economic issues that lay behind every international grievance. The aim was a new League of Nations, which would have a universal membership and be governed by a "peace mentality." At the same meeting, Roosevelt and Hull, the secretary of state, had a good deal to say about their passion for lowering tariff barriers and their desire for a reciprocal trade agreement with Great Britain. King, as we know, was a disciple of the freer trade religion, and he was delighted at the prospect of closer Anglo–American ties, which had always been one of the great goals of Canadian external policy.

Peacemaking in the North Atlantic triangle (a term that would soon come into use to describe the Anglo–American–Canadian relationship) was a pre-occupation in the dominion. English Canadians, in particular, always felt happiest when Great Britain and the United States of America were on a common course in world affairs, when they were not being asked to choose between their country and their next door neighbour and friend. Lester B. Pearson, then a diplomat and a future prime minister, said more than once that the great nightmare of Canadian governments "was a clash, or even a divergence, of policy between the two governments—American and British—with both of which Canada wished to keep in step." King believed, just as Borden and Meighen had believed, that Canada ought to do everything possible to encourage Anglo–American harmony. It was a staple of political speeches in Canada at the time that the dominion was the linchpin between the two great Anglo-Saxon powers, the ideal interpreter of one to the other.

The Imperial Conference of 1937 was held in London in the late spring, coinciding with the coronation of a new king. Mackenzie King attended with Anglo–American goodwill at the top of his

agenda. He vigorously promoted both the permanent peace conference that he had discussed with Franklin Roosevelt in Washington
and an Anglo–American trade agreement. King hoped that such an
accord would help to dissolve economic nationalism, lead to trade

William Lyon Mackenzie King, as seen by political caricaturist
Robert LaPalme (*LaPalme, 1930–1950*) (Montreal: Le Cercle du Livre de
France, 1950), 69

agreements with European countries, and bring Germany back into the family of nations. Canada would do everything possible to help achieve this world economic disarmament, the prime minister said.

It was made clear, however, that to make room for an American agreement, the Canadian government must forego some of its advantages in the British market, where it competed with the United States to sell certain products such as apples and timber. At this, King drove a hard bargain. He insisted on and won, over the objections of both the British and the Americans, a separate negotiation with the United States if he were going to modify the existing Anglo–Canadian trade arrangements. As he pointed out, it was "hardly customary or to be taken for granted that when two countries are negotiating a trade agreement for their joint advantage, a third country should be called upon to provide a great part of the quid pro quo" without compensation.

Thus a major Anglo–American–Canadian commercial negotiation took place. When Great Britain and the United States signed a trade agreement on 17 November 1938, a Canadian–American accord was completed simultaneously. It was much more comprehensive than that of 1935, and Ottawa won many concessions in the American market while conceding tariff cuts that they were about to make anyway. This time King had not rushed into a deal with Roosevelt; there was no doubt that Canada had negotiated shrewdly and well. The linchpin theory was applied to stunning effect, and although King claimed a great victory for world peace, the real victory was Canadian. Perhaps, though, his initial peacemaking goal had been advanced as well. The British and Americans were bound closer together for the tough times that were sure to come. Canada had played its part in that, even if it was not quite "the big and generous" role that King had promised at the Imperial Conference of 1937. The idea that Canada was crucial to the Anglo–American relationship was largely a fiction, but on this occasion at least the theory meshed with reality.

After the Imperial Conference of 1937, King had gone straight from London to Germany, where a meeting with Adolf Hitler had been arranged. This was not the prime minister's finest hour. Like so many other Western leaders who made the pilgrimage to Berlin,

King was completely mesmerized by the Führer: by the "liquid" eyes conveying "keen perception and profound sympathy," by the "very nice, sweet smile," by the calm, moderation, and logic of his words. "He impressed me as a man of deep sincerity and a genuine patriot. I felt increasingly in the course of my stay that there were conditions in Germany itself which accounted for much that had been done there which it was difficult to understand beyond its borders."

King, even so, delivered a warning to Hitler that the British Empire was indivisible. If "the time ever came when any part of the Empire felt the freedom which we all enjoyed was being impaired through any act of aggression on the part of a foreign country, it would be seen that all would join together to protect the freedom which we were determined should not be imperilled." Hitler for his part promised that there would be no resort to war "so far as Germany was concerned," although he quickly added that his country had too little land for its population and needed to secure sources of supply and markets. Reading King's notes of his encounter with Hitler, which he proudly sent to London, a high-ranking official from the British Foreign Office scrawled a protest: "It is curious how easily impressed & reassured Hitler's visitors are when Hitler tells them that Germany needs to expand at somebody else's expense but of course does not want war!"

Hermann Goering, Hitler's air minister, asked King specifically whether Canada would support a British effort to prevent the union of Germany with Austria, a country full of fellow Germans. The reply was that Canada would judge the case when it arose and on its own merits. In other words, an attack on Britain was one thing as far as Canadians were concerned, a conflict in Central Europe quite another. Goering quickly added that he did not wish King to jump to the conclusion that there was going to be any German aggression against its neighbour, but that is precisely what happened in March 1938, when Austria was brought into the German Reich.

Even the German–Austrian *Anschluss* did not discourage King or make him repent of his optimism about Hitler:

> I am convinced he is a spiritualist—that he has a vision to
> which he is being true . . . his devotion to his mother—that

Mother's spirit is I am certain his guide. . . . I believe the world will yet come to see a very great man-mystic, in Hitler. . . . [M]uch I cannot abide in Nazism—the regimentation—cruelty—oppression of Jews . . . but Hitler . . . the peasant—will rank someday with Joan of Arc among the deliverers of his people, & if he is only careful may yet be the deliverer of Europe.

Hating war and the thought of what it might do to his country and his political future, King had a deep-seated need to convince himself that Hitler might be reasonable, despite mounting evidence to the contrary. The boy from Berlin, Ontario, genuinely believed that he might be the linchpin between the British Empire and Germany, just as Canadians had long claimed to be the "golden hinge" between England and the United States.

THE DOGS OF WAR

King's wishful thinking about Hitler never affected the core of Canadian foreign policy. The country would go to war at Britain's side if the English "homeland" were threatened. In the meantime, the government would make no commitments that were likely to be criticized for compromising the right of Parliament to decide Canada's fate. King held the touchy external affairs portfolio tightly, discouraging Ernest Lapointe's ambition to become the minister and wherever possible preventing discussions of foreign affairs in the House of Commons. The 1937 defence debate was one of the few times such issues were aired in Parliament during the interwar years, and that occasion produced views the government would have preferred the country had not heard.

At the imperial conference that same year, King and his team had refused to give the British any guarantee of concrete assistance in some future crisis, and they had cleansed the meeting communiqué of all hints of co-operative empire defence schemes. Controversy was to be avoided at all costs. "It is sometimes well to allow sleeping dogs to lie," King told a friend. "This, I believe, is especially true when they happen to be the dogs of war."

King never doubted that Canada must fight for Britain if necessary—he promised his hosts at the imperial conference that "there would be great numbers of Canadians anxious to swim the Atlantic!"—and he quietly did what he thought he could to assist the cause of Commonwealth unity. As we know, that had been part of his motive in improving Canadian defences and paying court to Hitler. The government also sanctioned and encouraged a wide range of Anglo–Canadian military co-operation: uniform organization and training, standardized equipment, and agreements allowing Britain to use Canadian facilities in the event of war. Some of King's advisers, notably the arch anti-imperialist Skelton, thought that these arrangements would inexorably draw Canada into a European conflict. In 1939, the government included British pilots in an expanded Royal Canadian Air Force training program. King refused, however, to train Canadians for the Royal Air Force. The British badly wanted such an arrangement but King was convinced that it "would be certain to provoke a discussion on Canada contributing to forces overseas for war purposes, as contrary to [the] basic principle of Canada's autonomy and the right to reach her own decision on peace and war." The prime minister probably thought that if both Skelton and the British were annoyed with him, he had the balance about right.

After Austria, Hitler next threatened the Sudetenland, the German-speaking part of Czechoslovakia, and this time a general European war seemed unavoidable. As British prime minister Neville Chamberlain engaged in shuttle diplomacy to Germany in the hope that he could find a peaceful solution, he naturally had the Canadian government fully behind him. But if Chamberlain's efforts failed, what then? Speaking for the Quebecers in the Cabinet, Lapointe advised from Geneva, "Public opinion will have to be prepared, not aroused by irrevocable steps. . . . Submit that Parliament should be summoned, if war declared, and no definite commitment made meanwhile." A Canadian government press release sounded the same notes as Lapointe's telegram. Parliament alone would decide Canadian war policy if and when the time came, and only then. Nothing could be gained by creating dissension through precipitate action.

Behind the scenes, ministers were taking a firmer line. King was more worried about a major French–English split than ever before in his career but the Cabinet held together, agreeing that ministers would have to take the country into war if Britain became involved in an armed clash over Czechoslovakia. For King, in the lead and now very critical of Hitler, it was a question of international morality. "I would stand for Canada doing all she possibly could to destroy those Powers which are basing their action on *might* and not on *right*. . . . I would not consider being neutral for a moment." It was also a question of survival. Were Britain "worsted in a world struggle, the only future left for Canada would be absorption by the U.S., if we were to be saved from an enemy aggressor."

War, however, even a just and necessary war, would be a horror. Canadians, none more than King, were immensely relieved when the Munich Conference of 30 September 1938 resolved the crisis, although at the expense of giving Hitler what he wanted. The Sudetenland was his final territorial demand, the Führer said, and as part of the Munich agreement he promised to leave the rest of Czechoslovakia intact.

The promise, like so many in that dishonest decade, proved hollow. On 15 March 1939, the German army grabbed Prague, the Czechoslovak capital, and the rest of the country was quickly dismembered. Chamberlain's policy of compromise and patient negotiation was in tatters. The famous British cartoonist, David Low, depicted a Nazi tiger having devoured all of the British prime minister except his famous umbrella, a symbol of his desire for "appeasement." Britain put in place a tough new policy of containing Hitler. It increased defence spending, introduced conscription, guaranteed assistance to Poland, Romania, and Greece, and began to woo the Soviet Union in an effort to pre-empt the sympathies of that great and brooding power.

In Canada, King had already given a powerful public signal of his own sympathies in a House of Commons speech on 16 January. On 20 March, in the wake of the German march on Prague, he gave another: "If there were a prospect of an aggressor launching an attack on Britain, with bombers raining death on London, I have no doubt what the decision of the Canadian people and parliament

The end of appeasement (David Low, *A Cartoon History of Our Times*
(New York: Simon and Schuster, 1939), 173)

would be. We would regard it as an act of aggression, menacing freedom in all parts of the British Commonwealth."

Yet King was too careful and too clever to allow such unequivocal
language to stand for long. He spoke again in Parliament on 30
March, dispensing a bone to each segment of the Canadian spectrum of opinion on foreign policy: the isolationists and neutralists,
such as J.S. Woodsworth, McGill University legal scholar F.R. Scott,
University of Toronto historian Frank Underhill, and many French
Canadians; the imperialists, represented by former prime minister
Arthur Meighen, now perched in the Senate; the collectivists, such
as J.W. Dafoe of the *Winnipeg Free Press*, who still hoped that the
League of Nations would be able to mobilize the world against
aggression, using force if necessary; and the silent, cautious majority,
willing to prepare for the worst but anxious to stave off an irrevocable judgment. Seeming to contradict his words of just a week and a
half before, King refused to predict what government policy would
be "under conditions which cannot now be foreseen." There could
be no "automatic commitments to possible or actual participation in
war." Furthermore, in the event of a war, the conscription of young
Canadians for overseas service was out of the question.

Then, the next day, the prime minister launched his secret weapon, confusing or clarifying the government's stance, depending on the perspective of the listener. Earlier in the year Ernest Lapointe had toyed with the idea of resigning from the Cabinet if Canada committed itself to "possible or actual participation in war." Events had moved in such a threatening direction that he was no longer to be counted among the undecided or the uncommitted. The minister of justice delivered a powerful address urging that the "ostrich policy" of refusal to face the increasing international dangers would not keep them at bay. Military technology, he said, was bringing the country within reach of attack by any military power of the first rank (a view that Mackenzie King was beginning to share). Canada was part of the global community, and "this planet unfortunately cannot be considered today as an earthly paradise inhabited only by benevolent and rational beings of an altruistic frame of mind." Moreover, Canada was by its own free will part of a tightly knit British Empire. If Britain was at war, it was simply not possible for Canada to stand aloof. "It is contrary to international principles to recognize the possibility of one country being neutral and another a belligerent when they are not separate sovereignties."

King and Lapointe were pursuing a deliberate, co-ordinated strategy with their speeches of 30 and 31 March. From one end of the country to the other, a great debate turned around the issue of Canada's role and responsibility in the event of a big European war. It was necessary to give cautious leadership, the prime minister told the British high commissioner, "to show Canadians how serious the situation is, how vitally it affects Canadian interests and how Canada must be prepared to play her part which cannot be the part of the neutral." If King had made Lapointe's loyalist speech, the reasoning went, Ontario would have been pleased but Quebec outraged. If Lapointe had made King's apparently disinterested address, it might be popular in Quebec, but perceived outside the province as more of the same old Quebec unco-operativeness. The two Liberals were acting together as "two props of a bridge," King said, "sustaining the structure which would serve to unite divergent parts of Canada, thereby making for a united country."

National unity sometimes took a depressing precedence over international responsibility. As King well knew when he was in Berlin with the German leader in 1937, Hitler had embarked on a campaign of brutality and persecution against the Jewish people. Hundreds of thousands of them sought to escape, many looking to Canada as a spacious safe haven. In March 1938, King had claimed that he could do little for these refugees: "My own feeling is that nothing is to be gained by creating an internal problem in an effort to meet an international one." He was referring generally to powerful anti-immigrant biases in tough economic times and specifically to widespread anti-Semitism, which was particularly notable in the Catholic Church and the Liberal fortress of Quebec.

Later, in November 1938, King did make an effort to have his Cabinet adopt what he called a "liberal attitude" and act as the "conscience of the nation" even if it was not the "politically most expedient" course. Nevertheless, a principled stand received little support in the government or the bureaucracy, and King himself did not feel strongly enough to press the matter or to hold to his position in later Cabinet meetings. The way out was to let the provinces decide their own immigration entry levels, thus distancing the federal government from the problem. As the Liberal leader pointed out to members of the Canadian Jewish community on 23 November, the country was still wracked by unemployment. His job was to avoid strife, maintain unity, and counter "the forces of separatism."

Precisely the same argument had justified rearmament in 1937, a policy that was patently right for the time. Now unity was being used in the name of something very wrong, or so it seemed to King when he allowed himself to think about it. Perhaps the prime minister and his colleagues were simply political and moral cowards, or worse, out-and-out racists. Perhaps they were reacting to a feeling that Canadians, as immigration historian Irving Abella has written, "had already done their share":

In the first thirty years of this century, just under five million immigrants had arrived. In the next 15, barely 200,000 came, far less than previously arrived in one good year during the previous three decades. The arrival of so many new settlers of so many different languages, races, religions, and ways of life had obviously been traumatic to a nation that was itself just finding its feet. To integrate, assimilate, and educate these millions was both essential and enormously difficult. Those who for so long had been calling for a halt, for a period of digestion in which the country could finish absorbing those immigrants who were already here, finally got their wish.

It is also possible that the Cabinet's policy on Jewish immigration ought to be seen as a genuine attempt to hold the national fabric together against the day when another great war would make unity crucial to the country's survival. Wherever the truth lies—and all of these explanations carry some weight—Canada admitted only 748 Jewish refugees in 1938 and 1763 in 1939. As if to symbolize Canadian government indifference, 907 European Jews aboard the liner *St. Louis* were turned away from Canadian shores in mid-1939. The United States and Cuba had been no more generous to the unlucky ship but, as Abella says, "Of all the countries in the western world, Canada had perhaps the worst record of providing sanctuary to the hapless Jewish refugees."

In May and June 1939, as the *St. Louis* was searching the Atlantic for a home for its passengers, King George VI and Queen Elizabeth visited Canada to a rapturous greeting in every part of the country. The king and queen, with Mackenzie King in tow every step of the way, also went to the United States. There they were entertained by President Roosevelt, who dispensed beer and hot dogs at his home in Hyde Park, New York. The American president guaranteed all the assistance he could give "short of actual participation" in a war against Hitler. He even declared that the United States would join in if London were attacked. When the time came, Roosevelt was able to arrange for the first but not the second. American isolationist opinion, embodied in a series of Neutrality Acts prohibiting dealings with countries at war, was simply too strong.

The next great international crisis hit in August–September 1939, and this time there was no avoiding the war the world feared. On 24 August the Soviets, not sufficiently impressed by British attempts to interest them in an alliance, turned to Germany. The two countries signed an agreement pledging not to attack one another, thus freeing Hitler's hand to deal with Poland, the next of his expansionary targets. Poland lay between Germany and the Soviet Union, and the Nazi–Soviet Pact envisaged carving the country up between them. Chamberlain renewed his pledge to Poland but Hitler forged ahead nevertheless. Germany attacked Poland on 1 September, eliciting a warning and then an ultimatum from Britain. When Germany failed to respond by 3 September, Chamberlain declared war. Following Lapointe's logic about the British Empire as a single international unit, Canada was also at war.

What might have been true constitutionally was not true politically. Canada had been automatically committed to a European war in 1914, and King had always promised that Canadians would make their own decision the next time around. Parliament was summoned, and in an eloquent speech Lapointe repeated that there was no option but to participate. Most Quebecers, noting the solemn promise that there would be no conscription, seem to have followed the justice minister, while in the House of Commons only four members of parliament dissented. On 10 September, King George signed a separate Canadian declaration of war against Germany.

The prime minister wanted to make it clear that going to war was an entirely Canadian exercise. He emphasized to the British high commissioner in Ottawa, "we . . . take this stand on our own, not in any colonial attitude of mind, simply following the lead from Britain." King had always known that Canada would stand with Britain when "a great and clear call of duty" came. The war would be fought for nation, however, not for empire: for unity in a country where one out of every two citizens was of British origin, and for the survival of a nation that depended on British and European cultural, political, military, and economic ties to dilute the power and attraction of the United States.

For O.D. Skelton and some of his articulate young recruits in the Department of External Affairs, the decision to enter a British war was a triumph of loyalism and colonialism over autonomy and reason. The first casualty of World War II, Skelton asserted, was Canada's claim to independent control of its own destiny. The undersecretary of state for external affairs and his neutralist friends in the government missed the point, however, as did Professors Scott and Underhill and the politician J.S. Woodsworth. If Canadians were not yet fully independent, they had made that decision entirely themselves. Put another way, Canadians were as independent as they wanted to be, or felt they could afford to be.

In the final analysis, the opinions of Skelton and other would-be advisers to the prime minister did not really matter. Although he consulted people within a very narrow circle, Mackenzie King made the major Canadian foreign policy decisions alone. His peacetime leadership was often and probably excessively cautious and devious. He had hoped against hope that war could be averted, even to the extent of making a couple of further and rather foolish attempts to act the peacemaker with Germany in 1939, once right on the eve of war. Now he was ready to do what he knew had to be done.

CHAPTER FIVE

If Britain
and France
Go Down, 1939–1945

I N SEPTEMBER 1939, the memory of the sixty thousand dead in World War I and of domestic strife over compulsory service was still powerful, and Canada remained trapped in a grinding, seemingly endless economic depression. There was no enthusiasm for this new war, no cheering crowds in the streets, no overwhelming rush to the colours.

Anxious to shore up its restless Quebec support, Mackenzie King's government repeated the pledge it had made well before war broke out: it would never impose conscription for overseas military service. Indeed, Ottawa only grudgingly agreed that recruits might be enlisted for service overseas. Canada would contribute a single division of infantry, confining the major national effort to the air. This decision was given flesh in December 1939, when Britain, Canada, and the other dominions joined in the British Commonwealth Air Training Plan (BCATP). The expansive and expensive scheme to train aircrew for imperial air forces was to cost hundreds of millions of dollars and was to be directed by the Royal Canadian Air Force on behalf of Britain and the dominions. No one in 1939 could conceive the idea that war in the air might produce aircrew casualties to rival those suffered by the army on the ground.

AT BRITAIN'S SIDE

The BCATP negotiations were characterized by a lengthy, bitter dispute over costs that pitted King's government against the British. An almost equally bitter disagreement arose in November 1939 between a Canadian financial mission and Treasury officials in London. The British wanted cheap wheat from Canada; the Canadians insisted on a price that would give prairie farmers a decent return after a decade of drought, dust storms, and low prices. At the same time, the negotiators haggled over the size of a Canadian loan to pay for British purchases in Canada. The governor of the Bank of Canada refused to allow the sum to exceed a paltry $200 million. As Britain, naturally concerned to help expand employment and profits in its own factories, had placed only £7 million ($35 million) in Canadian orders thus far, the governor's figure seemed to be all Canada could do. All this left bad feelings on both sides of the Atlantic. In London, Mackenzie King was seen as shifty and his government as unreliable. To Ottawa, the British seemed willing to fight the war to the last Canadian dollar. It was not a happy augury for wartime relations with London.

Most strikingly, however, London assumed the right to direct the Commonwealth war effort and Ottawa, for all practical purposes, acquiesced. It was almost as if Sir Robert Borden's valiant efforts to secure Canada a voice in decisions a quarter-century before had never occurred; it was almost as if King's own struggle for autonomy had been blown away by the first shots of World War II. So fearful was King of being perceived by French Canadians to be in direct consultation with London that he avoided any suggestion of a Commonwealth prime ministers' conference, and even delayed his own first visit to London until the summer of 1941. In his careful, balanced view, abandoning any effort to increase Canadian autonomy was in the interest of the greater good: Quebec's continued acceptance of war. Even the appearance of going to Britain looked bad in Quebec, although not to do so, ironically, reduced Canadian decision making. The balance, however, always had its other scale. For English-Canadian consumption, the prime minister's first collection of wartime speeches appeared under the rather grandiloquent title, *Canada at Britain's Side.*

King also had his difficulties with the American position on the European war. He wrote caustically in his diary that Franklin Roosevelt's statement announcing American neutrality on 3 September was "all words, words, words. America keeping out of this great issue which affects the destiny of mankind. And professing to do so in the name of peace. . . . I was really ashamed of the attitude of the u.s." King did more than carp in his diary a few days later when he spoke bluntly to American opinion in his major address in Parliament during the short September session that decided to take Canada into the war. Talking to the neutral states, King said "I tell them if they remain neutral in this struggle, and Britain and France go down, there is not one of them that will bear for long the name it bears at the present time. . . . And if this conqueror . . . is able to crush the peoples of Europe, what is going to become of the doctrine of isolation of this North American continent?" The prime minister concluded, "It is for all of us on this continent to do our part to save its privileged position by helping others."

None of King's complaints and criticisms would ever be offered directly to President Roosevelt. The prime minister always paid due deference to the American chief executive, and King ensured that his government, obliged to impose controls and restrictions on trade, foreign exchange, and movements across the border, did as little as possible to irritate American sensibilities.

The course of the war soon made clear that the United States was sorely needed. The stunning German blitzkrieg swept over Poland in a matter of days. The "phony war," a hiatus in action after the end of September 1939, gave a brief respite, but that lasted only until spring 1940. The Germans took Denmark and Norway in April and the next month moved against the Low Countries and France. By mid-June, France had surrendered ignominiously and Britain's main expeditionary force, rescued from the cauldron only by grace of a miraculous evacuation at Dunkirk, was desperately trying to re-equip itself at home. The Canadian division had largely escaped the debacle on the continent, and it was the best-equipped formation left in Britain as people braced themselves for the Nazi invasion.

The shocking events in Europe electrified the Canadian people, and opinion in English Canada, and to a lesser extent in Quebec, quickly solidified behind the war effort. The neutralists of the 1930s who had accepted the idea of war in September 1939 with great reluctance now enthusiastically advocated doing everything possible to help Britain resist. A similar sea-change galvanized the government. The "limited liability" war of September 1939—the war that the government hoped to use to restore the depression-wracked Canadian economy—was forgotten. In its place was "total war," and now all the financial stops were pulled out. Even that national shibboleth "conscription" began to be uttered; compulsory service for home defence was put into place in the summer of 1940, initially for thirty-day training periods.

Almost never mentioned, though it dominated the thinking of the Canadian government, was the possibility that Germany might conquer Britain. This offensive would cost Canada much of its trade, causing serious dislocation in agriculture and industry. Canadian soldiers and aircrew in Britain, now constituting two divisions and almost every trained pilot, would also be lost, removing most of the country's trained military at one fell swoop. Depending on the course of battle and the terms of surrender that Hitler might impose, the Royal Navy could fall into Nazi hands, thus exposing North America to a credible threat of attack from across the Atlantic for the first time in the modern era. Canada itself might be subject to invasion.

Horrified by the wholly unexpected turn of events, Mackenzie King found himself uncomfortably in the middle when President Roosevelt asked him to sound out the new British prime minister, Winston Churchill, about the future of the Royal Navy. On 19 May 1940, even before the evacuation at Dunkirk, Roosevelt told Canadian diplomat Hugh Keenleyside that he was deeply concerned about "certain possible eventualities which could not possibly be mentioned aloud." Instructed by the American president to say the words "British fleet" to Mackenzie King, the diplomat was well aware that Roosevelt wanted King to strike an arrangement with Churchill under which the Royal Navy would cross the ocean to North America rather than be surrendered. A week later, with the situation on the continent more desperate still, Roosevelt again saw

British Columbia goes to war, 1940 (National Archives of Canada,
C 38723)

Keenleyside and expressed his fear that the British might accept a
"soft peace" and use the navy as a bargaining counter to get the best
possible terms. Roosevelt hoped instead that the Royal Navy would
fight to the end and then disperse its surviving remnants to the rest of
the empire, even if it meant the occupation of Britain and ruination

similar to that visited on the other Nazi conquests. The U.S. president wanted Mackenzie King to tell this to Churchill.

The very thought appalled the Canadian leader. To King, it seemed that the United States was trying to save itself through British sacrifice. "I instinctively revolted at such a thought," he wrote in his diary. "My reaction was that I would rather die than do aught to save ourselves or any part of this continent at the expense of Britain." But he could not deny the request from Roosevelt and after exquisite care in the drafting, he dispatched a telegram to Churchill on 31 May.

A few days later, the British prime minister told Parliament, "We shall never surrender." Even if the British Isles were lost, "our Empire beyond the seas, armed and guarded by the British Fleet, would carry on the struggle, until, in God's good time, the New World, with all its power and might, steps forth to the rescue and liberation of the old." King believed that these magnificent phrases were a direct reply to his message on behalf of Roosevelt. Privately, Churchill said only the truth when he wired King that he could not guarantee what a pro-German government might do, put into place either in succession to his or through occupation. To convey that realistic but despairing message to Roosevelt cost King dearly, and further exchanges made very clear that the middleman's position was uncomfortable indeed.

FRIENDLY AGREEMENTS

Worried as he was about the fate of Britain, King was the Canadian leader and his first thought had to be for the fate of his own country. In the summer of 1940 few thought Britain could survive much longer. The defence of Canada therefore had to be the top priority for Ottawa, however much and however quickly aid was sent overseas. In the circumstances, only one option stood open to the Canadian government: a military alliance with the United States. No such alliance had ever existed before. After-dinner orators in the two North American states had long bragged about the "undefended border," but military co-operation had been largely non-existent.

The Canadian and American chiefs of staff had met briefly in 1938 to talk about continental defence, but that was the extent of it.

Now more was needed, and opinion makers in Canada had begun to meet, talk, and write about the new situation. The new American minister to Canada, the canny professional diplomat Pierrepont Moffat, quickly became aware of the trend in opinion, and as early as mid-June 1940 he recommended military staff talks. These took place in July in great secrecy. Meanwhile, King's bureaucrats in the Department of External Affairs prepared their memoranda, pointing out that the Americans "will expect, and if necessary, demand, Canadian assistance in the defence of this continent and this Hemisphere." "The negotiation of a specific offensive–defensive alliance," Hugh Keenleyside wrote, "is likely to become inevitable."

President Roosevelt, whose intense interest in North American defence we have noted in the previous chapter, had clearly reached the same conclusion. In mid-August, after conversations with the Canadian minister to the United States and with some of his key advisers, he called Mackenzie King and invited him to meet the next day at Ogdensburg, New York, a little town across the St Lawrence River from Prescott, Ontario. There, in an almost casual discussion, the two leaders agreed to set up a Permanent Joint Board on Defence (PJBD). King leapt at the opportunity to secure his country, to guarantee Canada against invasion, and he did not even query Roosevelt's insistence that the board be permanent. The president explained that the board would "help secure the continent for the future" and King readily agreed.

Roosevelt displayed a hint of the steel inner core that had made him the shrewdest American politician of his century when he also talked about the "destroyers for bases" deal then being negotiated between Britain and the United States. The Americans were to give Britain fifty desperately needed destroyers in return for bases in the West Indies and, in a separate arrangement, in Newfoundland. Roosevelt remarked that he had not been able to understand British reluctance to lease bases, "that as a matter of fact, if war developed with Germany and he felt it necessary to seize them to protect the United States, he would do that in any event. That it was much better to have a friendly agreement in advance." The assertion contained an implicit threat that Roosevelt might have acted the same way towards Canada, but the PJBD had given him his "friendly agreement in advance." King responded that Canada had no intention of selling or leasing bases, a comment the president acknowledged by saying that all he wanted was to be able to get troops quickly into Canada in case of invasion. That was "all right," King said, as were annual manoeuvres on each other's territory.

Nonetheless, the Canadian government did not roll over supinely to do whatever the United States wanted. When negotiations for the Joint Canadian–United States Basic Defence Plan began in the autumn, the American military sought strategic control of Canadian forces in the event of a British defeat, and Canada agreed. After the summer of 1940 that made sense. The next spring, however, Britain was still fighting and had won a victory in the air war that Churchill had called the Battle of Britain. Negotiations for a second plan designed to come into effect if and when the United States joined in the war (the so-called ABC-22 plan) were thus much more difficult. Again the United States sought strategic and tactical control, asking for the integration of eastern Canada into its Northeast Defence Command and of British Columbia into its Northwest Defence Command. This time the Canadians resisted fiercely, the Americans backed off, and all that was agreed upon was the "coordination of the military effort . . . to be effected by mutual cooperation."

The British lion's bite had been diminished, but so long as Winston Churchill was in power it continued to roar. After King and Roosevelt had reached their agreement at Ogdensburg, Churchill aimed his wrath at the Canadian prime minister. King had told the British leader of the PJBD, stressing what he believed to be almost self-evident: that with its home territory secure Canada could now do even more for Britain's defence. A man with a long view of events, however, Churchill believed that Canada had now passed into the American orbit. After discussing the Canadian–American deal in his War Cabinet, he fired off a telegram to King: "I am deeply interested in the arrangements you are making for Canada and America's mutual defence. Here again there may be two opinions on some of the points mentioned. Supposing Mr Hitler cannot invade us and his Air Force begins to blench under the strain all these transactions will be judged in a mood different to that prevailing while the issue still hangs in the balance." Churchill had accused King and Canada of scuttling for safety under the American defence umbrella. This message deeply disturbed Mackenzie King, who had genuinely believed that he had done a good day's work for the empire by binding the neutral Americans closely to one of the belligerents.

In fact, King recognized the fundamental truth of 1940. Britain's military weakness had forced Canada to look for its own security to the United States. There was no option. Moreover, without American military assistance, Canada could not have continued to assist Britain. For the short term, for the war's duration, King was right, but in retrospect there is no doubt that Churchill had foretold the future. The Ogdensburg Agreement of 1940 definitively marked Canada's move from the British to the American sphere of influence. Under the weight of Nazi military victories, military and strategic power had shifted and Canada had shifted with it.

This was quickly evident in economic areas as well. Before the war, Canada had maintained a state of economic balance with its two main trading partners. The country had a regular trade surplus with Britain and an annual trade deficit with the United States. The two were ordinarily in rough balance, and there was no difficulty in taking a pound sterling earned by Canada in Britain and converting it into American dollars to pay for the deficit with the United States. The war changed all this. The British forbade the conversion of sterling, now a weak currency, into dollars for a start. Canadian exports to Britain began to increase under the stress of war, but the sterling earned for these transactions could not be brought back to Canada. At the same time, the war greatly increased crucial imports into Canada from the United States. Every truck and tank and artillery piece and aircraft engine made in Canada for Britain needed American parts or specialty steels or components.

The government tried to cut non-essential trade with the United States and strictly limited the amount of money that Canadians could spend in the United States. These measures were mere stopgaps, however, and they proved completely ineffective in the face of the growing shortage of American dollars. As early as the fall of 1940 the problem was severe enough that the government had begun to contemplate seizing American securities held by Canadians, blocking the payment of dividends from Canadian companies to Americans, and rationing American imports. Such measures would have undoubtedly caused a firestorm in the Canadian and American business press, and they were not implemented. By early spring 1941 the deficit had reached close to half a billion dollars.

In the early months of 1941 the Lend-Lease Bill was making its way through the u.s. Congress. A product of Roosevelt's fertile brain, the legislation would permit the United States to lease or lend war equipment to Britain, itself desperately short of American dollars with which to pay for supplies. There was, however, one serious problem for Canada inherent in the lend-lease proposal. If Britain could lease war matériel from the United States without putting cash on the barrelhead, why should it buy dominion goods for which it had to pay sterling or Canadian dollars? Lend-lease was a potentially war-winning lifeline to Britain, and no one doubted that. Unfortunately, the generous measure might have the unintended effect of destroying the Canadian economy. Factories and jobs could disappear, and the munitions industry with them.

King met Roosevelt at the president's New York home in April 1941 to find a way out of the dilemma. Canada itself would not accept the lend-lease arrangement, but wanted some way to get the benefits of the bill without having to sell off Canadian assets in the United States or sacrifice the country's postwar bargaining position with Washington. The lend-lease proposal was generous indeed, but for a country sharing a continent with the United States it could lead to an uncomfortably beholden position. Well-briefed by his officials, the prime minister hit on just the right approach. "Why not," he asked Roosevelt, "buy from Canada as much as Canada is buying from the u.s.—just balance the accounts?" There it was, and the Hyde Park Declaration issued on "a grand Sunday in April" stated that "in mobilizing the resources of this continent each country should provide the other with the defense articles which it is best able to produce." The declaration anticipated that Canada could provide between $200 and 300 million of war matériel over the next year, the sale of which "would materially assist Canada in meeting part of the cost of Canadian defense purchases in the United States." The key clause stated simply, "In so far as Canadian defense purchases in the United States consist of component parts to be used in equipment and munitions which Canada is producing for Great Britain, it was also agreed that Great Britain will obtain these parts under the Lend-Lease Act and forward them to Canada for inclusion in the finished articles."

At one stroke, King and Roosevelt had resolved Canada's shortage of American exchange. At one stroke, the Canadian economy was liberated from fear of economic collapse and permitted to do its utmost to pour out goods for the war. Roosevelt had acted on his own, the declaration falling within his presidential prerogatives. The Cabinet later confirmed Canadian agreement to the deal, but King too had acted informally.

This was a major agreement. Its wartime consequences were wholly positive, and Canada soon acquired large surpluses of American dollars as American companies and the u.s. government made large and continuing purchases north of the border. There was a drawback, however, and Mackenzie King seems to have been aware of it. As he told Parliament, the "Hyde Park declaration will have a permanent significance in the relations between Canada and the United States. It involves nothing less than a common plan for the economic defence of the western hemisphere." Canada was now just as firmly in the economic orbit of the United States as it was in its defence sphere of influence. British economic weakness had forced Canada to turn south for assistance; assistance had been freely and generously offered; and another major shift had occurred. After only eighteen months of war, Canada could never be the same again.

Along with the change came a new recognition in Washington of Canada's importance. With Europe under the Nazi heel, with Britain in great danger, and with Japan under the control of militarist elements seemingly bent on war, the Americas seemed all that the United States could count on. And in the Americas only Canada was a truly democratic state. That made Canadians important to the United States; it gave Canadian questions fast consideration at the State Department and even at the White House, and it meant—for a brief period—that the best minds in the American administration focussed on Canada. This had rarely been the case in the past, when the United States had had trouble understanding that Canada was

an autonomous dominion rather than a British colony. It would seldom be the case in the future.

The new Canadian status lasted only from the summer of 1940
through to the first secret American negotiations with Great Britain
in the spring of 1941. The Roosevelt administration, now actively
planning to enter the war at some as yet unspecified time, found
dealing with London easier than with Ottawa. More to the point,
once it had entered the war, the Americans much preferred to deal
with Whitehall as the representative not only of Britain but of all the
dominions.

The new situation was immediately apparent to everyone when,
in August 1941, Roosevelt and Churchill met for the first time in the
war. Aboard ship at Argentia, Newfoundland, the two leaders produced the Atlantic Charter, an idealistic statement of war aims, and
they did it without Mackenzie King. The prime minister was kept in
the dark even though Canadian troops garrisoned Newfoundland.
King was not amused at failing to receive an invitation to the
Anglo–American wedding, and the omission drew critical comment
in Canadian media conditioned to view Canada as the essential link
between London and Washington. He immediately flew to Britain
to see Churchill in an effort to re-establish his place and prestige
with the Canadian public. During wartime, it seemed, situations
changed with astonishing rapidity.

CARRYING ON AFTER SKELTON

The Department of External Affairs was changing under the stress of
war. Its de facto creator, Undersecretary of State for External Affairs
O.D. Skelton, had been a consistent nationalist throughout the
1930s, and could even be considered a neutralist. His suspicion of
British wiles and contempt for British policy had often boiled over
during the crises that preceded Hitler's invasion of Poland. If he had
had his way Canada would not have gone to war. His views certainly
were not those of the prime minister, who otherwise considered him
his most valuable adviser. Nor were they shared by all his department's officers. The neutralists of the 1930s—Hugh Keenleyside,

Loring Christie, Jack Pickersgill, and others—had changed their minds in the light of the first terrible year of war. Other officers such as Norman Robertson, Lester Pearson, and Hume Wrong had understood from the first shot over the German–Polish border that Canada's only option was to fight at Britain's side. The differences of opinion tended to disappear as the war unfolded, though officers such as Skelton, Keenleyside, and Pickersgill, for example, were probably keener on striking an alliance with the United States in 1940 than were some of the others.

Skelton had held the war operations of the department together. Hard-working, cerebral, and much admired by his superiors and juniors despite the administrative shambles that prevailed around him, he had seemed completely indispensable. Then, driving home for lunch on 28 January 1941, he suffered a heart attack and died behind the wheel. The prime minister was shattered, and he bemoaned his own lack of the "unselfishness and selflessness" that had characterized his faithful undersecretary.

The business of government had to go on and a replacement had to be named. There were contenders aplenty. Lester B. (Mike) Pearson believed himself to be the logical choice but he was overseas, performing work as the effective head of the diplomatic operation at the high commission in London while Vincent Massey, the high commissioner, handled the social side. The frequently disgruntled and ambitious Hume Wrong, stationed in Ottawa, had complained too often and too loudly about too many things for the prime minister to relish the prospect of working with him. Hugh Keenleyside had been entrusted with delicate missions to Roosevelt, and he had handled them well. King had perhaps been annoyed, however, by the idealistic Keenleyside's overt championing of Japanese Canadians in British Columbia while on the Special Committee on Orientals, struck to calm west coast fears in 1940. The prime minister did not think of him as up to the task of succeeding Skelton. Instead, his eye fell on Norman Robertson, a thirty-six-year-old British Columbian who had been a Rhodes scholar.

Robertson had joined the Department of External Affairs in 1929. He had worked mainly on trade matters, from the Ottawa Conference of 1932 to the 1937–1938 agreements with Britain and the

United States. His mind, character, and gravity had impressed both Skelton and King, who were comfortable dealing with him. After informing the Cabinet of his choice, King called Robertson on the evening of 28 January, only a few hours after Skelton's death, and told him to take over. Shocked by his chief's death and his unexpected promotion, Robertson scrawled a note to his parents in Vancouver: "Skelton had more of the qualities of greatness than anybody I've ever known," and the "request to try & carry on in his shoes came therefore as rather staggering & frightening." Robertson added, "The job is a big one & calls for a number of qualities I simply have not got."

The new acting undersecretary (the post would not be confirmed until 24 June at a salary of $10 000) was no better at administration than Skelton, but Robertson knew his weaknesses. He had Keenleyside sketch out a new organization for the department, with functional or geographical divisions and assistant undersecretaries to direct the work. The plan was a sensible one and the prime minister accepted it. Pearson, unhappy at being passed over for his friend Robertson, came back to Ottawa to become one of the assistant undersecretaries; Keenleyside, no less unhappy, became another; and Hume Wrong, unhappiest of all, went to Washington as minister-counsellor, the number two post at the legation. There he served under Leighton McCarthy, a Toronto businessman and Liberal who succeeded Loring Christie as Canada's chief diplomat in the United States after the latter's death in 1941. McCarthy had been picked for the post because he was a friend of Roosevelt's.

If there were hard feelings, there was no reason to sulk. Everyone recognized that Robertson had not intrigued for the job, and all understood that the war was more important than personal ambition. Pearson, Wrong, Keenleyside, and all the other officers in the rapidly expanding but still small department had too much to do to find time to grumble. Robertson and his three closest colleagues were left on their own most of the time by Mackenzie King, who had his own terrible responsibilities in running the war effort and attempting to keep French and English Canadians on the same side. Together, these four external affairs personnel gave Canada a foreign policy.

The needs of war, the extra business involved in being part of a great alliance, demanded that diplomatic missions be exchanged with additional governments. Before the war, Canada had kept a representative in Geneva with the League of Nations and envoys only in London, Washington, Tokyo, Paris, and the Low Countries. By the end of 1945, high commissioners had been dispatched to Australia, New Zealand, and South Africa, Commonwealth countries all. Canada also established diplomatic links with the Soviet Union, China, Mexico, Brazil, Chile, Peru, Greece, Ireland, Cuba, and Argentina. Ottawa also accredited an office to the Nazi-occupied countries that maintained governments-in-exile in London. In 1943, Leighton McCarthy in Washington became the first minister abroad to be raised to the status of ambassador, and this was followed by a similar change in a number of other countries before the war was over.

The Department of External Affairs had too few personnel to provide professional diplomats for all these posts. Moreover, the professionals were needed to do the hard work of diplomacy in Ottawa and in the key missions abroad. Military officers, business leaders, and Liberal Party supporters were therefore pressed into service, sometimes with less than satisfactory results. Major-General Victor Odlum, for example, became high commissioner in Canberra, Australia, at the end of 1941 when his superiors decided that his command of the 2nd Canadian Infantry Division in Britain was no longer satisfactory. A militiaman, a strong B.C. Liberal, a friend of Cabinet minister Ian Mackenzie, Odlum could not have been shunted into sedentary retirement. Instead, fired with enthusiasm for his new post and roused by danger after Japan attacked in the Pacific, he began promising the Australians Canadian military assistance. The Cabinet War Committee, horrified, had to slap him down. Diplomats, it seemed, could be created more easily than diplomacy learned.

A DIFFERENT KIND OF WAR

The war spread inexorably over the globe. In June 1941, Hitler launched his panzers against the Soviet Union, the erstwhile ally with whom he had divided the corpse of Poland in October 1939. Britain and its allies—incredibly, Canada was the strongest among them at this point—had all looked with disfavour on Moscow for its alliance with Germany, its share in the conquest of Poland, its long history of subversion, and its aggressive war against Finland. Suddenly Moscow was an ally, and the democracies hastened to strike links with the Soviet government and people. Canada offered what governmental aid it could (6.8 percent of all Canadian aid given during the war), and individuals and charities did their bit, stirred by the Russian people's vigorous resistance to the German invaders. Canada established a legation in the Soviet Union in late 1942, and Dana Wilgress became the first minister to Moscow, a position soon upgraded to ambassador. He had hitherto served as deputy minister of trade and commerce and was a genuine expert on the U.S.S.R.

The Soviets were at war with Germany, but they were not at war everywhere. When Japan launched a brilliant and co-ordinated series of attacks against American, British, and Dutch possessions in the Far East in December 1941, the Soviet Union remained neutral in the Pacific. Much of the American fleet was put out of action at Pearl Harbor, and American airpower in the Philippines was destroyed on the ground. Hong Kong was attacked from the north and fell in less than three weeks. Its garrison had included a Canadian brigade headquarters and two battalions of troops, and those who survived became prisoners of war. Malaya, the Philippines, and the Dutch East Indies held out longer but were swallowed up into Tokyo's Greater East Co-Prosperity Sphere all the same, while the Commonwealth countries of New Zealand and Australia lay exposed to the Japanese.

The stunning Japanese successes reinforced already existing fears and prejudices in Canada. Japanese immigration into British Columbia, underway on a small scale for over fifty years, had been generally resisted by the white majority, but it was particularly resented by those on the coast employed in small businesses and in such industries as logging, fishing, and berry farming. Not even the adherence of Japan to the Anglo–Japanese alliance of 1902 and the co-operation of the imperial Japanese Navy in World War I had eased feelings. Yet so long as Japan and Britain were allies, Ottawa could at least attempt to diminish harsh provincial treatment of the west-coast Japanese with an appeal that such actions were embarass-ing to Britain. When the alliance lapsed in 1922, this moderating influence was lost and British Columbian concerns about the "yel-low peril," the supposed threat to the white race, were only strength-ened. The war that began in December 1941 caused near panic along the Pacific coast of both Canada and the United States.

In September 1940, the U.S. army's Signal Intelligence Section cracked Japan's top secret diplomatic code. Five months later, word reached Ottawa via High Commissioner Vincent Massey in London that Tokyo was attempting to recruit agents on the west coast. The information was discussed and instantly discounted by the Cabinet War Committee. The records provide no evidence either that precau-tions were stepped up in British Columbia or that any Canadian Japanese had been persuaded to spy for Tokyo. Immediately following Pearl Harbor, about forty Japanese aliens were picked up by the RCMP and interned with other Axis aliens in military camps. They were a dis-parate group of coastal or Vancouver Island farmers, fishermen, and school teachers—roughly half of whom would be released in early 1943. In February 1942, as Singapore fell to Japan and after President Roosevelt had signed an executive order placing over one hundred thousand American Japanese under military control, all those of Japanese origin—Canadian citizens or not—were ordered off the coast and sent eastwards in a massive civilian evacuation.

Over the next eight months, some twenty-three thousand Canadian Japanese were displaced and dispossessed. In 1943 their seized property was sold off at fire sale prices. Ottawa actually interned only seven hundred Canadian Japanese under military guard. The entire community was, however, dispersed across the country in isolated camps and hostels and put under the watchful eye of the RCMP until 1949, when by law Canadian Japanese were permitted to return to the west coast.

At the end of the war, the federal government moved to transport all the Canadian Japanese who could be persuaded, with a good deal of arm-twisting, to sail for Japan. Close to four thousand, more than half of whom were Canadian-born, participated in the government's offer of transportation "home." Of these, over 33 percent were the dependent children of adult transportees. This postwar treatment of

Evacuation of the Canadian Japanese, 1942 (Tak Toyota, National
Archives of Canada, C 47066)

Canadian Japanese was perhaps the most shameful aspect of the
whole miserable affair.

Severe as these wartime measures were, they were kept under
constant review by the Department of External Affairs. The reasons
were eminently practical. Although External Affairs had repeatedly
warned Canadians to leave Japan and an increasingly unstable Far
East during 1940–1941, at the outbreak of war, more than two thousand ended up in Japanese hands, including 534 teachers and missionaries in China, Korea, the Philippines, and Japan, as well as
merchant seamen, other strandees, and almost seventeen hundred
surviving soldiers in Hong Kong. There was little public sympathy
in British Columbia for Canadian Japanese in early 1942—there
would be some in central Canada later in the war—but the government had no desire for harsher action against them for fear of what
Tokyo might do. As far as one can tell, Japan paid little attention to

its present and former nationals in Canadian hands. Imperial Japanese authorities were so brutal to prisoners of war, and even their own citizens, that they could not have been mindful of retaliatory measures.

The beginning of the war in the Pacific posed a clear threat to North America, especially because the sudden attack on Pearl Harbor had devastated the American fleet. The entire west coast of North America was thought to be under threat, and both countries rushed new forces to the West. The United States at once began to press Canada for permission to build a land route through Canadian territory to Alaska, and in the circumstances there was no choice but to agree. American construction battalions began the job forthwith, tens of thousands of workers and machines having an enormous impact on the small native and white populations and fragile environment of the North.

By 1945 the Americans had built airfields, an oil pipeline, weather stations, and a host of additional installations on Canadian territory. Their presence was so powerful that the federal government—spurred perhaps by the rumoured greeting, "Army of occupation," given by telephone operators at u.s. Army headquarters in Edmonton—began to fear for Canadian sovereignty. After British High Commissioner Malcolm MacDonald reported alarmingly on matters, Ottawa appointed an army general to show the flag in the North, to remind the Americans that they were in a foreign country. That helped, as did the government's decision to pay in full for every u.s. installation at the end of the war. The Americans were friends, and their help had been greatly appreciated. With the end of the war, however, it was time for them to depart.

VICHY "AIN'T"

More difficult, more frustrating than dealing with the United States was dealing with France. Under German sway after June 1940, France had a nominally independent government led by Marshal Pétain and administered from Vichy. Surprisingly, perhaps, Canada continued to maintain diplomatic relations with the puppet state, doing so at British request and on the assumption that the more Vichy was reminded of its former allies still in the war the better. Pétain's slogan of "travail, famille, patrie" had special resonance in Quebec, where the religiosity of the Vichy regime was much appreciated.

The Vichy legation in Ottawa was widely thought to be a centre of subversion in French Canada. The Canadian government responded by spying on the mission's officers and intercepting its wireless transmissions to Paris. In the process, the Examination Unit came into existence to intercept radio messages and crack codes. (The country's first spy agency worked under the nominal direction of the National Research Council.) Complicating matters still further were the French islands of St Pierre and Miquelon, located off Newfoundland very near to the main convoy routes to and from Britain. The Canadian government strongly suspected that the Vichyite government there was passing details of convoy movements to the enemy.

This fishy stew of obligations and fears simmered for more than two years. At times Ottawa was very close to sending troops onto St Pierre, but it hung back because of worries about Washington's reaction. At Christmas 1941, finally, a small Free French force seized the islands, acting under the orders of General Charles de Gaulle.

Furious at this intrusion of the European war into the hitherto sacrosanct Americas, Washington leapt to claim that Ottawa had connived at the attack, and ordered it to remove de Gaulle's force and restore the status quo. No hard evidence has yet surfaced to support this accusation. De Gaulle and Ottawa both bluntly refused the American demand, and although relations were very strained for a few weeks, the crisis blew over. St Pierre and Miquelon remained under Free France. The coup nonetheless increased American suspicion of de Gaulle, making it very difficult for Ottawa to recognize him as the representative of France.

Meanwhile, Pierre Dupuy, the Canadian representative to Vichy, made several trips from his base in London to see what was happening in France. His highly coloured, optimistic reports about the attitudes of Marshal Pétain's government were influential with the British government but only for a time. Churchill's advisers soon concluded that he could not be relied upon. Ottawa at first continued to put its trust in the worth of his reports but eventually, like London, reached the regretful conclusion that Dupuy's sanguine reporting from Vichy was simply wrong.

Nobody trusted the Vichy government. When Anglo–American forces landed in French North Africa in November 1942 and Hitler responded by sending his troops into hitherto unoccupied areas of France, thus eliminating any lingering appearance that Marshal

Canadian troops in France, 1940 (National Archives of Canada, PA 116510)

Pétain's government was independent, Ottawa seized the opportunity to sever ties with Vichy. The problem was to do so in a way that would minimize the political damage in Quebec, and Norman Robertson found the way. The undersecretary concluded that Canada was not breaking relations with Vichy because the Vichy government had for all practical purposes ceased to exist. As Roosevelt put it to Mackenzie King, "In other words, [Vichy] ain't." Exactly, the prime minister replied. In August 1943, Canada recognized Free France as the administrator of French overseas territories and in October 1944 as the provisional government of France. It had been a long road, and Charles de Gaulle would not forget Canadian tardiness in according his movement its rightful status.

"A VOICE . . . PROPORTIONATE . . ."

The entry of the United States into the war, first against Japan and shortly thereafter against Germany, pushed Canada into the background. Ottawa had a mixed response to developing events. On the one hand, the country's leaders were genuinely overjoyed that from the spring of 1941 Britain and the United States were secretly discussing American participation in the war. On the other hand, they felt left out of the new Anglo–American unity. After Churchill visited the United States in December 1941, the two great powers set out to co-ordinate their war effort. A combined chiefs of staff committee was to run the military war effort, while a series of combined boards co-ordinated the economic struggle.

No Canadian seriously thought that Canada's generals were entitled to a place on the Combined Chiefs of Staff Committee. By early 1942 the Canadian army consisted of five divisions and two armoured brigades overseas. The air force was shortly to consolidate its bomber squadrons in a separate group within the Royal Air Force. The Royal Canadian Navy, despite teething troubles as it contended with a fiftyfold increase in strength since 1939, had responsibilities stretching from the Caribbean to European waters, and it took over command of a crucial sector of the northwest Atlantic in 1943. This was a major effort, to be sure, but it paled beside the huge

American and British military forces. Canadian military leaders were, for the most part, learning their trade in Britain and struggling to do so. So too were the rank and file members of the forces.

When it came to the economic war effort, however, Ottawa was much less diffident. Canada produced vast quantities of food and raw materials. Its factories were now hitting their stride and war production was moving out of the shops and across the Atlantic in a torrent. So great was the flow that in 1942 the Canadian government felt able to give Britain a billion-dollar gift, testimony both to support for the war effort and to recognition that England simply could not pay for everything it needed. Nevertheless, the combined boards operated on the assumption that an Anglo–American directorate could dispose of Canadian production as it chose, an idea that Ottawa could not abide.

Hume Wrong conceived the outline of the Canadian response to this seemingly high-handed usurpation. The minister-counsellor at the Washington legation was the most clear-headed member of the Department of External Affairs, and he understood, as he told Lester Pearson privately, that Canada had been shut out because "the Government has hitherto adopted in these matters what may unkindly be called a semi-colonial position." Ottawa, after all, had acquiesced to British direction of the war effort, and the country had been relegated to the sidelines as a result. Wrong suggested a dictum to challenge this: "The principle . . . is that each member of the grand alliance should have a voice in the conduct of the war proportionate to its contribution to the general war effort. A subsidiary principle is that the influence of the various countries should be greatest in connection with those matters with which they are most directly concerned."

As yet there was no name for this, though it would come to be known as the functional principle. Its formulation clearly marked the gestation of the "middle-power" concept that Canada would champion during the later stages of the war and into the postwar era. Canadians began to employ Hume Wrong's line regularly. The prime minister, for example, told a British visitor in July 1942 that "we felt we were not getting the representation to which our country was entitled . . . that I thought our people expected in view of the fact they had been in the war for nearly 3 years while the Americans had not been in a year as yet. . . . Also of the fact that we were one of the large producing countries . . . [and] had provided Britain with a gift of a billion dollars."*

The first Canadian demand under the functional principle came in July 1942, when Ottawa sought a place on the Combined Food Board, the agency designed to control the allocation of food supplies. Canada based its claim on the simple fact that, next to the United States, it was by far the most important producer and contributor of foodstuffs to the allies. London, consulted first, responded with the argument that Canadian membership "would not make for technical efficiency," a suggestion that made Ottawa furious. The King government began to hint that unless Whitehall developed a more accommodating attitude, there was little chance of Canada making another billion-dollar gift in munitions and supplies.

This was a bluff, of course, for public opinion simply would not have tolerated an end to Canadian generosity. Nonetheless, French Canada demonstrated sufficient opposition to aid to Britain that in 1943 the scheme was renamed Mutual Aid, and assistance was deliberately offered to other countries as well. The overwhelming bulk of the aid continued to go to Britain, however, and by the end of the war the United Kingdom had received the original billion-dollar gift, $2.043 billion in Mutual Aid, and the forgiveness of $425 million owed for the British Commonwealth Air Training Plan. To put these sums into perspective, the whole federal budget in 1939 was $550 million.

British officials worried enough about Ottawa's threats over aid to suggest that they would support a Canadian request for membership

---

* King's confident exposition of what the people expected may not have been sound. The Canadian Institute of Public Opinion regularly asked Canadians their views after 1941, revealing sharply divided attitudes. In June 1943, it found that 49 percent wanted Canada to stay part of the Commonwealth after the war, 21 percent to join the United States, and 24 percent to become totally independent. In another poll, in March 1944, 47 percent of Canadians wanted Canada to have control of its own foreign policy, while 46 percent thought there should be a common imperial foreign policy.

on the weak Combined Production and Resources Board (CPRB) but, they regretted, not on the potentially powerful Combined Food Board (CFB). The prime minister accepted the offer, though Pearson complained that once again Ottawa had caved in. Canada became a member of the CPRB, a board without much of a role.

In March 1943, Canada renewed its claim for a seat on the CFB, arguing that its absence from the board was hampering its efficient operation. Again the British were reluctant, claiming that if Canada got a seat Australia and Argentina would each want one too. The infuriated Canadians responded that when those countries produced as much food as Canada they too would be entitled to a place. By October, after a long struggle and some hard feelings, London and an equally reluctant Washington finally conceded the justice of the Canadian case. Canada accepted membership on the board, the clear winner in the clash and the only smaller nation to win such status.

Victory here did not mean victory everywhere. First proposed in 1942, the United Nations Relief and Rehabilitation Administration (UNRRA) was organized by the allies in 1943 to distribute aid to liberated territories. The great powers—the Soviet Union, China, the U.S., and Britain—assumed that Canada would be one of the major contributors; they also determined that Canada would not have a place on the senior directing committee. London argued that the "Americans might not like the British side overweighed by Canadian representation." That response was guaranteed to exasperate Ottawa. Canada was a nation in its own right, not a British satellite. In a note dispatched to London and Washington in January 1943 the Canadians argued,

> We are confident that no workable international system can be based on concentration of influence and authority wholly in bodies composed of a few great powers to the exclusion of all the rest. It is not always the largest powers that have the greatest contribution to make to the work of these bodies or the greatest stake in their success. In international economic organizations such as the Relief Administration representation on such bodies can often be determined on a functional basis and in our view this principle should be applied wherever it is feasible.

The principle had been spelled out clearly, and Canada continued to argue its case with vigour for another three months. British Foreign Secretary Anthony Eden pressed King to yield, offering a place on the UNRRA supplies committee and representation on the key policy committee when supplies were discussed. The prime minister agreed. He feared that continued resistance could only incur the ill will of the great powers, and he had never been as keen as his officials on a special position for Canada.

The functional principle, very simply, meant that if Canada contributed a significant share of world food or mineral production or came to occupy a crucial place in postwar civil aviation, for example, the great powers could not deny it a say on the grounds that the country was not itself a great power. Canada produced more food than Britain, the argument ran, and was therefore the great power in this area; its voice had to be heard. The size of their military contribution—a million men and women in all—gave Canadian leaders strong backing for their claims, although no major voice in allied military decisions was sought or would have been given.

Thus when Winston Churchill and Franklin Roosevelt met in Quebec City in 1943 and 1944 to plot their strategy against the Berlin–Rome–Tokyo Axis, Mackenzie King acted as host and little more. The prime minister was present for the photo sessions, he provided the Scotch and the accommodations, and he was permitted to attend anodyne meetings. Whenever important matters were under discussion, however, there was no place for Canada.

It could not have been otherwise. Great as the Canadian contribution was, the country was still only a spear carrier in the next to last row. King himself understood this and was not upset. The functional principle was to be used to support Canadian claims when they were just and appropriate; it could not be pressed into service to try to seize a role that was beyond the dominion.

Functionalism was nonetheless a clear sign that Canada was ready to assume an independent place in the world. Accordingly when Lord Halifax, the cadaverous British ambassador in Washington, flew a trial balloon on the subject of imperial co-operation in a Toronto speech in January 1944, Mackenzie King quickly shot it down. In his address, which was unauthorized by London, Halifax correctly

A genial threesome at Quebec, 1943: King, Roosevelt, and Churchill
(National Archives of Canada, C 14168)

posited a postwar world in which China, the Soviet Union, and the United States would be unquestioned great powers. Britain, he said, could not continue to be a great power on its own; the dominions and Britain and its colonies should collaborate in promoting Commonwealth influence. The prime minister was outraged by this speech, delivered in the presence of his political enemies and in the heartland of imperial sympathies in Canada, and thus calculated to do him the most damage.

In a speech in Parliament, King squashed Halifax's suggestion like a bug. How could Canada, a Commonwealth country located between the United States and the Soviet Union, support such an idea? Moreover, it ran "counter to the establishment of effective world security, and therefore is opposed to the true interests of the Commonwealth itself." The only possible course for Canada, King said, was to participate in a regional or global scheme of international security, a United Nations. He made the same points at a Commonwealth prime ministers' conference in London in May

1944. After five years of war, Canada was no more willing to be a partner in imperial schemes than it had been in the 1920s. The only surprise was that Halifax, having watched Canada develop during the war, should have thought any such course was ever a possibility.

The functional principle was the way of the present. Ottawa had some success in getting this position understood, but the British, Americans, and Soviets refused to accept it in toto, to no one's surprise. Still, the very fact that Canada was arguing against common foreign policies and for functionalism was striking. Just as Borden's Canada had changed and grown during World War I, so too did the nation under Mackenzie King during World War II. And King, unlike his predecessor, had the enormous advantage of a first-rate cadre of public servants to produce ideas and to argue for them with skill in the councils of the world. Canada had entered the war as an autonomous dominion but its government had still thought and acted in a semi-colonial fashion. By the end of the war the nation had begun to transform itself into a middle power and the leader in defining just what that term would come to mean. The test would be to convert this new status into a proper place in the United Nations and in the postwar world.

CHAPTER SIX

The World Is Now So Small, 1945–1949

C ANADA EMERGED FROM THE CRUCIBLE of war strengthened. For one thing, the depression that had sapped the nation for a decade had ended in full employment in booming munitions plants. Though many Canadians feared that the economy might turn down again with the peace, they could not overlook the gains made during the war. The gross national product had doubled to over $11 billion, there were jobs and overtime for everyone who wanted work, and Canadians' savings swelled. The factories and farms produced vast quantities of goods; Canadian war production had amounted to 10 percent of the British Commonwealth total. Such abundance had helped to give Canada influence in wartime negotiations, as had the nation's military contribution. Canada had done its full share in fighting and winning the war. All this more than justified its claim to be a "middle power."

PEACEMAKERS AND POWERBROKERS

A middle power was, as Canada defined it, a nation of middling strength. In the areas in which a middle power was strong, the great powers had to ensure that they consulted it. In return, the middle power implicitly provided assurance that it would not meddle—too much—in great-power concerns.

To Canada, but not necessarily to others such as Australia or the Netherlands, a middle power was also just that: smack in the middle, a nation that sought to explain antagonists to each other, that sought compromise. There was never any doubt that Canada would align itself with the United States and Britain on any major issue, but Canadian diplomats also took it upon themselves to scurry through the halls of power carrying carefully crafted compromise resolutions on the thorny questions of world diplomacy. In other words, the wide streak of moralism that had always run through Canadian foreign policy was translated whole into Canadian middle-power rhetoric.

Unfortunately, as the long and difficult negotiations to create the new United Nations organization showed, Canadian claims for a special place were not destined to be given much weight by the great powers. The United States, the Soviet Union, Britain, and China had their own axes to grind, and the claims of the lesser states were not foremost in their minds.

The Department of External Affairs first seriously began to consider the postwar organization of the world in 1943, when London asked Ottawa for its views. To determine just what those might be, a working group headed by Hume Wrong was established as a precursor to a Post-Hostilities Planning Committee. Wrong's working group was to appraise the broad subject of postwar problems under the most flexible mandate possible; it was to consider postwar defence relationships with Britain and the United States, the place of Newfoundland in Canada and of a defeated Germany in Europe, and the advantages or disadvantages to Canada of regional or universal world security regimes.

The central question, however, was world organization, and it did not take long to decide what was wanted: a new world body in which Canada, though a North American member of the British Commonwealth, would have independent representation. Canada had represented itself in the old League of Nations but now the functional principle demanded that its special strengths be specifically recognized on any new bodies designed to deal with such subjects. Canadian bureaucrats did not therefore hesitate to produce plans for reordering civil aviation or establishing a new regime to govern international monetary policies.

Ottawa made no attempt to take the lead in postwar political organization. That was beyond its capacity. On the other hand, the government had no desire simply to accept what London or Washington wanted either. When Churchill told the prime ministers of the Commonwealth in May 1944 that he sought a postwar regional organization, a well-briefed Mackenzie King disagreed with the proposal: "We should not forget that a major lesson of this war is the truth that the seas do not divide and that the peace and prosperity of the world are indivisible." Canada had no wish whatsoever to see the Commonwealth as a single power with the dominions represented in the councils of the great by Britain. Canada, Norman Robertson said stoutly, "was not in favour of the division of the world into regional Power groups," for such schemes would only encourage American isolationism. "Canada's interests would not fit into a regional form of organization, nor would Canada be willing to represent the Commonwealth" in the American region. The Churchillian scheme was dead, though the British were slow to recognize this fact.

The great powers were still determined to shape the postwar world and the future United Nations (UN) to suit their concerns. At a meeting of great powers in September 1944, at Dumbarton Oaks near Washington, DC, proposals wholly unacceptable to Ottawa emerged. All the great powers were to be given permanent representation on the Security Council of the UN, which did not trouble the middle-power principles of Ottawa. Non-permanent members of the Council were to be elected by the General Assembly, however, and Canada expected that Central and South American states could form half the Assembly and might therefore secure up to half of the non-permanent slots on the Security Council. As the UN was intended to be a collective security organization, able to fight wars against aggressor states, that balance of forces posed problems. "The central Canadian difficulty," Wrong said, "will arise from the imposition of permanent and indefinite obligations which might, in the extreme case, require Canada by order of a Council on which Canada was not represented, to impose heavy burdens on the Canadian people." Canada and some other states toyed briefly with the idea of trying to organize a boycott of the UN by secondary powers, but the idea went nowhere. Nor did Ottawa's efforts to find some way round the Dumbarton Oaks proposals.

The final attempt to win concessions from the great powers came at the United Nations Conference on International Organization, held at San Francisco in April 1945. The Soviet Union proved a troublesome ally at the conference, so much so that Norman Robertson remonstrated with his colleagues at one meeting that "I wish to God somebody would come back into this room and not start his report by saying 'those Goddamned Russians.'" The Americans and the British were both difficult, and Canada's eight pages of amendments to great-power proposals for the UN Charter found little support. General Maurice Pope, Mackenzie King's military aide, maintained his usually sardonic view of his external affairs colleagues, noting that a few were filled with "the idea that we are about to participate in a great plan for the regeneration of the world," while at least one other, suffering from "bloody-minded Pacifism," seemed "prepared to fight Russia should she prove to be recalcitrant" in setting up the United Nations. Pope's remarks suggest that idealism remained strong despite the difficulties in protecting the national interest.

There was some success. Article 44 was put into the Charter after strenuous Canadian efforts to ensure that non-members of the Security Council would be invited to attend Council sessions on the use of those countries' forces. As General Pope put it, "It is impossible for us to grant to a Council on which we may not be represented the right to order us about without our having participated in the decision." Moreover, the Canadians, their functional principle firmly in mind, insisted on the Charter specifying that in electing non-permanent Security Council members, "due regard" was to be paid to the "contribution of Members of the United Nations to the maintenance of international peace and security and to the other purposes of the Organization." That too was a victory, but unfortunately Australia, not Canada, won the first election to the Security Council spot "reserved" for a Commonwealth nation.

Canada did not succeed in winning most of the points it had sought. Everyone wanted to keep the Soviet Union, still bleeding from its wartime wounds and suspicions of the intentions of the West, happy enough to join the organization. To accomplish this, it was imperative not to challenge great-power unity—hard won at Dumbarton Oaks—on important points. Robertson understood this:

> It seems clear to us that, in this year of grace, there cannot be a World Organization established, with Russia a member, unless it provides for voting rights in the Security Council substantially as set forth in the Great Power memorandum. . . . The effective choice appears, therefore, to be between such an Organization and an Organization from which the Soviet Union . . . [is] excluded. Our view is that it is better to take the Organization that we can get and, having come to that decision, to refrain from further efforts to pry apart the difficult unity which the Great Powers have attained.

The self-denying ordinance rankled, though it was probably necessary, and the long, acrimonious discussions at San Francisco managed to erase most of the Canadian idealism noted by Pope. The political gains that Canada had made from its wholehearted participation in World War II—a contribution vastly greater in every way than that in the earlier war—paradoxically received much less recognition than in 1919.

A large proportion of the population, recognizing that Russian troops had done the lion's share of defeating the Nazis, were confident that Canada could get on with the u.s.s.r. after the war, or so they told pollsters. The diplomats were already much less certain. Much of the reporting from the Canadian embassy in Moscow had been full of foreboding since 1944. After 1945, the chorus of almost unrelieved pessimism about the future continued from virtually every mission abroad. Diplomat Escott Reid, initially a true believer in the worth of the United Nations, wrote after watching the Soviet Union's performance at the first General Assembly in 1946, "The tactics of the Soviet delegations were to use the proceedings for purposes of propaganda." He added that it was "apparent that talk of turning the United Nations into an agency of international government . . . is in present conditions wholly unrealistic."

"RED SCARE"

Thus it was the Soviets who troubled officials and politicians in Canada the most. Reporting from the embassy in Moscow during the war, Dana Wilgress had noted the "desire of the Soviet Union for a long period of peace in order to recover from the ravages of the war." He had also understood clearly, however, that the U.S.S.R. would "continue to represent a distinct social and economic system to that of the United States," which might "lead in the more distant future to a conflict of interests if the system of collective security does not function effectively."

In 1944–1945, the Post-Hostilities Planning Committee, considering the same questions that worried Wilgress, had looked at the prospect of a Soviet–American war. It had found the possibility unlikely for the immediate future, but not something that could be neglected. Moreover, should such a war occur Canada had no option but to side with the Americans from the outset. As the drafters of the study, "Post War Defence Arrangements with the United States," delicately noted, "This closer tie-up with the United States need not conflict with the Canadian tradition of basing military policy and training upon British practice. However, if Canada and the United States are to be efficient in the defence of North America, common experience between the national forces will be desirable." The Cabinet War Committee, soon to go out of existence as the directing brain of the Canadian war effort, decided in July 1945 that defence ties with the United States had to be maintained in the peace. The reason was clear: the glowering presence of the U.S.S.R.

The Soviet presence in Ottawa was manifested in the embassy on Charlotte Street and other buildings scattered through the capital. The Russians gave cocktail parties, attended others, and did the usual work of diplomacy. So it seemed until 6 September 1945, when Igor Gouzenko, a cipher clerk in the embassy, turned up at newspaper and government offices claiming to have documents that proved the Soviet NKVD (precursor of the KGB) and intelligence organizations of the Soviet military forces were all running spy rings in

Canada. Initially, poor Gouzenko found himself treated as an embarrassment. No one took his story, presented in broken English, very seriously. When word reached Norman Robertson, however, he went to see the prime minister. King too wanted to do nothing, but British intelligence officials offered succinct advice: "take him."

The next day, after security officials from the Soviet embassy had broken into Gouzenko's apartment, the Canadians hid the clerk and his family away under protective custody. The documents that Gouzenko had spirited out of the embassy were hastily translated, and Robertson told the prime minister "that everything was much worse than we would have believed. . . . They disclose an espionage system on a large scale. . . . [T]hings came right into our country to a degree we could not have believed possible." There was a spy in the Department of External Affairs code room, one at the British high

Igor Gouzenko in 1975 (*The Globe and Mail*, Toronto)

commission, and another at the Canadian scientific laboratory involved in work on the atomic bomb. The bomb was then much in the news because of its use against Nagasaki and Hiroshima the previous month (something hailed by 77 percent of Canadians, according to the polls) and its major role in forcing Tokyo to surrender. Before long, Ottawa came to realize that the Soviet espionage networks had suborned scientists and sent samples of Canadian uranium to the U.S.S.R. Others involved in the rings included military officers, civil servants, and even a Montreal MP, Fred Rose of the Labour-Progressive Party, the name adopted by the banned Communist Party during the war.

The prime minister was horrified by the disturbing news. "I think of the Russian Embassy being only a few doors away," a despairing Mackenzie King wrote, "and of there being there a centre of intrigue. During this period of war, while Canada has been helping Russia and doing all we can . . . there has been . . . spying." Canada had fought World War II on the assumption, the naïve assumption, that its allies were united in a common cause. The government had similarly believed that its civilian officials and military officers were united by a shared belief in democracy and conviction that the enemy had to be beaten. To that end, it was essential that Canadians rallied to defend their nation. Suddenly, communist ideology was shown to have been strong enough to divert Canadians from their loyalty.

This realization led the government over the next few years to institute a system of security checks within its own bureaucracy and to compartmentalize information so that only those with a "need to know" received sensitive material. It also strengthened the role of the Royal Canadian Mounted Police in protecting the state. The Examination Unit, the wireless interception team built up during the war to listen in on Vichy, German, and Japanese communications (and, according to some historians, on Free French and other friendly states' secrets), also benefited from the Gouzenko case. Instead of being shut down, as had been the plan, the unit lived on, its targets now the U.S.S.R. and countries soon to be labelled its "satellites" in Eastern Europe. The ingredients for a "Red scare" were in place and, although the Canadian version was never as pronounced as the

American one, a small number of bureaucratic careers would be ruined because of political beliefs and past associations.

For the first time, perceived security risks also obliged Canada to attempt to screen prospective immigrants in a methodical way. The traditional barriers to other racial and cultural "undesirables" remained in place in the first years after the war, and Mackenzie King told Parliament that the people of Canada "do not wish, as a result of mass immigration, to make a fundamental alteration in the character of our population." It was nothing new that the so-called undesirables included those considered politically unacceptable. Before World War I, when Indian militants had been fighting British rule, spies had kept watch over the few Sikhs who managed to make it to Canadian shores. After World War II, the process of screening was systematized to try to keep out Nazis and, increasingly important, communists.

This was a horrendously difficult task as immigration swelled. In the first postwar decade, 1.3 million immigrants came to Canada— first from "displaced persons" camps in Europe and then from virtually every European country—almost twice as many as in the previous twenty years. As governments in Eastern Europe and the U.S.S.R. were rarely provided information of any kind on prospective migrants to Canada, especially on "DP"s, as the postwar refugees were known, screening was made even more difficult. It is significant that the mesh used to sift out those on the political left became finer as the concern about Nazis and their supporters gradually declined. The atmosphere of the day, the building public fear of the "Reds," fuelled this policy.

The Gouzenko affair—known in the government as the "Corby case" because the secret files were held in a whisky box in Undersecretary Robertson's office—played out in Canada in a royal commission and in a series of widely publicized trials. Internationally, it led to a substantial degree of co-ordination between Britain and the United States, because public servants and scientists in those two countries had been fingered in Gouzenko's documents or in the course of his interrogation. Many on the left in Canada, then and since, argued that the whole affair had been trumped up but, surprisingly, Moscow admitted that it had run spies from its embassy.

The impact of the case was sharp. Opinion polls in Canada showed increasing suspicion of the U.S.S.R., and of domestic communists. Fifty-two percent of Canadians took a dark view of the Soviet Union in the spring of 1946, just after the Gouzenko case became public, versus only 17 percent who expressed any sympathy. Well over half supported the government's actions in the spy case.

In London the Gouzenko revelations were also followed closely, most notably because of the way civil servants had been seduced into betraying their country. The disclosures played a part in shaping one of the seminal speeches of the era, Winston Churchill's "Iron Curtain" address, delivered in Fulton, Missouri, in early 1946. That speech, delivered with President Harry Truman sitting on the platform and after consultation with Lester Pearson, the ambassador in Washington, was a signal that the Cold War had begun. Washington, too, was profoundly affected by the Gouzenko case. The American government was made very nervous because Alger Hiss, a senior State Department official, and Harry Dexter White, the key official in the Treasury Department, had been named by the Soviet clerk.

For the Canadian government, the spy case left a mood of reinforced apprehension. From Ottawa, an American diplomat reported that "the Canadians are like the brave little boy who has talked back to the bully and is wondering what is going to happen to him."

CHANGES

While the Canadian government continued to worry about Soviet actions abroad and spies in Canada, the country and its foreign policy were going through changes of their own. In the first place, the government recognized the nationalism created by war and seized the opportunity to promulgate its own citizenship law. Canadians had been British subjects; being "Canadian" was merely a minor variant of local importance. Now, however, thanks to the Canadian Citizenship Act of 1946, Canadian citizenship was primary and basic, and British nationality secondary and derivative. The "common code" of the British Empire, a member of the House of Lords lamented, had been "completely shattered." After that, it was but a minor step to install Vincent Massey, the country's first minister to the United States and the long-serving high commissioner in London, as governor general in 1952, the first Canadian to hold the post. Slowly, the ties that bound Canada to Britain were being eroded.

Another fillip to nationalism came when Newfoundland, a separate dominion still run by a British-appointed commission of government, decided after a constitutional convention and two referenda to join Confederation on 1 April 1949. This was the fulfilment of a long-cherished Canadian dream, though many Newfoundlanders, feeling they had lost their own nationality, were not as happy. There had been no conspiracy, but Britain had nonetheless helped push St John's in the direction of joining Canada. London had been motivated primarily by the desire to reduce expenditures and commitments abroad but was also concerned to keep Newfoundlanders out of American hands, something that the war and postwar years made less far-fetched than it now seems. American troops and sailors had been stationed in Newfoundland since 1941, and the United States had acquired military bases there on a ninety-nine-year lease. The island's location far out into the North Atlantic was a valuable asset, especially in the age of intercontinental bombers. Now Newfoundland and Canada were one nation.

The Department of External Affairs had played a large part in the negotiations that brought Confederation to fruition. The department continued to grow, and by 1947 the number of officers had increased to 175, among them the first six women to work as foreign service officers. The number of missions abroad also increased. In 1947 alone, an embassy opened in Turkey, legations established shop in Sweden, Poland, Switzerland, Denmark, and Italy, a high commission opened in New Delhi, and a consulate was set up in São Paolo, Brazil. There were now twenty-eight diplomatic missions and seven consulates, as well as a permanent delegation to the United Nations, a military mission in Germany, and a liaison mission in Japan. Almost half of external affairs officers were posted abroad, a very high proportion indeed, especially as delegations had to be found for the ever-increasing number of international conferences: eighty-six in 1947 alone.

Striking changes were made at the top too. In September 1946, Mackenzie King gave up the post of secretary of state for external affairs, which he had held through all his years as prime minister. To replace him in the position that he had always considered to be the most important in the Cabinet, King turned to Louis St Laurent. St Laurent was a Quebec City lawyer who had entered the government at the end of 1941 as minister of justice, replacing Ernest Lapointe. Fluently bilingual, very intelligent and decisive, and a man of great rectitude and high principle, St Laurent intended to leave politics soon after the end of the war, but King persuaded him to remain with the offer of the external affairs portfolio and an implicit suggestion that even higher office might soon follow.

At the same time, Lester Pearson, hitherto ambassador in Washington, became undersecretary to replace Norman Robertson, who went to Britain as high commissioner. Pearson, always known as Mike to his friends, was enormously affable, a charming man and a masterly conversationalist. His persuasive talents hid his superb intelligence and his understanding of just how far his country's limited resources could be committed to costly courses of action. No administrator, Pearson relied on others for the day-to-day work and to generate ideas that he then sold abroad. Pearson and St Laurent had a happy combination of talents.

The two were different and similar at the same time. One was a French Canadian, the other an Ontarian, but both believed that Canada had to play an important role in the world and could not, must not, retreat into isolationism. Pearson was adventurous, sometimes almost rashly so; St Laurent was calm and collected but also capable of erupting in anger. For the next two years, they would work together very closely, form a deep affection for each other, and significantly advance Canada's role in foreign policy. When St Laurent succeeded King as prime minister in late 1948, it would seem almost natural for the civil servant Pearson to replace him as minister of external affairs. Had King remained prime minister, Pearson would not have left public service for the more chancy world of politics. With St Laurent in office, however, with assurances that the course of government would be sensible and progressive in foreign policy (providing the Liberals won re-election), he would be prepared to take the big step.

St Laurent and Pearson were both very different from Mackenzie King. The old leader remained fundamentally suspicious of the world, ever fearful of the ways in which foreign entanglements could divide Canadians. For St Laurent and Pearson, World War II had demonstrated that Canada could play an international role, and they wanted it to do so. As St Laurent put it in a lecture he delivered at the University of Toronto in 1947, the growth of the foreign service during the war had been "a natural development. We are preparing ourselves to fulfill the growing responsibilities in world affairs which we have accepted as a modern state."

Mindful of his situation as a French Canadian speaking in Toronto, the secretary of state for external affairs was careful to say that he was not proposing to have Canada turn its back on Britain and the Commonwealth. Nonetheless, the country was committed to the United Nations for "constructive purpose[s]," and had to work with the United States in this new postwar world, obviously implying that this was now the country's single most important relationship. The minister also showed that he understood realities, delicately but correctly stating the case: "There is little point in a country of our stature recommending international action, if those who must carry the major burden of whatever action is taken are not in sympathy." His cautionary phrases were necessary, but there could be no doubt that St Laurent's lecture was a call for Canada to accept its international commitments and to play its proper role as what would later be labelled a "moderate mediatory middle power."

THE "AMERICAN HAND"

The immediate problems facing the new guard were distressingly familiar: American dollars and British trade questions. At the end of the war, Canada and the United States were prosperous and powerful. By contrast Europe and Asia were in ruins, desperately deficient in almost all the necessities of life. Countries such as Britain, France, and the Netherlands were also short of hard currency to pay for the Canadian and American goods necessary to rebuild. Canada tried to do its bit to help its friends—and to keep up its export markets and employment at home—when in 1946 it gave the British a $1.25 billion loan at 2 percent interest and forgave all war debts to boot. The loan was huge, representing more than 10 percent of the Canadian GNP in that year. Considering that the American GNP was about fifteen times larger, the Canadian loan was proportionately far greater than the $3.75 billion lent to Britain by the United States. That the credits were so large attested to Canadian affection for Britain, to be sure. Much more, however, it reflected the Canadian need for markets overseas. The British took almost all Canada's exports of bacon, eggs, and canned salmon and high proportions of its wheat, newsprint, and timber. If the United Kingdom didn't take these products, who would? Additional very substantial sums amounting to another billion dollars went in loans to other European countries to encourage the development of export markets.

In the immediate postwar years Canadians were tired of privation. Money saved during the war burned holes in their pockets, and they wanted to buy all the necessities and luxuries that had been denied them since the 1920s. They wanted refrigerators and radios, automobiles, jukeboxes, and winter trips south. Businesses wanted to upgrade their capacity to meet postwar needs. All these demands increased American imports into Canada to $1.4 billion in 1946, the highest peacetime total ever, and simultaneously increased the trade deficit with the United States to $500 million, depleting Canadian holdings of U.S. dollars to $1.6 billion. A deficit with the United States was usual, but not so usual was the continued British ban on conversion of sterling into dollars. Canada was prevented from converting its trade surplus of $460 million in 1946, thus recreating the wartime situation that had forced it into the 1941 Hyde Park agreement. Worse still, the struggling British (and other Europeans too) tried hard to avoid purchases in Canada unless they could use their Canadian credits and loans to pay for goods. Once again, Canada had tried to assist Britain; once again, this intention had helped to push the dominion into a crisis that demanded American assistance.

Throughout 1947, officials in the Departments of Finance and External Affairs worried about their American situation. Imports continued to rise towards the $2 billion level, causing a collapse of the country's American dollar holdings to $480 million by the fall.

In desperation by November the government had to slap special tariffs and restrictions on American imports, embarrassingly just as Canada signed on to the General Agreement on Tariffs and Trade (GATT), a global trade liberalization organization. At precisely this time, the marriage of Princess Elizabeth to Philip Mountbatten distracted the public's attention from the fiscal crisis, fortunately for the government. Officials scurried back and forth between Ottawa and Washington, seeking a way out of the crisis with the help of the United States and trying to find some way to get Canada a share of the great new assistance package for Europe that American Secretary of State George C. Marshall had begun to talk about in June 1947.

The European Recovery Program, almost always called the Marshall Plan, was approved by the U.S. Congress in spring of 1948. Thanks to intensive Canadian lobbying it permitted "off-shore purchases," a device that gave recipient European countries American

President Truman and Mackenzie King, Ottawa, 1947
(National Archives of Canada, PA 113240)

funds to purchase goods outside the United States, and specifically listed Canada as one of the allowable sources of such goods. This let Canada secure almost $1.2 billion in American dollars by the end of the first half of 1950, one-eighth of the total the United States expended, to cover European purchases of Canadian goods. This inflow of dollars went a long way to ease the country's shortage of American exchange. So too did a temporary loan and the tariff measures.

At the same time, the dollar shortage led naturally into discussions on trade, which soon ballooned into a full-fledged proposal for free trade between the two North American nations. Prime Minister Mackenzie King was consulted and gave the negotiators his blessing.

The argument for free trade went like this: Europe was not recovering from the war and the rise of communism in countries such as Italy and France seemed almost unstoppable. The only two democratic economies with high standards of living were Canada and the United States. The choice for both, Canadian negotiator John Deutsch said, was between "a relative[ly] free enterprise world with the highest existing standard of living and a government controlled world with a lower standard of living. Which we did not want." The solution was "meshing our economy as much as possible with that of the United States." The U.S. officials could see the situation clearly. As Woodbury Willoughby of the State Department wrote in a key memorandum,

> Canada is at the parting of the ways. Either she turns toward Europe or the United States. If she takes the former way she must undo the progress made during the war toward economic integration with the United States and, by controls and restrictions, force a permanent reorientation involving less dependence on trade with us. The present Canadian government would prefer the latter. They tend to the view that Canada's ultimate destiny is inevitably linked to ours.

The arguments, the needs, were powerful on both sides and, negotiating under the tightest security, the Canadians and Americans had produced a scheme for free trade by the beginning of 1948.

The plan called for the immediate removal of all duties. In effect it was a modified form of customs union. Both Canada and the

United States, however, were to be allowed to put quotas on some goods for a five-year transition period. Canada's leeway in this area was greater, to allow the smaller economy more protection during the transition. Canada could impose permanent quotas on American fruits and vegetables, while the United States could permanently limit imports of Canadian wheat and flour. The agreement was simple and dramatic. Deutsch felt certain that Canada would gain huge economic advantages from the plan while continuing to set its own tariffs against the rest of the world. The Americans took a longer view: the deal would eliminate British preferences in Canada, a long-term American goal, and would effectively bind Canada forever into the American economic sphere.

Before the deal could pass into law, political approval had to be secured. This seemed certain to be a problem in the United States in the election year of 1948, but to everyone's surprise, the deal stopper was in Ottawa. Mackenzie King was seventy-three years old in 1948 and clearly nearing the end of his long reign of power. Indeed, he had already announced his intention to retire later that year. King's policies—and circumstances—had brought the two North American nations close together in economics and defence. Most recently, in 1947, he had struck a defence agreement to continue military co-operation between the Canadian and American armed forces into the postwar years. Even so, King never ceased to worry about American influence, and during the war he had fretted about the "American hand" reaching over Canada. His government had refused to take advantage of the Lend-Lease Bill in 1941 for fear of postwar complications, and at the end of the war Ottawa paid full value for every American wartime installation in Canada to ensure that no subsequent claims could arise. Now faced with a free-trade package, King was concerned.

The support for free trade seemed strong. Opinion polls during and just after the war had found substantial majorities in favour of it; his bureaucrats wanted it; the few ministers who knew about the secret negotiations waxed enthusiastic. King worried nonetheless. He had lived through the 1911 reciprocity election when public opinion, initially favourable, had been swung around by a massive business-sponsored campaign. He had lost his own seat when Laurier was destroyed by charges that he wanted to sell out Canada to the

Yankees. The Tories in 1948 were no different than Borden's lot had been, and King feared a charge of disloyalty that would end his days as leader in acrimonious controversy. In his study while he agonized over the question, King reached up for a book on his shelf, and it fell open at a chapter called "The Soul of Empire." The fortuitous omen confirmed in the prime minister's mind that free trade would destroy British ties and allow the opposition to portray his last act as the betrayal of Canada to the Americans. "I would no more think of at my time of life and at this stage of my career attempting any movement of the kind than I would of flying to the South pole," he wrote in his diary.

Free trade was dead, stopped cold by a leader who retained total control over his Cabinet and party even in his final days of power. Supporters of the deal tried again to persuade him of its benefits, but King remained unbending. Free trade was bad for Canada, bad for the prime minister, bad for the Liberal Party.

Embarrassed officials had to tell the Americans that the deal was off, their uneasiness made more complete by the knowledge that Canada had initiated the push to free trade with the prime minister's earlier consent. Hume Wrong, the ambassador to the United States, laid out for the Americans the difficulties that had blocked consummation of the deal, and then he turned to another issue:

> It is probable that the proposal for a security pact for the North Atlantic area may be made public within a few weeks. This is a matter of such great importance in relation to the present international situation, which will arouse so much attention and discussion . . . that to confront the Canadian people at the same time with this issue and with the problems involved in the proposed economic arrangements would be of doubtful wisdom. . . . It is believed, therefore, that at the moment the energy and attention of the Canadian government should be concentrated on the problems involved in the security pact and on the necessity of rallying Parliament and public wholeheartedly around that pact and the policy which it embodies.

Perhaps, Wrong said, the trade discussions could begin again after the security pact was signed. Indeed, the economic discussions could be related to the security pact, "since they are concerned with measures for economic defence against aggression." They might even be broadened to include the United Kingdom. The Americans were not happy with any of this, especially the suggestion that Britain might be brought into the free-trade talks, but their attention too had focussed on the negotiations that would lead to the North Atlantic Treaty.

PUTTING TEETH INTO
COLLECTIVE SECURITY

The reasons for a North Atlantic security pact seemed very clear to those guiding Canadian policy in the first few years after the war. The Soviet Union was an aggressive state; it had already gobbled up most of Eastern Europe and seemed on the verge of ingesting the rest. The Soviets had created satellite governments with communists in charge and, increasingly, democratic anti-communists in jail. Once China joined the communist monolith, its present and potential power became enormous.

The West was frightened; almost no one in the late 1940s saw the nationalist cracks in the unitary ideology directed from Moscow. Soviet pressure on Greece, where communist guerillas fought against royalists, and on Iran, where Moscow nibbled at the borders, also disturbed the West. Every state on the periphery of the Soviet Union seemed to be at risk of coercion, even countries such as Norway. The last straw, however, was the Soviet capture of Czechoslovakia. Perhaps guilt over the 1938 Munich Conference, in which Britain and France had handed the Sudetenland to Hitler, played a part. Perhaps the popularity of the Czech democratic leaders in the West made an impression. Whatever the reason, when the communists staged a coup in 1948 and put paid to Czech democracy, the alarm bells rang loudly.

The growing fear was compounded by concerns for Western Europe. It was not so much the idea that Cossack hordes might cross the Elbe—the river marking the boundary between the Soviet and Western zones of Germany—and strike for the English Channel, though some fear of that existed. Instead, Western nations worried that the weariness of spirit in Europe would paralyse resistance. The democracies of Europe had been savagely fought over during the war; their industries, their housing stock, their people had been ravaged. Recovery was slow, hampered by hard winters and a terrible shortage of hard currency. The Marshall Plan, beginning in 1948, was an imaginative and generous American attempt to help Europe get back on its feet, but many feared it was too little too late. Communist parties in Italy and France were powerful enough that it seemed possible, even probable, they would win power in an election.

Germany, too, was wracked with economic turmoil. It had been divided into four zones at the end of the war and into two separate "countries" by 1949, one on each side of the Iron Curtain. Berlin was the flashpoint for East–West tensions and intentions in Germany. Occupied by the British, Americans, French, and Soviets but located deep within the Soviet sphere in East Germany, the city was very vulnerable. The Russians could cut off access to Berlin, if they dared. They did, throwing up a blockade in 1948, and the Americans, British, and others (but not the Canadians, who cautiously hung back) mounted a massive airlift that fed the city until the Soviets finally relented.

These crises occurred at a time when the democratic spirit was low in Europe. A moral malaise afflicted the continent, a sense that the failures of democracy had created the Hitlers and Mussolinis who had conquered Europe and the Pétains and Quislings who had helped them rule it. The circumstances also bred a sense that communism might be the wave of the future. Many intellectuals who had suffered in Nazi concentration camps or lived under German occupation felt a great revulsion both at the way their societies had surrendered to Hitler and at the way the old ruling élites had come back to power in 1945. The political left doubted the existence of Stalin's concentration camps, but many in its ranks might have said that sending the bourgeois to the Gulag was no loss. As for North American aid, many Europeans would take it but without much thanks. The cultural élite did not want to be Coca-colonized, to become the satraps of a new American empire.

This was the atmosphere hanging over Europe by 1948. Fear presided: fear of the Soviets, fear of domestic communists, fear of the Americans. Was there any will to organize and resist the inevitable march of Stalin and his cohorts towards the Atlantic?

Some emerged in Washington. In 1947, President Harry Truman had proclaimed the "Truman Doctrine," pledging support to "free peoples who are resisting attempted subjugation by armed minorities or by outside pressures." The Canadian embassy in the American capital reported that Truman's address had laid aside the conception of "one world." The president's policy recognized the reality created by Soviet expansionism and divided the globe "between the Soviet sphere and the rest."

Some spirit emerged in Western Europe, too, when Belgium, France, Luxembourg, the Netherlands, and Great Britain signed the

Continuity: St Laurent (left) and King at the national Liberal convention, 1948, with Laurier looking down on his successors
(National Archives of Canada, C 23278)

Brussels Treaty in March 1948. This agreement called for the creation of a common defence system and the strengthening of political, economic, and cultural ties to help resist Soviet pressure.

Officials in Ottawa had already reached the conclusion that the United Nations could not operate as an effective vehicle for collective security so long as the Security Council was paralysed by the Soviet Union's use of its veto. Escott Reid, Pearson's chief aide at the Department of External Affairs, made a speech at the Canadian Institute of Public Affairs' Couchiching Conference that August (a speech sometimes rather grandiloquently claimed by Canadian historians as the real origin of the North Atlantic Treaty). In it he raised the idea of a military alliance of democratic nations. Reid was a great progenitor of ideas, some brilliant, others not, but this was one of his best, and he had taken the time to get his words cleared by his superiors in the department. The West, he said,

> was not debarred by the Charter of the United Nations or by Soviet membership in the United Nations from creating new international political institutions to maintain peace. . . . Nothing in the Charter precludes the existence of regional political arrangements . . . and these regional agencies are entitled to take measures of collective self-defence against armed attack until the Security Council has acted. The world is now so small that the whole of the Western world is in itself a mere region. If the peoples of the Western world want an international security organization with teeth, even though the Soviet Union is at present unwilling to be a member of such an organization, they . . . can create it consistently with the United Nations Charter. . . . [E]ach member state could accept a binding obligation to pool the whole of its economic and military resources with those of the other members if *any* power should be found to have committed aggression against any one of the members.

Secretary of State for External Affairs Louis St Laurent reiterated that theme in the next several months, at the UN General Assembly and at home. He told a Quebec City audience that "if theory-crazed totalitarian groups persist in their policies of frustration and futility, we will not, for very much longer, allow them to prevent us from using our obvious advantages to improve the conditions of those who do wish to co-operate with us." No one had any doubt just which nations he meant.

At much the same time, the Labour government in London proposed secret talks with Canada and the United States on defence questions. In April 1948 the talks successfully concluded with a decision to broaden them to other like-minded states including, but not limited to, signatories of the Brussels Treaty. By this time, one of the deepest thinkers in the Department of External Affairs had begun to see how a North Atlantic grouping might bring very real benefits to Canada. Norman Robertson was high commissioner in London, one of the very few officials informed of the secret discussions, and he set out his views in a message to Ottawa: "Ever since we have been in a position to shape our own policy abroad, we have had to wrestle with the antinomies created by our position as a North American country and as a member of the Commonwealth, by our special relationship with the United Kingdom and at the same time . . . with other countries in western Europe." Some way to protect those special relationships and simultaneously to involve the United States economically and militarily would be "such a providential solution for so many of our problems that I feel we should go to great lengths and even incur considerable risks in order to consolidate our good fortune and ensure our proper place in this new partnership."

It was striking that Robertson did not mention the Soviet threat to Western Europe in his rationale. Perhaps he simply considered that his colleagues took it as a given, but even so he saw the North Atlantic Treaty as necessary for more important political and economic reasons. If handled correctly, such a treaty could increase access to Western European markets, solidify links with Europe, and even ease the difficulties of sharing a continent with the United States. Robertson made a North Atlantic Treaty sound like a wonder drug, the general Canadian view at the time. His interpretation of the benefits helped to ensure that Canadian negotiators fought hard to see an economic clause included in the treaty.

The Canadians argued that if trade wars occurred among the alliance partners they would inevitably weaken efforts at defence.

Although they saw the sense of the Canadian argument, American negotiators were already worried at the prospect of getting through Congress a defence pact that obliged them to fight if any European members were attacked, and feared endless complications if an economic clause were included. Hume Wrong, handling Canada's side of the bargaining out of the Washington embassy, thought that the treaty ought to be about defence alone, but both his political and his bureaucratic superiors disagreed. Condemned to battle for something he opposed, Wrong nonetheless did his very able best while Robertson and other ambassadors overseas lobbied their host governments. In the end, the Americans and the almost equally reluctant British conceded the Canadian case. When signed in April 1949 the North Atlantic Treaty included Article II, the "Canadian article," pledging the signatory states to make every effort to eliminate conflict in their economic policies and to develop their trade with one another. It was a Canadian triumph but like so many such victories it ultimately came to mean very little.

More important was what the treaty did in practical political terms. During the war, Canada had had to struggle to win the right to representation on the policy committees running the war effort. The Canadian government believed that the North Atlantic Treaty guaranteed it a place at the table in any future conflict, a definite gain.

When Canada signed on there was no suggestion that Canadian troops might have to be stationed in Europe as a contribution to the military organization to be formed under the treaty. It was up to the European nations to re-arm their military forces and revivify their spirits. North America would assist economically and pledged support in the event of war. The United States had occupation forces in Germany as part of the North Atlantic Treaty Organization (NATO) forces. General Dwight D. Eisenhower, leader of the wartime alliance, was designated supreme commander of NATO. Even so, American involvement on the ground in Europe was not expected to be great.

The North Atlantic Treaty had to be sold to Canadians; the government was especially concerned about Québécois attitudes to the new organization. French Canadians had never been enthusiastic about overseas commitments, even in wartime. Would they perceive

a defence alliance in peacetime as different, or as an even greater violation of their position and rights by English Canadians? It helped
greatly that St Laurent was in charge, first as secretary of state for
external affairs and then as prime minister.

The leader was very persuasive about the advantages and necessity of the treaty. At one speech to a service club in St-Jean-sur-
Richelieu, he pointed to a senior cleric at the head table and said
that he did not want to see him suffer the same fate as Cardinal
Mindszenty, the Hungarian prelate who had been jailed and tortured
by the Communist regime. Such arguments were interpreted as scare
tactics by Canadians on the left, but they had great potency, especially in Catholic Quebec. The Gouzenko case had alerted all
Canadians to Soviet machinations, and a succession of news headlines stretching from 1945 and each more alarming than the last had
shaped a tougher mood in Canada. Only the small and relatively
insignificant Labour-Progressive Party actively opposed Canadian
adhesion to the North Atlantic Treaty. In Parliament, the treaty
passed in a single day—28 March 1949—with two Quebec *national-
iste* MPs providing the only opposition.

THE END OF MACKENZIE KING

Meanwhile, other issues were rousing passions in Canada. One was
the desire of Jews to have a state of their own, a need that had
become especially urgent after near total German destruction of
European Jewry in the Holocaust. The new state, Israel, was to be
located in Palestine, which had been under a British mandate since
the end of World War I and for years the scene of sharp skirmishes
between Jews and Arabs and Jews and the British army. By the
beginning of 1948, the question of a Jewish state had been seized by
the United Nations, where the United States and United Kingdom
were seriously divided on policy, and the Canadian government
found itself torn.

Undersecretary of State for External Affairs Lester Pearson, a
minister's son raised on Bible tales of the holy land and sympathetic
to the Jewish position, wanted Canada to take "a strong independent

stand for what we thought was the proper and right solution, and to have dismissed the British and Americans with 'a plague on both your houses.'" Mackenzie King was still prime minister, however, and he had a natural desire to support Britain and not to move out ahead of the United States, which was pressing for the establishment of a new state. Britain itself was anxious to escape its mandatory responsibilities in the area and was suffering casualties as it strove to keep the peace. Jews believed strongly that Britain favoured the Arabs, however, and Canadian Jews, most of them long-time Liberals, put pressure on the government to take the lead in helping to create the state of Israel.

In the end, Ottawa supported the establishment of the new state in May 1948. Nonetheless, when war erupted between Jews and Arabs the Canadian government hung back and forebore from providing Israel with arms. That did not stop Canadian Jews from raising substantial sums of money and a few recruits to assist the new state. The birth of Israel was an indication that ethnic groups in Canada had continuing interests abroad and that such interests could often pose difficulties for the government.

More routine questions of foreign policy faced the old King government, not least the continuing definition of relations with Great Britain. To Ottawa's surprise, the Labour government of Clement Attlee seemed almost as imperially minded as Churchill's administration had been before it. There were pressures from London for increased co-operation in Commonwealth defence, and urgings that Canadians go slowly in increasing defence ties with the United States. Attlee told his Chiefs of Staff Committee that American requests for defence installations "would involve serious difficulties over Canadian sovereignty." Despite all the changes brought about by Canada's increased stature, despite wartime gifts and postwar loans, London instinctively felt obliged to act *in loco parentis*.

Nevertheless, the Commonwealth was changing. All the "white" dominions were playing independent roles in the world; indeed, Ireland had left the organization in 1949. India, Pakistan, and Ceylon, though they remained members, had become republics, and were soon to be followed by dozens of other nations in Africa and Asia. These wanted as little control as possible from London and as much foreign aid as they could get from everyone. Moreover, the confidential relationship between London, Ottawa, Canberra, Wellington, and Pretoria, in which members of the old club shared secrets and talked frankly, did not seem as possible to them in an expanded and increasingly non-white Commonwealth. The group quickly became too large, and some of the newer members, such as India, seemed to be too friendly with the Soviet Union.

Even so, Ottawa continued to look to the Commonwealth as a valuable organization and, for a time perhaps, even more so once its exclusively white character vanished. Its attitude arose from a mixture of idealism and the Cold War instinct to prevent the Third World from falling under the influence of the u.s.s.r. At the 1948 Commonwealth Prime Ministers' Conference, the last Mackenzie King attended, Canadians played a crucial role in finding a form of words to let India join the club as a republic. Cranky, difficult with his staff, and seriously ill with heart strain, King had to take to his bed, and Louis St Laurent, already anointed as his successor by a Liberal Party convention, flew over to take the old chief's place. Soon after his return to Ottawa, King finally resigned. St Laurent was in charge.

Before he departed into history, Mackenzie King had one last blow-up over foreign policy. The subject was Korea, of which few Canadians other than missionaries had ever heard. Korea had been divided at the end of the war against Japan between the Soviet Union and the United States, and the two great powers had installed regimes friendly to them in their parts of the divided land. The United Nations, already on the verge of paralysis because of East–West divisions, had unaccountably managed to secure agreement on one issue. In 1947, it set up a temporary commission on Korea—always known by the acronym UNTCOK—to supervise planned elections in both the North and the South.

In December of that year, St Laurent recommended Dr. George Patterson for membership on the committee. St Laurent had committed Canada to participation in UNTCOK at the United Nations in New York while the prime minister was in Britain for the royal wedding in November 1947. Arguing that Cabinet had not been consulted, King was furious when he learned of the decision. The time had come to speak out, King said to his astonished Cabinet. "I did not see how I could support the recommendation. That I thought I ought to say I felt a great mistake was being made by Canada being brought into situations in Asia and Europe of which she knew nothing whatever, of interfering with Great Powers without realizing what consequences might be." If a war broke out in Korea, Canada would be drawn into it via its membership on UNTCOK. The UN had become a snare and a delusion just like the old League of Nations. Worse, it was a useless organization that served only as a forum for Soviet propaganda.

King's vehemence grew as he expressed his traditional view that Canada had to stay out of trouble by turning its back on the world and—adding a new wrinkle that had been on his mind since the Gouzenko affair—avoiding situations in which it could be blamed for triggering a new world war. Later, writing in his diary, he blamed the contretemps on the young staff members in the Department of External Affairs, especially Pearson, who, "with his youth and inexperience and influenced by the persuasion of others around him, had been anxious to have Canada's External Affairs figure prominently in world affairs. . . . I am sure if Skelton had been alive, he would not have advocated our going afield in that fashion."

Not only Pearson and his officials wanted Canada to play its part globally. St Laurent was as much an internationalist as his undersecretary, and he was tough enough to resist the prime minister. Resist he did, bolstered by the support of some of his Cabinet colleagues. Over the course of several days, the crisis between King and St Laurent escalated as aides looked desperately for a solution. King threatened to resign, and St Laurent pointed out that it was almost ridiculous for the government to break up over such a question. A few days later, St Laurent told King quietly and firmly that he and J.L. Ilsley would resign. (Ilsley was the minister who had been representing Canada at the United Nations when the UNTCOK invitation had been accepted.) Brooke Claxton, the defence minister, was also thinking of resignation if the UNTCOK decision was reversed. The prime minister had the right to disavow their actions of course, St Laurent said, but their influence in Cabinet would be destroyed if he did so. Now it was King's turn to be horrified; St Laurent was the one he wanted to succeed him. Both then turned to find a compromise that would satisfy St Laurent's firm intention to keep Patterson on UNTCOK, and the crisis blew over. Patterson could stay, but in typical Mackenzie King fashion, he was to be permitted no leeway.

The UNTCOK affair was significant nonetheless. It embodied a straight-out confrontation between King's foreign policy of non-involvement and the new era of responsible internationalism. Cautious, fearful, worried about the impact of every issue on national unity, the prime minister had not changed as Canada had changed. St Laurent and his department recognized that international affairs had become the route towards responsible nationalism, and they were determined to forge ahead. The compromise over UNTCOK kept Canada on the commission and kept St Laurent and Pearson at the helm. The old era had passed, and the nationalist-internationalists were in charge with, very significantly, a French-speaking leader.

Yet King had been on to something. Somehow the old chief's exquisitely sensitive antennae had picked up the first inklings of trouble in Korea. Later, journalists made suggestions that a spiritualist medium in late 1947 had brought him into contact with the shade of his old friend Franklin Roosevelt, dead since April 1945. FDR's ghost had alarmed King with warnings of trouble in Korea. Whether this mystical explanation was correct is immaterial. There would in fact be enough trouble in Korea to bring the world to the verge of nuclear war. Still, Mackenzie King had been wrong on the broad issue. The Canadian government could not avoid international trouble by ignoring it; the lessons of the 1930s had made that clear to everyone with eyes to see.

CHAPTER SEVEN

End of Empire,
1950–1956

A SIA WAS NOT a part of the world that ordinarily attracted Canadians, who usually fixed their gaze across the Atlantic on Britain and the European continent. Canadian Protestant and Roman Catholic missionaries had served in Japan, Korea, China, and the Philippines for at least a half-century, and their churches at home had long raised money for spreading the gospel among the "heathen Chinee." These links had never translated into a government policy thrust, however. The experience at Hong Kong in December 1941—when an understrength brigade of troops was lost in eighteen days of combat against superior Japanese forces—left a searing memory that restrained the government from showing enthusiasm for the war against Japan and from forging effective postwar diplomatic links with the East. "Canada had not an acre of land or property in the Orient," said Prime Minister King. Except for British Columbians, studies showed, Canadians cared not a whit about the Pacific. Nevertheless, the Far East was becoming vital as one of the main battlegrounds in the Cold War between the West and Soviet communism.

POLICY MOVES FAR EAST

The victories seemed to belong to communism, at least initially. In August 1949, the Soviet Union exploded a nuclear device, demonstrating that Stalin's regime had the power to match the United

States in harnessing technology to destructive force. That blow was more than matched in the same year when Chiang Kai-shek's Nationalist government was driven off the Chinese mainland and into refuge on Taiwan by the People's Liberation Army, led by Mao Zedong. "Who lost China?" was the question asked in Washington, as Red-baiters sought scapegoats in the Democratic administration and in the State Department. They avoided the obvious answer: Chiang lost China.

Ottawa was caught up in the struggle against communism in Asia. The new prime minister, Louis St Laurent, sympathized with the nationalist aspirations of Asian peoples, particularly those in former parts of the British Empire that, like India, had asserted their independence. His secretary of state for external affairs, Lester Pearson, fresh from a 1949 election victory in the constituency of Algoma East, similarly hoped to help bind the huge, fledgling democracies of India, Pakistan, and Ceylon into the Commonwealth family. Other colonies were struggling towards independence as well, and the West believed that the resources and population of Asia and Africa could make Moscow and Beijing invincible. It was far better to help turn former colonies towards democracy.

In January 1950, therefore, Pearson paid his first visit to Asia to attend the Commonwealth Foreign Ministers' Conference in Colombo, Ceylon. Lester Pearson had been a Canadian diplomat for more than twenty years; that he had not visited the East before spoke volumes. The voyage gave him the opportunity to talk at length with Pandit Nehru, the impressive but baffling Indian leader, to visit Pakistan, Nepal, Malaya, and Hong Kong, and to see General Douglas MacArthur, the American proconsul in Tokyo. But the highlight of the long trip was the government's proposal for a Colombo Plan, an early effort in what is now called development assistance, aimed at helping Asian countries to modernize and to follow democratic means in so doing. The Cabinet was more than a little dubious about pouring money into this part of the world, especially at a time when re-armament was beginning to absorb so much of the national revenues. Nevertheless, Pearson and others successfully made the case, mixing anti-communist arguments with ones pointing to the humanitarian benefits and the potential advantages for Canadian business. In 1951–1952 Canada donated $25 million to the Colombo Plan. This was Canada's first venture into aid for Asia; it would not be the last.

Asia already dominated the thoughts of both Pearson and the rest of the country. On 25 June 1950 the North Korean army crossed the 38th parallel, the 1945 demarcation line between Soviet and American occupation zones, and invaded South Korea. The United States immediately moved in the United Nations to condemn the North's aggression and to put troops into South Korea to assist its demoralized forces.

The initial response in Ottawa was cautious. Pearson said privately that he did not think the conflict was anything but a civil war, that the principle of collective security did not seem to be involved, and that he doubted the United States would become involved. The government condemned the invasion, and three Royal Canadian Navy (RCN) destroyers, hurriedly provisioned for action, sailed to Asian waters, a contribution scorned in Washington as a token. When Canadian officials protested that three destroyers were far from a token, a harassed and quick-witted American spokesman said bluntly, "Okay, let's call it three tokens." The retort stung, and soon a Royal Canadian Air Force (RCAF) transport squadron was ferrying supplies from North America to Japan. The war went from bad to worse, and the Koreans and their American allies were hemmed into a shrinking perimeter around the port of Pusan.

Then, on 22 July, Mackenzie King died and government business ceased to allow the old leader to be buried in Toronto while his former colleagues stood at grave side. On the return trip to Ottawa, the key members of the Cabinet met in the prime minister's railway car to discuss the war in Korea. A certain symbolism could be discerned in the movement at this informal meeting towards the dispatch of Canadian troops. King was dead and with him some of the old caution. Even the socialist CCF wanted Canadians on the ground in Korea. Nevertheless, Quebec remained wary of international commitments, as St Laurent knew well.

Before the full Cabinet discussed committing troops to Korea, Pearson paid a quick, quiet visit to Washington to see the American secretary of state, Dean Acheson. Acheson made clear that however vital it was to resist the Soviet-sponsored aggression in Korea, the real threat lay in Europe. Korea demonstrated, he believed, that Stalin had been emboldened by his possession of nuclear weapons to use military means to expand the communist empire. NATO had to be made ready, and at the same time Korea had to be defended. Moreover, the American people had shed their isolationism and were ready to take up the struggle but, Acheson said, it would be easier for them if the democratic nations of the world co-operated in the fight against communism.

Pearson made the same arguments to his colleagues. Canada announced that it would raise a brigade of troops, some eight thousand recruits, for UN service in Korea or for employment with NATO in Europe. The final agreement to send ground troops to Korea came in September 1950. A further decision was made to send another brigade, as well as an air division of interceptor aircraft, to Europe. For the first time ever in what was still technically peacetime, Canada prepared to send soldiers abroad.

The Canadian forces in 1950 were not in good working order. The great army, navy, and air force of 1945 had melted away like winter snow before the spring sun. Instead of the force of a million men and women raised during World War II, Canada at the end of September 1949 had a navy of 8900, an air force of 16 400, and an army of 20 000. The defence budget was $375 million in that year, up from $195 million in 1947–1948, but still a derisory sum. The country received what it paid for, as might be expected. The army had a Mobile Striking Force, designed to repel enemy lodgments in Canada, but in fact it was almost incapable of mounting any effective defence whatsoever. The navy in December 1947 had only ten ships in commission: an aircraft carrier, two cruisers, and a handful of destroyers and minesweepers. The air force was similarly unready for action, though it did consist of two squadrons of Vampire jet interceptors and a maritime squadron. Most flying was done by transport squadrons. All three services had reserve units, but they lacked equipment and training.

Korea galvanized military spending in Canada. Where no money was available prior to 1950, suddenly the government allocated funds to purchase equipment in wholesale lots. By 1953, Canada was spending $1.9 billion annually on defence, an extraordinary 7.6 percent of its gross national product. The RCN numbered just under 17 000 recruits, the RCAF 45 600, and the army 50 000. It was an amazing transformation, the more so because the forces were well equipped with the best of modern weapons. The navy had begun to acquire Canadian-designed destroyer escorts, specially built for anti-submarine warfare. These ships of the *St Laurent* class (named after the river, not the prime minister) were state of the art. RCAF fighter pilots flew F-86 Sabres, with powerful, Canadian-made Orenda engines; the Air Division in NATO, with twelve squadrons, was one of the keystones of Western European defence. The army also had punch, its troops equipped with Centurion tanks and its infantry regiments fit and ready. By the mid-1950s the Canadian forces were well equipped and well trained, much more so than had ever been the case in peacetime before.

Thanks to fighting in Korea, the three services had also received a taste of warfare. The RCAF saw less action than the others, with a combat role limited to experience gained by fighter pilots on exchange with the United States Air Force. The RCN rotated ships from Canadian to Korean waters throughout the war, destroyer crews developing great skill at "train busting": shooting up rail traffic along the North Korean coast. Navy crews also discovered that U.S. rations, procured from American bases in Japan, were far better than the old mutton that Royal Navy provisioners tried to palm off on the dominion sailors.

That discovery was part of a new pattern. Great Britain was no longer a major military power and the United States was. American weaponry and equipment were almost always the best available and, not unnaturally, the Canadian forces began to want them. British influence remained strong in the navy, however, where officers raised in the Nelson tradition still ruled the quarterdeck, much to the annoyance of many sailors. Shortly before the Korean War, in fact, mutinies broke out on a few ships and the resulting soul-searching began the long, slow process of Canadianizing the RCN. The army, too, had close ties with the British Army, honed during the world wars and preserved by the regimental system and links with sister units. The Canadian air force harboured resentment over its treatment by the Royal Air Force during World War II, however, and its leadership was much more amenable to Americanization than that of the other services. These issues would not be played out until later in the decade, yet significantly, only the Canadian ground effort in Korea and in NATO would be executed in association with the British.

The major effort in Korea fell to the 25th Canadian Infantry Brigade. Recruited from volunteers in the late summer of 1950, the group included veterans, adventurers, and, because of the haste with which it was put together, not a few of the aged and the infirm. The brigade underwent its preliminary training in Canada and its final preparations in the spacious confines of Fort Lewis, Washington, in the United States. One of its units, the 2nd Battalion, Princess Patricia's Canadian Light Infantry, sailed to Korea in November 1950, completed its training, and went into action in February 1951. While reinforcement and replacement units began to get ready in Canada, the remainder of the 25th Brigade arrived in Korea in April 1951 and went into the line in May as part of the Commonwealth Division.

The war had changed complexion dramatically by then. The early North Korean successes of the summer of 1950 had been reversed completely after an amphibious landing by u.s. forces at Inchon, near Seoul, in September, and by November the North Koreans had been driven well into the north of their territory, close to the border of Chinese-controlled Manchuria. Chinese communist forces then intervened in massive strength. In a vicious campaign in sub-zero conditions, they drove the surprised United Nations Command troops pellmell towards the south where, with great difficulty, a defence line was finally stabilized south of the 38th parallel.

By the time the Canadian brigade arrived on the scene, the UN forces, mainly American and Korean but with contingents from many other European and Asian nations, had moved to the offensive again. For the next two years fierce fighting for limited objectives saw the United Nations move the front back over the 38th parallel once more. An armistice was signed in 1953, signalling the division of Korea into two competing nations. Canada had suffered 1557 casualties from among the twenty-two thousand soldiers who had served in the fighting.

CONTAINING THE AMERICANS

Canada had done its part in the Korean war, and the war memorials in towns across the land added new names to those already engraved from the country's earlier wars. Even so, Ottawa had serious concerns both about the way the war was directed from Washington, rather than from the United Nations in New York, and about the war aims that shaped the direction of the American-led United Nations effort. These worries had become more pronounced when General MacArthur's troops had crossed the 38th parallel after the Inchon invasion. Was the role of the United Nations to free South Korea of the invaders from the North or to conquer North Korea? The question had been answered when UN troops kept on going towards the Manchurian border, thus posing a threat to China, or so the Beijing government must have believed. The Chinese intervention at the end of 1950 had demonstrated that Canadian fears had been legitimate, but nations, much like individuals, often dislike those who have been proven correct.

Canada wished to secure a ceasefire to stop the killing, and to prevent the Korean War from escalating into an Asia-wide war or, worse still, a nuclear World War III. These goals were co-ordinated from Ottawa by Pearson and also pursued by Canadian diplomats at the United Nations in New York, in London, in Washington, and in other foreign capitals. The Canadian tactic, in scholar Denis Stairs' phrase, was to essay the "diplomacy of constraint," a policy of trying to control the untrammelled desire of the United States for victory over Chinese communism. Americans were much like Canadians, the line went, except when they had the bit in their teeth; then they were rash, impetuous, and positively dangerous. Americans, naturally enough, resented Canadian preaching, which applied the superior morality of the relatively weak and powerless against them. It was American soldiers, after all, who were dying in Korea in large numbers, not Canadians. Secretary of State Dean Acheson, whose father was Canadian-born and who knew Canada well, later characterized Canada as "the Stern Daughter of the Voice of God," an unflattering reference to the tendency of its government to act as if it alone always knew best.

Eisenhower and St Laurent meet in Washington, 1956
(National Archives of Canada, C 90466)

Other Canadians also fell under suspicion, among them Herbert Norman, the American-desk officer at the Department of External Affairs in Ottawa at the beginning of the 1950s. The Norman question disappeared for a time but it was not forgotten. To Canadians, it seemed to be another example of the American lack of perspective and balance when faced with the slightest suggestion of communism. They seemed too ready to forget that an individual's democratic rights had to be protected.

During the same period, Canada found itself embroiled in various disputes over trade and tariffs. These were very often with the United States, with which ever-increasing percentages of Canadian imports and exports were exchanged. As a founding member of the General Agreement on Tariffs and Trade (GATT), Canada always loudly claimed to be in favour of freeing trade by lowering tariffs, a protestation that often hid a web of domestic subsidies and non-tariff barriers. No one was fooled by this excessive moralism, of course, but at GATT meetings Canadian representatives often continued to take the holier-than-thou attitude that if only other countries followed the rules of the world trade organization, as Canada did, all would be well. At one 1955 session, a blunt Australian chairing a session summed up his own country's position in a stinging way: "Unlike Canada, Australia is not without sin." Fortunately, perhaps, the United States had much the same moralism, and the same hidden trade barriers and tariffs, so it was not in a position to judge.

The Soviet Union watched all these capitalist disputes and manoeuvrings with great interest, so much so that Pearson felt obliged to declare in brusque terms that Canada was firmly on the Western side. Disagreements over tactics were one thing; disputes over the broad principles, over the divide between democracy and despotism, were another matter entirely. There were, after all, only differences of degree between Stalin and his successors in the Kremlin. Aiming his words at Moscow, Pearson said pointedly that the United States was "our leader and we stick with [it] and we'll be solid and don't get any ideas you're splitting us." Still, in a speech at home delivered when disputes over policy in Korea were at their sharpest, Pearson did say that the age of "easy and automatic relations" with the United States had ended. Nothing could be easy and automatic in a world of Cold War and nuclear weaponry.

As the Cold War intensified through the early 1950s, Canada and the United States continued to co-operate closely, if sometimes warily, in defence questions. Both North American nations worked closely in NATO, joining in the formation of an integrated military force under the command of General Dwight Eisenhower in December 1950. Both stationed troops in Europe and both joined in naval defence in the North Atlantic. In North America itself, the growing menace of Soviet long-range bombers led to increased co-operation between the air defence commands of the RCAF and the United States Air Force and to construction of sophisticated air warning systems.

Radar lines, designed to provide early notice of any attack, were established across the continent. By 1954, the Pinetree Line—running roughly along the 50th parallel—had been put in place at a cost of $450 million, two-thirds paid by the United States and one-third by Canada. The search for more warning time was unending, however,

and construction of the Mid-Canada Line, another expensive system*
along the 54th parallel, started in 1955. Finally, the Distant Early
Warning Line (DEW Line), located in the high Arctic along the 70th
parallel, was begun. Weather and terrain made these radar sites enormously expensive to erect, and Ottawa and Washington struck a deal:
if Canada paid for the Mid-Canada Line, the United States would
pay for the DEW Line. Unfortunately, zealous American security officials sometimes forgot that the sites were still on Canadian soil, even
if the United States was picking up the tab. Canadians were forbid-
den to visit the DEW Line sites, except with U.S. agreement. Military
security was involved, of course, but the American rules seemed high-
handed, drafted with the aim of rousing Canadian ire. They did,
although no one in Ottawa forgot that the radar lines were intended
to detect a Soviet nuclear attack on North America, a possibility that
seemed frighteningly real in a world divided into two competing
blocs. American high-handedness seemed a small price to pay for the
co-operation of a superpower that was spending far more to defend
Canada than its own citizens were.

POST-STALINISM

Threat that it was, the Soviet Union nonetheless remained an
enigma. The successors to Stalin, after his death in 1953, were new,
little known in Ottawa, and there were some indications that they
hoped to break out of the self-imposed Soviet hostility to the West.
One such sign came at the tenth anniversary celebrations of the
founding of the United Nations, when Soviet foreign minister V.M.
Molotov invited Pearson to visit the U.S.S.R. As Pearson's biographer,
John English, noted, the Soviets knew that Pearson was a founder of
NATO and certainly no pacifist, but "he was among the most prominent Western voices calling for more contacts and understanding
between East and West." That provided Moscow with sufficient reason to attempt to convince him that post-Stalinist communism had
"a more congenial face."

Certainly Nikita Khrushchev, who had emerged as the real power in
the Soviet Union, could be more congenial than previous leaders. Short

and squat, his expressive face capable of a beaming smile, he was about as different from Stalin as it was possible to be. When Pearson and his party arrived in Moscow in October 1955 they were wined and dined, and they also began the process of negotiating an agreement to begin Canadian grain sales to the Soviet Union. The pact would be immensely profitable to Canadian prairie farmers over the next decades.

The culmination of the trip was a visit to Khrushchev's holiday mansion near Yalta in the Crimea. There the parties engaged in formal talks about NATO plans to admit a re-armed West Germany to full membership. With their long memories of the death and destruction that Nazis had visited on the U.S.S.R., the Soviets were clearly upset by the subject. Pearson replied, weakly some observers said, that the move was defensive, and seemed stunned by the rapidity with which Khrushchev moved to the attack. Only Russians and Germans understood war, he argued, and the West did not know how to fight. In the event of a third world war Germany would not fight, and NATO would fall apart as soon as the first shot was fired. Moreover, Khrushchev said pointedly, "This time Canada would not be geographically secure."

While this somber discussion proceeded, the Canadians and their hosts dispatched much food and more vodka. They made toasts to peace and friendship, obligatory despite the bluster of the Soviet leader's denunciations, and the Pearson party finally made their escape after midnight, "with eighteen vodkas in each bloodstream." The experience had been, said George Ignatieff, the Russian-born diplomat who accompanied Pearson, like visiting Hitler at Berchtesgaden. Pearson's biographer added that the next morning, the car carrying Pearson swerved around the roads atop the Black Sea cliffs, stopping before a monument to a nineteenth-century military hero. There, the guide said, the Marshal lost an eye defeating the Turks. "Build another monument five miles back," Pearson said, "for that is where I lost my stomach."

The post-Stalinist Soviet Union was full of menace, or so Pearson concluded. The West could not afford to relax its guard, and there seemed little prospect that the huge sums being devoted to defence by Canada could be reduced in the near future. The world was going to remain a dangerous place; hopes for peaceful co-existence with the Soviets had been nothing more than a chimera.

The next year brought ample evidence of this. In October 1956, a democratic revolution erupted in Hungary, hitherto a docile Soviet satellite. Amid scenes of horrific bloodshed and great rejoicing, the secret police headquarters were stormed, statues of Stalin were toppled, and the Soviet forces stationed in and around Budapest began to withdraw. Hungary announced its withdrawal from the Warsaw Pact, the military organization formed by the U.S.S.R. and its satellites as a counter to NATO, and asked for the protection of the United Nations. But then orders from Moscow came for the tanks to move in and the cheering crowds met a bloody fate, their rifles useless against the armour of the Soviet T-34 tanks.

The old regime was back with a vengeance, and tens of thousands of Hungarians fled over the Austrian border. Countries around the world took in the refugees; Canada, after a hesitant start, absorbed thirty-seven thousand men, women, and children. There were some extraordinary stories. Cabinet minister J.W. Pickersgill, sent to Vienna to administer the crash program that Ottawa had eventually put in place to assist, heard that the entire forestry faculty of Sopron University and most of its students had escaped. Quick as a flash, the minister contacted a British Columbia colleague, who arranged to have a lumber camp turned into a reception centre to house the Hungarian foresters until the fall term opened at the University of British Columbia and the Sopron foresters could be admitted. The Hungarians proved of enormous value to their adopted country.

Twelve years later, Soviet repression of the "Prague Spring"—a program of political reform in Czechoslovakia—sent more refugees fleeing westward. With another mixture of altruism and self-interest, Canada moved quickly to scoop up the best qualified, taking in twelve thousand Czechs.

PEARSON'S SHINING HOUR

The Hungarian revolution and its bloody dénouement ought to have been an enormous propaganda coup for the West, a demonstration of the profound ruthlessness and moral bankruptcy of Soviet communism. Instead, most of the neutral states quickly forgot about the slaughter in Budapest because, shortly thereafter, Israel, Britain, and France invaded Egypt. The combination of military action by old colonial powers and the aggressive might of the Jewish state somehow over-rode the Soviet atrocities. In this greatest of postwar crises, Lester Pearson was at the forefront.

The crisis in the Middle East had been in the making for a decade. German slaughter of European Jewry had lent moral force and urgency to the long struggle for a Jewish state in Palestine. Britain wanted to be rid of its colonial possessions. Together, these factors prompted the creation of the state of Israel in 1948. Neighbouring Arab states had attacked the new nation as soon as it was formed and, to the world's surprise, had been thrashed despite numerical superiority. Israel's boundaries expanded as a result of the first Arab–Israeli war, and the United Nations stepped in to broker an uneasy armistice.

The drafters of the United Nations Charter in 1945 had envisaged large armies placed at the disposal of the organization by the great powers and directed by a general staff, but the Cold War had intervened to block any such moves. Instead, New York sent out observers to watch over the borders between Israel and its Arab neighbours, a small force called the United Nations Truce Supervision Organization (UNTSO). The job of UNTSO was to oversee violations of the various armistices and report on them. At much the same time, the United Nations Military Observer Group India–Pakistan (UNMOGIP) was created to keep watch over the disputed borders of Jammu and Kashmir, claimed by both India and Pakistan.

Canada had been asked to send officers to both UNMOGIP and UNTSO and had initially refused. The Canadian army was small and the government was also concerned about being caught in a war between the two Commonwealth nations on the Indian subcontinent. Eventually a few officer observers were dispatched to both forces in response to UN pleas. In 1954, Major-General E.L.M. Burns, a wartime corps commander in Italy and former deputy minister of veterans' affairs, became the head of UNTSO. The presence of a Canadian on the scene gave added impetus to Ottawa's efforts when the Suez crisis erupted in 1956.

Canadian policy leading up to the Middle East crisis had been cautious in the extreme. Ottawa had been hesitant in supporting Jewish efforts to create Israel for fear of adding to Britain's difficulties. Though Canadian Jews gave money and some served in the Israeli army in the 1948 war, the government had remained careful not to appear partisan. It had imposed restrictions on arms sales, for example, to both sides. Still, if sympathies of any sort existed within the federal government, they probably leaned towards the Israelis. The memory of the Holocaust, guilt about Western anti-Semitism, and admiration for the way in which Israelis had begun to make the desert bloom all combined to make Canadians as a whole sympathetic to Israel.

Initially, at least, these tendencies were reinforced when Egyptian President Gamal Abdel Nasser suddenly nationalized the Suez Canal in 1956. Run by British and French investors, the canal was still widely seen as Britain's lifeline, its route to the Far East, and the waterway by which Arabian oil made its way to Europe. Nasser was a vigorously anti-Western, pan-Arabian nationalist, and was being wooed by the Soviet Union with arms shipments. Under his control, the canal might not be a secure route any longer. Unstated but obviously present were concerns, at once self-satisfied and condescending, that the Egyptians could not run the canal effectively and efficiently.

The British and French convened international committees and mustered all the political pressure they could bring to bear. Their efforts apparently unavailing in the face of Nasser's obdurate rhetoric, the two countries began mobilizing troops for an attack on Egypt, sending ships, aircraft, and soldiers to a staging post on Cyprus. At the same time, secretly, Britain and France held discussions with Israel about co-ordinating their own attack with an Israeli strike across the Sinai desert. Although the negotiations were kept covert, there were whispers in London of the Anglo–French military preparations.

The Canadian high commissioner there, Norman Robertson, repeatedly tried to make clear to the British that they could not and should not count on Canadian support for military action. Let diplomacy work, Robertson urged. The British apparently assumed that such warnings would be brushed aside by a wave of popular feeling in the event of war. London calculated that it would be 1914 and 1939 all over again. The British were wrong.

In the last week of October, while world attention focussed on the Hungarian revolution and the United States was caught up in the presidential election battle between President Eisenhower and challenger Adlai Stevenson, Israel launched an attack on Egypt. As agreed in the secret plan reached with the Israelis, a joint British–French ultimatum demanding that both sides withdraw their forces to allow the Suez Canal to be safely used was delivered on 30 October with a twelve-hour time limit. The Egyptians refused the ultimatum, exactly as anticipated. British and French forces then began air and sea operations against Nasser and continued preparations for an assault by seaborne and parachuted infantry. The Israeli advance continued, completely smashing Egyptian forces in the Sinai.

The world reaction was one of shock and revulsion. At the United Nations Security Council, the Americans, incensed that their friends had launched an attack without consultation and in the closing days of a presidential election campaign, demanded the withdrawal of the invaders. Britain and France vetoed this American attempt and the crisis passed into the hands of the General Assembly. Little support could be found there for London and Paris. Asian Commonwealth members pointedly condemned the attack. Only Australia and New Zealand, still close to Britain (and worried about their links to Europe through Suez), lent the British unqualified support.

The Canadian position was awkward in the extreme. Public opinion in Canada was divided: some newspaper editorialists were quick to compare Nasser to Hitler and to applaud the Anglo–French assault; others bemoaned the use of force against an emerging state and called for UN action. The government, privately outraged at the British attack and at not having been consulted beforehand, was characteristically moderate in public. Prime Minister St Laurent stated publicly its "regret that . . . the United Kingdom and France felt it necessary to intervene with force on their own responsibility." The secret messages to London were much harsher, made more so by Prime Minister Anthony Eden's bald-faced lies in his telegrams that Britain had only acted to prevent the spread of fighting and to protect the canal.

Everyone knew that the Anglo–French–Israeli aim was to topple Nasser. In the Department of External Affairs, Eden's call for Canadian understanding and support was received with the contempt it merited as word began to be received of Anglo–French connivance with Israel. St Laurent's reply to Eden, much toned down from the white heat that had gone into the first draft, was still blunt. Without more information, he said, "we cannot come to the conclusion that the penetration of [Israeli] troops into Egypt was justified or that the probable resistance of the Egyptians necessitated the decision of the u.k. and France to post forces in the canal zone." Canada and Canadians "will endeavour to shape our course in conformity with what we regard as our obligations under the Charter of and our membership in the United Nations."

That historic message marked the de facto end of the British Empire in Canada. The response to Britain's call of 1899, 1914, and 1939 was history now, never to be seen again. The idea that Britain was an especially moral nation, and that Canada therefore owed it something, was ended at Suez. The British government now knew, if it had not before, that the Canadian course was dead set against it on this issue.

Nonetheless, the government in Ottawa still wished to try to save Britain and France from the consequences of their folly. Both nations after all were members of NATO, the keystones of Western defence in Europe. Both were allies and friends; indeed, they were Canadians' mother countries. Striking a pose that only pointed up the fundamental absurdity of the situation, the Soviets, their hands still reeking of Hungarian blood, soon threatened missile strikes against London and Paris and called on Washington to engage in joint action to liberate Egypt from the imperialist invasion. Some way had to be found to get the Anglo–French attackers off the hook on which their own actions had impaled them. Some way had to be found to restore the links between Washington and London and keep Canada's two great friends on a common course in world affairs.

When Lester Pearson flew to New York on 1 November, he took with him the idea that the Anglo–French forces might be transformed into a United Nations force, "not to give United Nations respectability to the Anglo–French intervention but to change its character and make it serve different ends." That idea soon proved a non-starter, so angered were the members of the United Nations and so intent on branding Britain and France as aggressors. Late that night, the Assembly passed an American motion calling for a cease-fire and immediate withdrawal behind the existing cease-fire lines. Pearson abstained for Canada on this vote. When he finally had the chance to explain his country's decision, Pearson told the General Assembly,

> I regret the use of force . . . but I regret also that there was not more time, before a vote had to be taken, for consideration of the best way to bring about that kind of cease-fire which would have enduring and beneficial results. . . .
>
> We need action, then, not only to end the fighting but to make the peace. . . .
>
> I therefore would have liked to see a provision in this resolution . . . authorizing the Secretary-General to begin to make arrangements with Member Governments for a United Nations force large enough to keep these borders at peace while a political settlement is being worked out. . . . I hope that even now, when action on the resolution has been completed, it may not be too late to give consideration to this matter. My own Government would be glad to recommend Canadian participation in such a United Nations force, a truly international peace and police force.

For the next few days, while Britain and France flouted the UN demand for a cease-fire and continued preparations for a seaborne invasion, Pearson worked to put flesh on the bare bones of the idea he had advanced. He had endless consultations with Dag Hammarskjöld, the United Nations secretary general, who, initially dubious about Pearson's idea, soon came to recognize in it the best hope of averting disaster. Pearson and his staff had deliberations with other nations, among them the United States, Britain, and France. The external affairs minister undertook hurried trips to Ottawa to keep the Cabinet on side, and received St Laurent's permission to introduce a resolution calling for the establishment of a UN force.

The resolution was duly presented on 3 November, requesting, "as a matter of priority, the Secretary-General to submit . . . within forty-eight hours a plan for the setting up, with the consent of the nations concerned, of an emergency international United Nations force to secure and supervise the cessation of hostilities." It passed in the early morning hours of 4 November by a vote of 57–0 with nineteen abstentions.

Now all that remained was to create the force. Again Pearson and his team, including military staff officers sent from National Defence Headquarters, played crucial roles. It was decided in the initial meeting to create a UN command headed by General "Tommy" Burns. As chief of staff of UNTSO he was already on the spot. Burns was authorized to form a makeshift staff for the new force from the officers serving under him in UNTSO. Infantry from contributing nations were to be sent to Egypt just as soon as Burns's staff was operating. The plan, requested in forty-eight hours, was ready in twelve.

The need was great. Britain and France, acting with incredible foolhardiness in the face of General Assembly actions and the tenor of world opinion, expanded their military operation on 5 November. Airborne troops jumped into Port Suez and additional troops followed by sea. Heavy fighting ensued as the Egyptian army tried to redeem itself from the military disaster it had suffered in the Sinai desert. At the United Nations, Pearson and Hammarskjöld raced to get their plan into place before the conflict spread. It was presented on 6 November.

The principles that were to govern peacekeeping for the next three decades were now put in place. The most important provision excluded permanent members of the Security Council from participation in the UN force; the British and French were thus barred from donning blue berets to camouflage the character of their aggression, and the Soviets and Americans were blocked from converting the UN force into a covert extension of the Cold War. Less opportunely, U.S. equipment and support were prohibited, constraining the ability of the United Nations to get its emergency force to Egypt as quickly as it might have wished. The secretary general was to have political control of the force, with an advisory committee to assist. As for the force itself, it was to be "more than an observer's corps, but in no way a military force temporarily controlling the territory in which it is stationed." The force was not intended to impose the will of the United Nations on the combatants. Its sole purpose, Hammarskjöld affirmed, was to assist in bringing about results desired by all the governments involved, and the report made clear that the sovereign rights of Egypt were to be respected. Egyptian consent, in other words, was necessary before the force could begin to function within the territory of Egypt.

The Suez crisis dominated the world news, and especially in Canada. Despite substantial support for the peace force concept, the Canadian initiatives at the United Nations were not uniformly well received across the country. Most notably in loyalist Ontario, many claimed that Canada had sold out its mother countries. Long-retired prime minister Arthur Meighen argued that Canada ought to have followed the "most exemplary" lead offered by Australia and New Zealand and offered the United Kingdom diplomatic support. "Ready, aye ready" remained the Meighen line, even when Britain was the aggressor. The Toronto *Globe and Mail* stated that the Canadian government "added nothing to its prestige—or to Canada's—by its conduct at this week's emergency meeting of the United Nations General Assembly." But polls discovered massive support for the UN peace force idea. Still, the issue divided Canadians very sharply.

One major criticism directed at the government was that its policy had been very similar to that of the United States. Britain and France were fighting and the United States was holding off, just as in 1914 and 1939. The situation struck emotive chords for many Canadians, whose anti-Americanism exceeded their good sense and understanding of history. When Eisenhower and St Laurent talked on the telephone on 6 November not only the warmth of good fellowship but also the prime minister's concern about anti-American sentiment was apparent:

> St Laurent: Things are happening pretty fast. . . .
> [Eisenhower]: Things are pretty encouraging. Never have I seen action on the part of a government that excited me more than the rapid way you & your government moved into the breech. You did a magnificent job & we admire it.

St Laurent: I very much appreciate that, & my Colleagues will, too. But we happened to be in a position that no one had any misgivings about it. But you just can't explain the vagaries of human nature. We have trouble up here, with people who look upon bigness as a sin.

FREEZING THE CRISIS

Meanwhile the efforts to create a UN force, now being called the United Nations Emergency Force (UNEF), continued in New York. The Scandinavian nations, some South American states, and others were being asked for troops, and Canada itself was scrambling to decide what units should form its contribution. The immediate need seemed to be for infantry, and the defence minister designated the 1st Battalion of the Queen's Own Rifles of Canada, along with service units, for the job. This was announced on 7 November, followed by a decision to fly the troops to the Middle East on RCAF aircraft. The aircraft carrier HMCS *Magnificent* was to carry the unit's heavy equipment and provide a "firm base to which we could evacuate quickly," said General Charles Foulkes, chairman of the Chiefs of Staff Committee. In the end, however, it was decided that the "*Maggie*" would carry the Canadian contingent's personnel as well as their equipment.

Then, suddenly, problems arose over the Queen's Own. It might have been expected that Egypt, its armies in disarray, its air force eliminated, would have welcomed UNEF. This was not the case. With the imposition of a genuine cease-fire on 7 November, Nasser's task now was to get rid of the invaders at the cheapest possible diplomatic price. Was UNEF just another way of putting pressure on Egypt to abandon the struggle? If so, the more conditions that Egypt placed on the presence of UNEF the better. Where would it be stationed? How long would it stay? Who would be part of it?

The last was the sticky question. Hammarskjöld believed that he had finessed the matter by accepting offers only from "non-controversial" countries such as Colombia, Norway, Denmark, Sweden, Finland, and Canada. But was Canada uncontroversial? The

Canadians certainly thought so. After all, UNEF was a Canadian idea, and Canada had turned its back on its historic allies in advancing the proposal.

Ah, the Cairo government said, that was immaterial. Canada was a NATO ally of Britain and France, and Canadian troops wore British-style uniforms and marched under a flag containing the Union Jack. The name of the Queen's Own Rifles was similar to that of British units attacking Egypt and reeked of British imperialism. Moreover, Britain's queen was Canada's too. The Egyptian people, those who had been bombed, strafed, and shot by the British a few days before, simply would not understand.

The Canadian public and its UN representation reacted with outrage, but the Egyptians had a point, as Pearson later agreed privately. (His decision as prime minister in 1964 to see Canada adopt a distinctive flag, without the Union Jack in the corner, seems to have been influenced by this incident.) Canadian ties to Britain had suddenly been revealed as an impediment to independent policy at the United Nations. In addition, as the Egyptians confidentially told Pearson, they felt some resentment that Canada had abstained on the initial resolution at New York on 1 November.

For days the wrangling between Pearson, the secretary general, and the Egyptian government continued. On 14 November, Cairo agreed to let UNEF into Egypt, the Canadian question remaining unresolved. Finally, Hammarskjöld, driven nearly to distraction by Canadian and Egyptian pressures on him, reached an accommodation. Egypt agreed that "Canada is welcome as a country from which elements of the UNEF may be drawn. It is felt that the most important contribution that could be given at the present stage . . . would be air support . . . and [units] for the current functioning of the UNEF in Egypt." General Burns also provided Lester Pearson with a letter suggesting that UNEF needed not infantry but air transport and non-combat troops "to help in organizing the administration at the base of the force in Egypt."

Pearson's retreat on the issue was now covered by the demands of military necessity. Canada would not send the Queen's Own Rifles but instead essential, if unglamorous, supply, transport, and medical units. The Queen's Own returned to barracks in the full glare of publicity and with opposition-leaning newspapers denouncing the surrender to Egyptian demands. The logistical units left for Egypt towards the end of November. Some of the glow created by Pearson's achievements had been removed by this unhappy dénouement. UN peacekeeping service, Canadians had discovered, was fraught with unsuspected political perils.

Before long, General Burns called for more troops from Canada. He desperately required more administrative support for UNEF, and National Defence Headquarters agreed to his requests in December. Ottawa provided a signals squadron, a field workshop, two transport platoons, and an RCAF communications squadron. Burns also asked for and received a reconnaissance squadron equipped with armoured cars, a unit that gave Canada some representation in combat troops.

Canada ultimately contributed more than a thousand troops to UNEF, the largest national contingent and one-sixth of the total force. UNEF was the first real peacekeeping unit: a large, multinational grouping with the task of separating two potential combatants, rather than simply observing. The UN troops carried weapons and, although they had to be circumspect in how they dealt with Egyptians and Israelis, they had authority to defend themselves.

The Canadian soldiers in UNEF soon settled down into a routine. Their jobs were prosaic, their adventures more bound up with trips to Beirut, Cairo, or Jerusalem—then the three most interesting cities in the Middle East—than with exciting military missions. Hauling groceries to El Arish, the Canadian base in the desert, was no more challenging after all than hauling them to Camp Borden, Ontario. Yet there were some differences. The squalor of Egypt was unparalleled; the heat had a wholly different character; and the corruption and incompetence of officials was something new. Even these contrasts faded into insignificance and all that remained was boredom. One junior officer with the reconnaissance squadron wrote home, "I have read so many westerns in the last while that I'm even talking like a cowboy."

In part the duty was tedious because the United Nations had no success in moving from peacekeeping to peacemaking, though it was in its mandate to do so. Israel and Egypt remained obdurate, despite the arm-twisting applied by the secretary general and other interested parties. The only accomplishment of UNEF was to freeze the crisis for a decade, an achievement of sorts but one far below the expectations of its creators.

PEACEKEEPER

Clearly the Egyptians had not wanted Canada to be part of UNEF for reasons both sound and peculiar. Nevertheless, Canada did form part of the force.

In the 1990s Canadians have the sense that their suitability for peacekeeping operations derives from their innate talents as a middle power, from their ability to be impartial if not quite neutral. Whether this is a real reflection of the Canadian character may well be doubted, but the sense of it is powerful. In 1956, these traits did not leap instantly to Canadian minds. Canada was a Western democracy, a member of NATO, an ally of the United States, a member of the British Commonwealth, and proud of all these things. Opposition within the country to the role that Pearson had played in New York reflected the confusion that Canadians felt at seeing their leaders speak and act against Britain and France, and Egyptian objections to Canada were not far off the mark.

When UNEF got on the ground, Canada was present. Canadian armed forces had always been constituted for service overseas. In 1914 and 1939, the country sent its divisions, pilots, and ships overseas, ready to serve the empire wherever it was threatened. The forces therefore had to have good communications, lengthy supply trains stretching back to North America, and substantial air transport capacity. Similarly, they needed to be mechanized, or mobile, a trait that demanded maintenance capacities of a high standard. After 1951, Canadian troops stationed in Europe had to be prepared to fight the Soviets on the German plain, and this also required high standards of supply, maintenance, and communications. Most national military forces simply were different. African and Asian states could provide infantry but none of the "administrative tail" necessary for a force to function. Scandinavian forces were trained to fight on their home ground, and this had shaped their organization.

The great powers, with armies possessing all the accoutrements necessary for a worldwide reach, were barred from UNEF. Almost no one else could have provided the administrative support for UNEF.

Somehow Canadians never grasped this. The success in establishing UNEF washed away public concerns, though not, as we shall see, until after the 1957 general election. The myth of Canadian impartiality began to grow in the public mind, and the people forgot that Canadians were needed in UNEF not because they were neutral but because they were Western and NATO, mechanized and efficient.

Lester Pearson understood these nuances, and he showed substantial political courage in recommending that the Queen's Own Rifles be returned to their home station and logistical troops be sent to UNEF in their stead. The job was to facilitate Anglo–French–Israeli withdrawal and move towards peace; whatever helped reach that end had to be done. Even so, the Liberals paid a price for Pearson's actions at the United Nations in those harried days of November 1956. The government brought some of its problems on itself, not least by Prime Minister St Laurent's unwise if truthful slip in the House of Commons that the British and French were "those supermen of Europe whose days are about over." Pearson did not help either when he told Parliament that the government was not willing to be "a colonial chore-boy" for Britain.

These comments did not sit well with Conservative MPs, who promptly blasted the Liberals for being the chore-boys of the United States, for stabbing Canada's friends in the back, and for putting London and Paris in the same bag as Moscow. In the election of June 1957, to the astonishment of virtually every observer, the Conservatives won a minority victory. The fiery eloquence of their new leader, John Diefenbaker, captured Canadians' hearts, and the tired Liberals seemed pale by comparison. Some of the electoral swing was certainly caused by Liberal actions during the Suez crisis, though how much cannot be definitively determined. The Liberals had committed a multitude of sins in twenty-two years in power; to some voters, Suez was one of them.

If many Canadians took a jaundiced view of their country's role in the crisis, the world community was more admiring. Pearson garnered plaudits everywhere for his actions at New York. Even the

British and French, still smarting from Canadian condemnation, which many saw as desertion, grudgingly began to concede that Pearson had helped rescue them from the hole they had dug for themselves. This international praise mattered in Canada. Once St Laurent announced his decision to step down as leader of the Liberal Party, Pearson was pressed to throw his hat into the ring, which he soon did. The accolades he had received were then capped by a Nobel Peace Prize in October 1957, an honour greeted by all Canadians, even those who had opposed his role during the crisis, as

On the rise (National Archives of Canada, C 138703)

an award to Canada. Pearson himself, told by a reporter that he had won the prize, offered only a heartfelt "Gosh!" His victory in the Liberal convention several weeks later was almost anti-climactic, pre-ordained as it seemed.

Peacekeeping became the one role Canadians performed better than anyone else. Although Ottawa had been reluctant to send observers to Palestine or Kashmir and unhappy about being pressed into service in Indochina, in the view of both the government and the public no peacekeeping force after UNEF seemed complete without Canadian participation. This became a political factor of some importance as successive prime ministers and foreign ministers ever after conducted themselves as though a peace prize were on the horizon. The Suez crisis changed Canada and its policy. Pearson himself remained puzzled by the attack at Suez. Writing privately to a friend, he wondered,

> How the British ever expected to get away with military action with the Americans strongly opposed, with the Asian members of the Commonwealth even more strongly opposed, with the certainty that the matter would be referred to the UN Assembly where the UK and France would be in the dock . . . and with the knowledge that the Communists would exploit the situation to their own advantage, is something I will never know.

Just as Suez elevated Canadians to unaccustomed heights, the suicide of Herbert Norman brought them crashing back to reality. A Japanese expert, Norman had served in Tokyo before and after World War II, and had performed his duties brilliantly. He had had leftist connections in the 1930s as a student in Britain and the United States, and when hard-line anti-communists in both Washington and the American mission in Tokyo began to worry about him, he had unfortunately obfuscated matters. Pearson and the government investigated the diplomat and, satisfied, backed him to the hilt.

After being fingered as a communist by American investigators at the beginning of the decade, Norman had been in both New Zealand and Egypt, where he was Canadian ambassador during the Suez crisis. His reporting from Cairo had been superb, all agreed,

EGERTON HERBERT NORMAN (1909-1957)

Shame (Reidford, *Globe and Mail,* 1957)

and he had worked with great effect to persuade President Nasser to allow Canadian troops into UNEF. Then renewed allegations against the Canadian diplomat surfaced in congressional committees in Washington. Distraught, Norman killed himself early in April 1957 by jumping from an apartment building.

His death provoked an extraordinary outburst of anti-Americanism in Canada, as politicians and newspapers of all stripes denounced the witch-hunting Americans. The Canadian ambassador in Washington delivered Canadian protests to the State Department, only to be told that Congress was a law unto itself. President Eisenhower told the ambassador the same thing; privately, senior American officials believed that Norman had earlier been a communist even if he had at some point ceased to be one. The sour mood after Norman's suicide reinforced a growing anti-Americanism in Canada. It was a powerful and emotional weapon, as John Diefenbaker would soon make all too clear.

CHAPTER EIGHT

A Great National Destiny, 1957–1963

THE ELECTION OF JUNE 1957 was expected to be a predictable bore. Opinion polls showed the Liberals well in the lead, Louis St Laurent was aging but remained popular in an avuncular way, and the competent management of domestic politics seemed to be appreciated by the nation as a whole. Not so, or not enough. The Progressive Conservatives stunned the political backroom operatives and editorialists alike by squeaking out a minority victory. It was a profound upset, and the new prime minister, John Diefenbaker, was virtually unknown both in Canada and in the capitals of Canada's friends and foes.

THE CHIEF

The Chief, as he was soon called across the country, was a westerner. Born in Ontario, he had moved to Saskatchewan with his family soon after the turn of the century. World War I had interrupted his university schooling, but 2nd Lieutenant Diefenbaker had escaped the slaughter of the trenches when a training injury in England led to his release from the army. Then it was law school, a successful career as a defence counsel in Prince Albert, and repeated, unsuccessful attempts to win political office. Not until 1940 did Diefenbaker finally win a race, securing election to Parliament despite Mackenzie King's Liberal landslide.

His views on foreign policy were predictably Tory. Perhaps because of sensitivity about his Germanic name, Diefenbaker was even more pro-British than most Conservatives, a firm supporter of the empire, of Winston Churchill, of British power. His Canadian nationalism, though always strong, was filtered through a British lens; he was suspicious of the Liberal Party willingness to treat with the United States. Like many others, Diefenbaker wanted Canada to support and help maintain Mother England as a great power. During the Suez crisis, for example, just before he won the Conservative leadership in convention, Diefenbaker vehemently denounced the St Laurent–Pearson turn away from Britain. He even more vehemently decried the apparent co-operation of Ottawa and Washington at the United Nations. Subservience, Tories called it. There was, in addition, more than just political opportunism in the way that Diefenbaker and his party observed the humiliation of the Queen's Own Rifles by Nasser. He considered the affair a Munich-like appeasement of petty dictators.

Strong nationalist and sometimes anti-American rhetoric flowed forth in the election campaign, the Conservative leader's biblical cadences captivating a nation jaded by the soporifics of the Grits. John Diefenbaker was rewarded with the highest office. As the new prime minister, he flew off to London within days of taking power to attend a Commonwealth prime ministers' conference and to meet the Queen.

Diefenbaker's vigour, his apparent forthright admiration for Britain and the Commonwealth, struck a responsive chord in Britain. The Saskatchewan agent general in London reported to Regina that the British popular press made it sound as if Canada under Diefenbaker "was almost going to amalgamate with the United Kingdom." Clearly the British believed that if Diefenbaker had been in power a few months before, the Canadian course over Suez would have been different. Diefenbaker responded delightedly to the adulation, and when he returned to Canada he enthusiastically described his reception to the press and people. As an expression of his earnest intent as a good Commonwealth member, he delivered a pledge: it was the government's "planned intention" to divert 15 percent of Canadian purchases abroad from the United States to Britain.

That promise ought to have sounded a warning about the future of the government. Diefenbaker had consulted neither his Cabinet nor his public service before speaking out and, as he was soon informed by alarmed bureaucrats, such a diversion in trade was almost impossible. To switch 15 percent of trade would mean increasing British imports into Canada to $625 million a year, a serious problem because the British share of the Canadian market had been declining continuously since the nineteenth century. Moreover, British goods—except for such well-known specialty products as Scotch whisky, shortbread, and Shetland sweaters—had acquired a poor reputation with consumers. British automobiles were notorious for failing to start in cold weather and for transmission problems, and British apartment-size refrigerators tended to vibrate so much that they moved around and had to be chained to the floor. Worse still, the General Agreement on Tariffs and Trade, which Canada had joined in 1947, forbade giving one country any special advantages in the market of another.

It was apparent within days that the trade diversion was a wholly uninformed promise by a leader who had been stirred emotionally by his reception in the old country. His ministers quickly backed away from the proposal, the Americans were reassured that their exporters would not suffer, and the British, who had tried to capitalize on the Chief's idea by proposing a free-trade agreement between the two countries, were unceremoniously shown the door. A small matter, to be sure, quickly forgotten by a Canadian public that, early in 1958, gave Diefenbaker the largest majority in Canadian history to that time. The Liberals under Pearson (chosen as leader at a party convention soon after he was awarded the Nobel Peace Prize for his efforts during the Suez crisis) were reduced to their smallest number of seats ever.

THE COMING CRISIS

Diefenbaker's trade diversion fiasco, minor though it was, reinforced concerns that had already begun to surface in the United States. The able and knowledgeable ambassador in Ottawa, Livingston Merchant,

Pearson, Diefenbaker, and Olive Diefenbaker in an apparently
happy moment (Duncan Cameron, National Archives of Canada,
PA 115202)

had been reporting for some time about the rising mood of Canadian
nationalism on which the Conservatives had ridden to power.
Pearson's success at the United Nations had fostered that mood in
some Canadians, but Herbert Norman's suicide had given it a nasty
edge. During Diefenbaker's campaign in 1957 he charged that Canada
had sold out Britain, and he attacked American foreign investment,
reinforcing the unpleasant tone. The abortive trade diversion, in fact,
had been an attempt to cater to the new feeling in the country.

Nevertheless, initial relations between the Diefenbaker government and the Eisenhower administration in Washington were good.
One pressing issue on the table when Diefenbaker took office was a
draft agreement to establish the North American Air Defence
Command (NORAD), a defence alliance much desired by the two
countries' air forces and one that made eminent sense in view of the
Soviet Union's growing long-range bomber fleet. The pact had

largely been ready for signature when the Liberals called the election, confident of their coming victory. Their defeat greatly troubled the military high command in Ottawa and Washington, and the chairman of the Chiefs of Staff Committee, General Charles Foulkes, was quick to express his concern to the new minister of national defence, George Pearkes, an officer with whom he had served during World War II. The Cabinet was scarcely in office and the Cabinet Defence Committee had not yet been formed when Pearkes took Foulkes to see Diefenbaker on 24 July. After a brief explanation, Diefenbaker said "of course" and signed on.

The Americans were gratified, but the Department of External Affairs, more than a little stunned, scrambled for months to get the language of the agreement clear and to define responsibilities and roles carefully, while critics in Parliament and out raised anti-American cries. Nonetheless, the two air forces had been virtually united in the defence of North America. Later Diefenbaker would argue that he had been pushed too fast by Foulkes, and Foulkes agreed, telling a House of Commons committee that "we stampeded the incoming government." Yet most of the fault, and all of the responsibility, was the Chief's.

Still, this seemed not to matter in the glow of the first months in office. Diefenbaker was eager to meet President Eisenhower and to make his mark. The affable president was older and a great war hero, and he played up to the Canadian leader. His letters were warm, always addressed "Dear John," and he made a show of seeking Diefenbaker's advice. In his memoirs, noticeably vitriolic about other u.s. leaders, Diefenbaker showed that the memory of Ike still lingered: he was "a warm and engaging person, and we became the best of friends. He had an appreciation of Canada and Canadians . . . a man that one could talk to [who] . . . was prepared to listen to my point of view."

Nonetheless, the Americans were beginning to feel alarmed at the nationalistic mood Diefenbaker had cultivated, exploited, and was continuing to foster. Prior to a 1959 meeting of the Ministerial Committee on Joint Defence, one of the many ministerial and bureaucratic committees that had been created in recent years to regulate relations across the border, a briefing paper was cautious and nervous. The general outlook of the Diefenbaker government, it said,

is strongly nationalistic and is based on a growing public consciousness . . . of a great national destiny. As a result Canadians
are developing a greater desire for recognition and self-assertion,
coupled with an understandable defensive reaction which takes
the form of sensitivity to any real or imagined slight. . . . [T]he
present Canadian government is not basically anti-American,
although in its appeal to Canadian national self-consciousness it
has come close at times to such a position.

Diefenbaker himself tried to reassure the United States. In a conversation with visiting Washington officials, he remarked that he
knew he was wrongly considered anti-American in the United States
but that in Canada he was portrayed as "dominated by United States
policy." The opposition Liberals would be quick to attack his government for not being strong enough in its protection of Canadian
interests. There was some truth in this, of course, and the fuss over
the NORAD agreement had shown Diefenbaker that the task of dealing with the superpower to the south was no easy task. This again
became evident on defence matters.

The initial issue was the Avro Arrow, the CF-105. The Arrow was a
Canadian-designed interceptor aircraft, built to fly high and fast over
the Canadian tundra to intercept Soviet bombers as far north of popu-
lated North America as possible. The Arrow had been in process of
development since 1953, the year in which the Royal Canadian Air
Force had asked for some six hundred aircraft to defend the country.
The St Laurent government had agreed to the construction of proto-
types, and after the U.S.S.R. unveiled long-range Tupolev bombers at
their 1954 May Day parade, the pace in Canada was stepped up. Pre-
production orders were placed for twenty-nine Arrows at a cost of
$190 million, and soon the Cabinet also agreed to finance the develop-
ment of a suitable jet engine. Similar decisions followed on armament,
all raising the cost. By the time Diefenbaker took office, the CF-105s
were to cost some $12 million apiece. Roughly comparable American
aircraft could be purchased for at most one-sixth that cost.

The government understood that cancelling such a major project
would have serious repercussions. Four thousand engineers and ten
thousand production workers were employed at the Avro factories in

Toronto, a highly skilled team unmatched elsewhere in the country, and the Arrow was the company's only aircraft in production. But the costs were so high, and the missile age could be seen to be fast approaching. In 1957, the Soviets had put a satellite into orbit, and the race to develop intercontinental ballistic missiles was on. Aircraft were useless against ICBMS.

The government agonized, delaying the decision for almost two years. The military chiefs meanwhile bargained. If the Arrow went ahead it would seriously constrain the budgets of the army and navy and scant funds would be left for other RCAF needs. Still, the Arrow was a "hot" fighter and would put the RCAF into the supersonic aircraft business. Perhaps Arrows could be sold abroad, lengthening the production run and lowering unit costs. Unfortunately, and despite the best efforts of government salespeople, the Europeans were indifferent and the Americans correctly believed that their own fighters were as good or better. American aircraft were lighter and, unlike the Arrow, compatible with the new generation of ground-based computer controls then coming into service. Most important, they were less expensive. Some American officials thought it might be possible to buy a few squadrons of CF-105s to give to the RCAF, but this smacked of charity and was not taken seriously. In the end, the military chiefs and politicians had no option except to face the inevitable. On 20 February 1959, the government announced the cancellation of the CF-105.

Avro responded by firing its workers the same day, and many Avro engineers were immediately snapped up by the U.S. space program. The press and the opposition flew into an uproar. The Conservatives had sold out Canadian technology, the charges went, and the Diefenbaker government suffered a blow in Ontario from which it never recovered. The charges continue to this day but the simple truth is that the decision was right: Canada had been priced out of the high-technology defence business. The investment required to develop major weapons systems was now too much for all but the largest countries.

Almost unnoticed in the uproar over the Arrow was the government announcement that Canadian air defences would now be centred around nuclear-tipped Bomarc surface-to-air missiles. Defence against bombers remained a continuing necessity, planners concluded, for until ICBMS were ready in large numbers, each superpower was forced to rely on crewed aircraft to threaten the extinction of the other. John Diefenbaker believed that the Soviet threat was real and he wanted Canada to do its part in defending the West. His Cabinet therefore decided to make an agreement with the United States for both "the sharing of Bomarc and S.A.G.E. [Semi Automatic Ground Environment] installations in Canada" and "the acquisition of nuclear weapons." Two bases were to be built in Canada, one in Ontario and one in Quebec, situated to defend the industrial heartland and to tie in with American Bomarc bases south of the border.

No attempt was made to mislead the Canadian public about the characteristics of the Bomarc. The prime minister told Parliament the day he announced the decision to acquire the missiles, "The full potential of these defensive weapons is achieved only when they are armed with nuclear warheads."

At much the same time, the government also decided to acquire Honest John surface-to-surface nuclear missiles for the Canadian brigade in NATO and CF-104 Starfighter aircraft to take a nuclear attack "strike-reconnaissance" role for RCAF squadrons in Europe. (This would involve first reconnaissance and then attack with nuclear weapons at enemy cities, troop concentrations, and so on.) Royal Canadian Navy anti-submarine warfare ships would also have nuclear depth charges to wage war against the expanding Soviet submarine fleet. The crisis that was to destroy the Diefenbaker government and bring Canadian–American relations to their absolute nadir had been set in train.

"THE POSSIBILITY OF GLOBAL SUICIDE"

The Department of External Affairs was not entirely happy with these decisions, nor was it pleased by the way it was perceived by the Diefenbaker government. Perhaps Tory suspicion was understandable. After all, opposition leader Lester Pearson had worked for almost thirty years with the senior officials in the department. Even so, Diefenbaker's scorn for the "Pearsonalities" was palpable, so much so that the department cast around for an officer to go into the Prime Minister's Office as a liaison. The choice was H. Basil Robinson, an able young man who won the prime minister's trust and kept that of his colleagues.

In his first few months in office, the prime minister retained the external affairs portfolio for himself. Then, in September 1957, he surprised the country by appointing Sidney Smith, the much respected president of the University of Toronto, to the post. Untried in anything but faculty politics, Smith got off to a bad start—in Diefenbaker's eyes—by indicating that he had admired Pearson's role at Suez, and he never really seemed to master the intricacies of his portfolio. In 1959, he died suddenly.

His successor was equally unlikely. Howard Green, a long-serving British Columbia MP, had been public works minister since the Conservatives came to power. As strongly pro-British as Diefenbaker, he had not been abroad since his World War I service, and although he quickly won affection for his kindness and decency, it took him a long time to learn the details of his new post. Strikingly, however, Green believed that nuclear weapons were a curse and had to be destroyed before the world was. It mattered not to him whether the weapons were American or Soviet, British or French; nuclear disarmament was his goal. The American administration was not amused at the way its friend and neighbour began to crusade against the only means the West had to counter the huge numerical advantage in armed forces enjoyed by the communists.

In his anti-nuclear advocacy, Green had the advice of Undersecretary of State for External Affairs Norman Robertson. Robertson had served King in this role, and he had twice been high commissioner to Britain, as well as clerk of the Privy Council and ambassador to Washington. Robertson understood power, and he knew where Canada ranked in the international pecking order. He had participated in the making of Western strategy as much as any Canadian. By 1959, however, he had become convinced that nuclear weapons were a snare and a delusion. The concept of deterrence "was a sad comment on our generation to envisage the possibility of global suicide." A way had to be found to avoid the consequences of nuclear warfare.

Robertson came to believe in unilateral Western nuclear disarmament. Because Marxist theory posited that the victory of socialism was inevitable, it was not in the interest of the Soviets to blot out the West. Why would intelligent people destroy what they intended to win? Of course, a mad leader in the Kremlin could wipe out everything, but the West would then be destroyed whether it had nuclear weapons or not. A great power strengthened itself, rather than the reverse, if it got rid of weapons it dared not use. The logic was clear to Robertson, and in Howard Green he found a minister who shared his concerns. As Green later recalled, "We were advocating in the United Nations that there should be control of the spread of nuclear weapons . . . and then to turn around and take them ourselves just made us look foolish." Nuclear disarmament advocates were in key positions of power in the Department of External Affairs.

It did not take long before the Department of External Affairs was sharply divided on the issue. Those officials who worked closely with the Department of National Defence wanted the nuclear weapons; those who understood Robertson's thinking did not. The ministers of defence and external affairs began to joust in the Cabinet Defence Committee, and slowly the public became apprehensive about nuclear war.

They had justification. The Soviet Union was bellicose at the end of the 1950s. Success in putting the Sputnik rocket into orbit in 1957 had seemed to demonstrate the superiority of Soviet science, and Chairman Khrushchev was quick to use his advantage to bully the world. He threatened to force Western powers out of Berlin, the divided city that lay within East Germany. An American U-2 spy plane was shot down over the U.S.S.R. by a surface-to-air missile, handing Khrushchev a heaven-sent opportunity to cancel a summit meeting with Eisenhower and to score propaganda points around the globe. Fidel Castro carried out a successful leftist revolution in Cuba at the end of 1958 and suspicious Americans quickly persuaded themselves that another country had fallen into the Soviet pocket. The threat of war was omnipresent; prudent people talked of building fall-out shelters in their basements. Organizations began to form to protest the possibility of nuclear war, and in Canada the Voice of Women began a campaign against the acquisition of nuclear weapons. Maryon Pearson, the Liberal leader's wife, was a prominent member.

HOISTING THE FLAG OF EUROPE

Other issues exercised Canadians too, the most important concerning Britain and the Commonwealth. The British had proposed free trade to Canada in 1957 but were soon contemplating the advantages of entry to the "Six," the European Common Market. The idea of Western European unity was in the air in the 1950s; six key nations had joined together in a great common market in 1958. Such a move posed some potential problems for Canadian trade, and these would be exacerbated if Britain joined the group. Despite years of maintaining sterling as an inconvertible currency and of restricting imports from hard currency countries such as Canada and the United States, Britain was still Canada's second largest market and the principal market for Canadian wheat. The European Common Market (ECM) was already showing signs of developing restrictive trade policies, and the new common tariff, it was feared, might be higher than existing national tariffs in some areas. If Britain joined a high-tariff Europe, the consequences for Canadian exports were not promising. There was one additional implication. Declining trade with Britain and Europe forced greater dependence on the U.S. market, not something that Diefenbaker could lightly contemplate.

In September 1960, Britain decided to renew its efforts to join the ECM. Diefenbaker and Canadian diplomats took every possible opportunity to argue against such a move, and the prime minister met British leader Harold Macmillan early in 1961. Macmillan admitted that Commonwealth trade preferences would be jeopardized if Britain joined the Common Market, and he also admitted that this did not trouble him very much. The choice between the short-run advantages of Commonwealth preferences and the long-run advantages in being part of the large, rich European market was no choice at all.

In fact, as Canadian government studies in 1961 demonstrated, the threat to Canadian exports really was not huge: 35 percent of Canadian exports to the United Kingdom would be completely unaffected by ECM membership, and an additional 25 percent would probably get free entry; a further 17 percent of the country's exports would be only slightly affected. Only semi-manufactured goods and agricultural products, especially wheat and barley, were at risk.

Nonetheless, for the next three years Canada and Britain sparred. A major row blew up at the Commonwealth Economic Consultative Council meetings in Ghana in September 1961 when, as the British press put it, Canadian finance minister Donald Fleming told London to choose Canada or Europe. George Drew, the former Ontario premier and national Conservative leader who was the high commissioner to Britain, also played a major role in trying to per-suade the British to change course. Indeed, his efforts to mobilize public opinion in Britain against Europe sometimes caused embar-rassment at the Department of External Affairs.

In other words, the issue was more emotional than economic, and no one was more emotional about the Commonwealth than Prime Minister Diefenbaker. Commonwealth ties were important, and they were also a way of staving off American domination. At the Commonwealth Prime Ministers' Conference in London in September 1962, the Chief let fly. The British press were astounded, the *Sunday Observer* remarking acidly that "Mr Diefenbaker, it was confidently expected, would be speaking for the benefit of the yokels back on the prairies." Instead of posturing, he had directly attacked the British government. With the support of the entire Common-wealth contingent, the Canadian prime minister blasted British unwillingness to see that Commonwealth trade was protected. "He would like to know whether it would be possible to maintain tradi-tional sales of Canadian wheat . . . [and] of canned salmon. . . . [T]he arrangements outlined did not provide a genuine assurance that Canadian trade would continue at satisfactory levels." Macmillan "had hoisted the flag of Europe," one British newspaper observed, but Diefenbaker had shot it down. A Ghanaian delegate, his country's exports even more exposed than Canada's, "was so moved that I thought I was going to cry," or so the London *Observer* quoted him.

The conference broke up with the British sent back to the ECM negotiating table to seek better terms.

In fact, the British application to join the ECM was already limping and soon died. President Charles de Gaulle of France declared himself "unbending toward any significant concessions designed to facilitate British entry." The negotiations in Brussels were duly torpedoed by a French veto on 29 January 1963, and Britain, much to Diefenbaker's relief, blamed only Paris for the rebuff.

The Canadian fight had been vigorous, but the trade in question was relatively small while the Commonwealth itself had already been revealed as weak and disintegrating. In a very real way it had been not Canadian trade at stake but Diefenbaker's conception of the Commonwealth as a British-led community that fought the good fight and co-operated on all things. Any such creature had long since ceased to exist, if it ever had, but John Diefenbaker and those who thought as he did found that impossible to admit. The power of the United States was the only alternative to the beneficence of the Commonwealth, and the prime minister could not abide that prospect. That Canada might be able to live and prosper as an independent nation in North America apparently never crossed his mind.

THE OLD COMMONWEALTH
AND THE NEW

If the debate over the abortive British attempt to join the ECM had shown Diefenbaker at his emotional worst, the question of South Africa probably showed him at his best. Diefenbaker believed in human rights, and he worked vigorously to persuade South Africa, a predominantly black country ruled by a white minority, to adapt to a new world order that put some stock in racial equality. On the other hand, he was also concerned that every effort be made to keep the Union of South Africa in the Commonwealth, and his role was far from easy.

The issue for the Commonwealth was whether to allow South Africa to retain its membership after it became a republic. The change in status from monarchy to republic provided the pretext for a vote that was really provoked by the South African policy of apartheid, or racial separation. The Commonwealth had changed from the old, all-white club into a world-spanning association that included newly independent Asian and African states. The Cold War had made the emerging Third World into an area of confrontation, and the West could ill-afford to be painted yet again as the home of racialist reaction.

At first, Diefenbaker did not want to join the controversy. When a delegation of Canadian trade unionists pressed him to take the lead in pushing South Africa out of the Commonwealth, the prime minister exploded that "the Commonwealth was an association of independent states each with responsibility for its own internal affairs." He would not even raise the question at the 1960 Prime Ministers' Conference; Basil Robinson, his external affairs aide, privately noted at the time, "[He] shrinks from expulsion." Even so, at the 1960 gathering Diefenbaker had two private conversations with the South African foreign minister in which he expressed his grave concern. "Your policies are not only wrong, but dangerous," he said. It was already evident that the non-white members of the Commonwealth were almost certain to oppose South African re-admission, and the Canadians worried about the implications of a black–white split in the Commonwealth.

Cabinet Secretary Robert Bryce, fresh from an officials' planning meeting before the conference, urged strong action. The Commonwealth might be able to do something to bridge the racial divide within its own ranks, but not if South Africa was allowed back in: "That action will be interpreted widely as implying some approval or at least toleration of South Africa's policies." If the decision went the other way, then the world would say that the Commonwealth actually meant what it said "from time to time in woolly phrases." His own view, Bryce said bluntly, was that at the next prime ministers' meeting "Canada should take the lead."

That was easier said than done for the prime minister. Though the Commonwealth Division in the Department of External Affairs strongly advocated taking every step required to preserve the "old, white Commonwealth" with South Africa as a part, by the fall of

1960 Diefenbaker seemed prepared to follow Bryce's advice and to press the issue to a conclusion, even if it meant forcing South Africa out of the Commonwealth. Nonetheless, early in 1961 he began to waver under pressure from Harold Macmillan, who contended that if South Africa were forced out any chance of liberalization there would disappear. The argument held some truth and Diefenbaker, as Basil Robinson noted, was "reluctant to be responsible for South Africa's expulsion from the Commonwealth at least until a further opportunity has been given for changes."

That was the prime minister's attitude when he went to London in March 1961, only to find the British arguing that South Africa was entitled to automatic re-admission once it became a republic. No government except London found that satisfactory. Diefenbaker

Schoolmaster Verwoerd and wayward pupil Diefenbaker (McNally, *Montreal Star*, March 1961)

struggled to find an acceptable formula, a declaration of principles, to delay the question. South African leader Hendrik Verwoerd, however, proved completely inflexible. Diefenbaker then allied himself with the Asian and African leaders against South Africa, the only white prime minister to do so. Finally, Verwoerd announced that his nation would not seek re-admission, and in his comments then and later blamed Diefenbaker, that "vicious fellow," for his "strong and hostile" position.

Public opinion in Canada hailed the Chief, and the prime minister soon forgot the agonizing he had gone through to reach a position. He had been on the right side, and his actions had helped to keep the Commonwealth together as a multiracial organization. There were few enough of those in a troubled world, and even if the Commonwealth had already become little more than an organization for dispensing aid to the Third World, its survival remained important to Canadians.

RESPONSES TO DECOLONIZATION

The Third World, and in particular Africa, was becoming a key arena of the Cold War. The debate surrounding South African membership in the Commonwealth had taken place with one eye on the Soviet Union. Communist preaching about human rights, rights never honoured within the communist world, had to be countered with a principled stand by the West. It was also important to assist African and Asian nations in their struggle for independence whenever possible, or else "freedom fighters" armed by Moscow or Beijing might seize control and spread propaganda about colonial repression around the world.

Third World independence movements could pose problems for Canada, sometimes in unlikely places. In 1960, the Belgian Congo, a huge, potentially rich tract in the heart of Africa, became independent, and almost at once order broke down. Belgian settlers were massacred if they did not flee, and the United Nations, striving to prevent the entire process of decolonization turning into chaos, decided to intervene. The secretary general, Dag Hammarskjöld, soon sought a Canadian military contribution for the largely French-speaking African state. Especially needed were bilingual army signallers.

Peacekeeping had become popular with Canadians after the 1956 Suez crisis. Ottawa had been applauded for sending small numbers of observers to Lebanon in 1958 to join the UN group established to watch that country's borders. The armed forces, however, were faced with decreasing budgets, and looked on peacekeeping as a drain and a distraction from their real task of preparing to fight the Soviet Union in central Europe. Bilingual signallers were in particularly short supply. National Defence Headquarters therefore advised the government to decline Hammarskjöld's request regretfully; instead of communications personnel a few aircraft and staff officers could be provided.

Ottawa quietly did as suggested, and soon newspapers and letter writers across the country got into the act. The *Globe and Mail,* usually a Tory newspaper, called the contribution "meagre" and the Ottawa *Journal* said that Canadians hoped and expected an "imaginative and wide-visioned and generous" response. The papers made further and increasingly sharp denunciations of the army's readiness. What *were* we getting for $2 billion a year in defence costs? Finally the government surrendered to the growing clamour and agreed to provide a maximum of five hundred troops, including two hundred signallers, for the UN Congo force (ONUC).

The Canadians ran into difficulty almost as soon as they arrived in the Congo. Their skin colour, their uniforms, their language, were not dissimilar to those of the hated Belgians, and in a number of incidents Congolese troops beat Canadians and threatened worse. Great forbearance was demanded, and shown.

Later the Congolese venture turned into a full-scale war, with UN troops fighting against mercenaries and others armed by the breakaway state of Katanga. The financial costs were horrendous and came close to bankrupting the United Nations. The greatly admired Hammarskjöld, urgently seeking a way out of the quagmire, died when his aircraft crashed in the Congo, apparently shot down from the ground. Canada stayed with ONUC until it closed down in June 1964, a wearying commitment at last reaching its end.

The affair was significant from the Canadian point of view in that Ottawa had been virtually forced into major participation by public opinion. Canadians evidently wanted their soldiers to engage in peacekeeping. It differentiated Canada from most other countries, it seemed more "peaceful" than NATO or NORAD service, and it appeared to strike a responsive chord in the Canadian psyche. Diefenbaker had seemed a laggard, and his hesitancy over the Congo force was just one of many areas of foreign policy in which his government managed to portray itself as both unsure and overcautious.

In one area, however, the Conservative government did move forcefully: immigration. Canadian policy had historically discriminated on grounds of race and sometimes of religion. The barriers against blacks, Asians, and Jews, however popular they had been in the past, now seemed an embarrassment and a violation of human rights, especially considering initiatives such as the Canadian Bill of Rights, put in place by Diefenbaker in 1960. In the early 1960s, therefore, with a nod to the courts and another to the newly emerging nations of Asia and Africa, the Cabinet lifted racial and ethnic restrictions on most types of immigration. This was progress even if the resources of the national immigration bureaucracy tended to be deployed only in Britain and Western Europe, the traditional sources of Canadian immigration. Soon, however, the horizon expanded. Immigration offices opened in Egypt in 1963, in Japan in 1967, and in Lebanon, the Philippines, the West Indies, and Pakistan in 1968. The colour bar had disappeared, and immigration criteria now focussed on skills and family reunification.

THE ANTI-AMERICAN YEARS

The American administration of John F. Kennedy, elected in November 1960, preached vigour—pronounced "vigah" in Kennedy's New England accent—in policy, and admired it in allies. Very quickly, it became apparent that the Canadian government was not one of those admired. The State Department briefing book for Diefenbaker's February 1961 visit to Washington to meet the new president already showed signs of American misgiving. The

Canadian chief was described as "self confident and shrewd"; he was "not believed to have any basic prejudice against the United States. He has appeared, however, to seek on occasion to assert Canadian independence by seizing opportunities for Canada to adopt policies which deviate somewhat from those of the United States." Such "deviance" was well within the bounds of diplomatic practice, but unless the president and prime minister had a strong relationship, the differences could escalate into serious tensions. The first auguries were favourable, and Diefenbaker returned to Ottawa singing Kennedy's praises. This would not last.

By the time Kennedy had left Ottawa after his first visit to Canada as president in May 1961, relations were chilly. The president had drawn too much adulation from Canadian crowds to please Diefenbaker, and the beautiful, poised Jacqueline Kennedy far outshone Olive Diefenbaker. Kennedy was too young to be so successful, the prime minister seemed to believe, and too rash, too pushy, too aggressive in trying to get Canada to follow the u.s. lead. The calculated deference of Eisenhower was gone. Instead, Kennedy had pressed Diefenbaker to enter the Organization of American States and although the prime minister had demurred, had nonetheless repeated his exhortations in an address to Parliament. The tactic rankled the older politician, who was sensitive to slights, real or imagined. Worse, a presidential briefing memo was left behind after one meeting, and the prime minister had taken umbrage at its urging that Canada be "pushed" to do certain things. There were even rumours that Diefenbaker had been called an "s.o.b." in a marginal note. The memo was not returned, a grave breach of protocol that caused anger in Washington. It also appalled the Canadian ambassador to the United States, who recorded his shock in his diary when the prime minister told him that "he had not so far made use of this paper but 'when the proper time came,' he would not hesitate to do so."

The real divisions between Kennedy and Diefenbaker nonetheless arose over policy, not personality or style. At their first meeting in February 1961, the two had sharply disagreed over an application by Imperial Oil of Canada to sell bunker oil to Canadian ships under charter to China. In so doing the company would violate the American blockade of the Beijing regime, or so the State Department saw it. Imperial Oil was a subsidiary of an American company, and the United States took the position that it had the right to enforce its laws outside American boundaries. Diefenbaker disagreed: extra-territoriality was not a position Canada could accept. The president backed down, but he remained troubled by the Canadian government's willingness, as he believed, to put more trust in communist governments than was merited.

Kennedy persisted in this view of Diefenbaker, even though the prime minister—who held very strong anti-communist and anti-Soviet attitudes—rallied behind him over the Berlin question after the failure of the president's first summit with Chairman Khrushchev. The status of Berlin again became a crisis point in the summer of 1961, as the U.S.S.R. pressed the West hard to recognize East Germany. The Canadian government announced plans to increase the armed forces from 120 000 to 135 000 and also sent a small number of additional troops to Europe.

The Americans were deeply worried about China and Berlin, but Cuba obsessed them. The Castro regime rankled Washington every day, its pro-Soviet government just a few miles offshore from Miami and a perpetual thumb in the eagle's eye. The small Caribbean nation soon became a major bone of contention between Canada and the United States. Officials in Washington felt increasing concern that Ottawa was "soft" on Havana (and some anxiety, too, that Canadian exporters might grab hold of traditional American markets there). They were genuinely annoyed at the sharp criticism levelled by Canadian ministers and officials at American threats to topple Castro with military force. The Eisenhower administration had decided by mid-1960 that Fidel Castro was a communist, and the Kennedy government enthusiastically seconded that view.

The United States cut off trade with Cuba early in 1961, and it wanted American subsidiaries in Canada and Canadian-owned companies to follow suit. The Canadians, however, were reluctant. Their reports from Cuba were far less alarmist and their judgment was clear; the only effect of such sanctions would be to force Castro inexorably into Soviet hands. Through his first few months in power, Kennedy kept up diplomatic and economic pressure on Cuba. Then in April 1961 he sanctioned an abortive invasion of the country by

Cuban exiles surreptitiously backed by the resources of the Central Intelligence Agency. The landing at the Bay of Pigs was a fiasco, and Castro's triumph gave his increasingly authoritarian regime a boost. There was not a little subdued gloating in the Canadian media—and in political circles—that the cocky JFK had been humbled so quickly.

For the next year and a half Cuba was like a chicken bone in the president's throat, and the Soviet Union, now openly aiding the Castro regime, rashly decided to go a giant step further. In October 1962, American U-2 spy planes discovered evidence that the Soviets were putting Intermediate Range Ballistic Missiles into Cuba. The nuclear-tipped IRBMs had sufficient range to reach most of the United States and constituted both an intolerable threat and a completely unacceptable alteration in the existing balance of power.

Secretly, Kennedy prepared his response, and on 22 October American emissaries flew into Western capitals to brief alliance leaders. To Ottawa came Livingston Merchant, the former ambassador, to tell Diefenbaker that the United States was putting a naval blockade around Cuba to quarantine the island and force the removal of the missiles. A letter from Kennedy to the prime minister said, "we are now in possession of clear evidence . . . that the Soviets have secretly installed offensive weapons in Cuba and that some of them may already be operational."

The world was close to war, as close as it had been since 1945. De Gaulle, Macmillan, and others pledged Kennedy their support, but the Canadian government's response was different—indifferent, thought Washington. Instead of instantly putting the Canadian aircraft in NORAD on the same state of alert (DEFCON 3) as those of the United States Air Force, instead of ordering its ships to sea to track Soviet submarines, the Canadian government did nothing. The United States had remarkable photographs that left no doubt of the Soviet missiles in Cuba, and these had been shown to Diefenbaker, but the prime minister appeared not to believe the evidence.

Instead, Diefenbaker told Parliament that a UN fact-finding mission ought to go to the Caribbean to provide an "objective answer" to the question of missile installations. This diplomatic device had been proposed by Norman Robertson at the Department of External Affairs as a "cooling-off" measure, and it infuriated Kennedy and his

State Department. It also greatly worried the Canadian military chiefs and Minister of National Defence Douglas Harkness. At last, after repeated confrontations with Harkness, Diefenbaker reluctantly and belatedly agreed to put the Canadian forces on alert on 24 October.

In fact, Canadian NORAD aircraft had already gone to full readiness. Harkness had given the order on his own authority, presumably knowing full well that he was acting improperly. At the same time, the Royal Canadian Navy's Atlantic fleet cancelled leaves and put all its ships to sea, relieving the United States Navy of responsibility for a critical and soon to be expanded sector of the northwestern Atlantic. One authoritative account summarized the reasoning of Admiral Kenneth Dyer, the RCN commander on the east coast: "North America was under direct immediate threat. That included Canada. All the long-standing arrangements and government-to-government agreements said if one partner boosted its defence [readiness] condition, the other followed." When Ottawa did nothing, Dyer simply acted on his own initiative. In countless NATO exercises over the years he had formed a relationship with his U.S. commanders that was so close and so trusting, and his assessment of the Soviet threat was so fearful, that he felt compelled to put to sea to assist an ally. As naval historian Commander Tony German wrote, the navy "honoured Canada's duty to stand by her North American ally," clearly implying that the prime minister had not wished to do so.

If anyone noticed this near mutiny in the Department of National Defence, no one said anything, then or later. The Cuban missile crisis was happily resolved for an anxious world by a Soviet agreement to pull its missiles out of Cuba and a quiet U.S. indication that some missiles would be removed from Turkey.

Nonetheless, the government's handling of the crisis quickly combined with an imbroglio over the acquisition of nuclear weapons to destroy Diefenbaker's administration. Since its cancellation of the Arrow and decision to acquire Bomarcs, CF-104s, and Honest Johns, the government had repeatedly put off negotiations with the United States to procure nuclear warheads for these weapons systems. The issue had not been urgent before the missiles and aircraft reached Canadian hands but by late 1962, with the Bomarc bases nearing completion and the CF-104s ready to enter service, it had become pressing.

Minister of External Affairs Howard Green's crusade for nuclear disarmament had stirred a popular response in Canada. Though a majority still favoured Canadian acquisition of nuclear weaponry, the decision to obtain the warheads was much less straightforward than it must have seemed a few years before. The prime minister, indeed, made speeches saying that nothing would be decided about the warheads so long as progress towards disarmament continued. Diefenbaker himself thus wavered uneasily between accepting the warheads he had ordered and yielding to the urging of the Department of External Affairs that he delay while peace was sought. Wearing his anti-Soviet hat, Diefenbaker wanted the weapons so that the Canadian armed forces could contribute to Western defence; but when he looked south at the aggressive, disrespectful Kennedy, the prime minister bridled at being pushed around by the Americans, and his disarmament leanings became ever stronger.

The Cuban crisis brought the issue to a head. To many Canadians, the possibility of disarmament now seemed a chimera in the face of an adventurist government in Moscow. Moreover, once they realized that Canada had not stood by its continental partner, the Canadian public and media were outraged. Cabinet ministers who had not paid attention to the nuclear issue suddenly realized that relations with the United States were at a critical point, and the opposition parties, scenting blood in the water, gathered their forces.

DIEFENBAKER IN DEFEAT

The 1962 general election reduced Diefenbaker's huge majority of 1958 to a shaky minority government. In January 1963, the retiring NATO supreme commander, General Lauris Norstad, told an Ottawa press conference that Canada had not met its commitments to the alliance. Within days Liberal leader Lester Pearson, avid for power, arbitrarily and on his own reversed his party's policy against taking nuclear weapons and promised that a government led by him would honour its commitments. His announcement shook the Conservative government, which began to lose the confidence of its own supporters.

Diefenbaker was brought down, however, by his own extraordinarily convoluted address in the House of Commons on 25 January 1963, in which he seemed both to say that Canada would take the weapons and to put obstacles in the way of so doing. The United States was furious at the prime minister's speech, which had revealed details of the negotiations for the warheads. It was equally unhappy with the Canadian position in those negotiations, finally begun in November 1962. The State Department responded with a press release a few days later that in effect called the prime minister a liar and stated crudely and bluntly that the Canadian government "has not as yet proposed any arrangement sufficiently practical to contribute effectively to North American defence." Within days, the defence minister resigned, the government was defeated in a vote of confidence in Parliament,

Off the protected list: Pearson dislodges Diefenbaker
(Reprinted with permission—The Toronto Star Syndicate)

further ministers left the government, and an election was called. American intervention and Diefenbaker's hesitancy had brought down the government and reduced Canadian–American relations to their absolute nadir.

It is also worth noting that the Canadian military played a key role in these events. Military officers worked together to lobby the media against the Diefenbaker policy and in favour of nuclear weapons. As one admitted later, "It was a flat-out campaign, because Diefenbaker was not living up to his commitments. [Air Marshal] Roy Slemon [Canadian deputy commander of NORAD] was going bananas down in Colorado Springs [at the NORAD headquarters]. We identified key journalists, business and labour people, and key Tory hitters in Toronto, and some Liberals, too, and flew them out to NORAD. It was very effective."

The American view of North American defence needs, as interpreted by the RCAF, was in this way put forcefully and clearly to key Canadian opinion makers. Significantly, the plan of attack on public opinion received authorization at the highest military levels in Canada. "You go ahead," the chairman of the Chiefs of Staff Committee reputedly said. "Just don't tell me the details." The Canadian forces wanted nuclear warheads, and they helped demolish the Diefenbaker government in their efforts to secure them. As political scientist Jocelyn Ghent put it, "the Canadian military perceived and acted on a threat that was defined not by their government, but by the transgovernmental group to which they felt much closer, the Canadian–American military." The campaign ran parallel to the efforts of the U.S. ambassador to Canada, the hard-nosed W.W. Butterworth, who ran anti-government briefings for Canadian journalists in the embassy basement in Ottawa. The tactics worked.

Defeated in Parliament, its relations with the United States in ruins, the Diefenbaker government ought to have been on the ropes. The Canadian media was in full cry against the prime minister. Disgruntled ministers, fleeing the Tory government wreckage, were as loud in their denunciations of their leader as the opposition.

Despite the odds, Diefenbaker ran a brilliantly shameless election campaign that nearly reversed a seemingly inevitable result. Using what a Kennedy administration official called "snide comments, insinuations, innuendoes or other anti-U.S. overtones," Diefenbaker became as openly anti-American as any Canadian party leader in modern times. He made oblique references to the misplaced "S.O.B." memorandum from Kennedy's May 1961 visit to Ottawa. He apparently gave credence to a forged letter, purporting to be from Ambassador Butterworth to Pearson congratulating the Liberal leader on his reversal on nuclear policy, and he was prevented only by the entreaties of advisers from using it in the campaign. Instead, the letter was leaked to the media, but too late to do much damage. Diefenbaker also took advantage of just-released secret congressional testimony by U.S. Defense Secretary Robert McNamara that pointed to what he called the primary utility of the Bomarcs: to draw Soviet missile fire onto Canada. This, Diefenbaker thundered, proved that the Liberals were both wasting money and attracting Soviet missiles onto Canada in their desire to put nuclear warheads on the Bomarcs. The prime minister seemed to forget that his government had accepted these weapons and the nuclear commitment originally.

Rational argument scarcely mattered in the 1963 election. Diefenbaker had tapped so deeply into the perpetual wellsprings of anti-Americanism in Canada that the election result, far from being the expected Liberal cakewalk, was another minority government, although this time with the Liberals in command.

It had been a near thing, but the Americans were delighted at the result. Ambassador Butterworth wrote privately that the election had been about fundamentals: "That is why facing up to them was so very serious and why the Pearson victory... was so significant.... At any rate, the outcome holds salutary lessons which will not be overlooked by future aspirants to political office in Canada." And not only in Canada. The Canadian ambassador in Bonn reported that Chancellor Adenauer had told him how alarmed he was by the American "hatchet job" against Diefenbaker and how he feared that someday he too might fall victim to an American coup. Allies like Canada or West Germany had to recognize that the Kennedy administration was ready to pay any price to prevail against communism. Laggards in the crusade for victory over Moscow and Beijing would no longer be tolerated.

CHAPTER NINE

The Shadow of Vietnam, 1963–1968

The public service greeted the return of the Liberals to power in April 1963 with a collective sigh of relief. Nowhere was this more evident than in the Department of External Affairs, whose diplomats had been uncommonly tried by the alternately wobbly and rigid policies of the Diefenbaker government. Their relations with colleagues at National Defence had been strained by the nuclear dispute. Their British counterparts had been unhappy with Canada's reaction to their failed attempt to get into the European Community, and their unhappiness was all the sharper because they had held high hopes for close co-operation with Diefenbaker. The Americans at the State Department and, even more important, in the White House had been furious over Canadian nuclear policy. A host of other issues had waited for decisions while Washington prayed for a change of regime in Ottawa. Most of the other Western states seemed reluctant to treat with Ottawa in the face of British and American unease over Canadian policies. The Diefenbaker–Green regime had made a mess of Canadian foreign policy.

Now things would change, everyone in Ottawa confidently believed; the professionals were back in charge. Prime Minister Lester Pearson, after all, was the same breezy "Mike" who had been the pre-eminent Canadian diplomat of the 1940s and the most successful secretary of state for Canadian external affairs ever. The country's new leader therefore clearly understood the international issues. The new Liberal external affairs minister was Paul Martin, an enthusiastic parish pump politician from Southwestern Ontario, to be sure: "Anyone here from Windsor?" was his standard opening line in a crowd. Nonetheless, he was also a long-time Cabinet minister with knowledge and scope who had led Canadian delegations to the United Nations in the 1950s and played an important role in, for example, brokering the deal that saw UN membership expanded to include a package of Communist, non-Communist, and neutral states. Martin, too, understood how the game was supposed to be played. The status quo ante Diefenbaker, everyone assumed, was shortly to be restored.

REMINDERS OF INTERDEPENDENCE

The initial signs were very favourable. A week after his swearing in, Pearson flew to London to see British prime minister Harold Macmillan, a leader who had soured on Canada while Diefenbaker was in charge. The two old acquaintances, John English wrote, "had the kind of conversation both loved, circling the globe, expertly settling on those parts where problems had erupted or would erupt, and then soaring again." For his part, President Kennedy had sent Pearson a warm message when the prime minister took office, making clear that "the early establishment of close relations between your administration and ours is a matter of great importance to me." A meeting at Kennedy's family home at Hyannisport, Massachusetts, in May went well. Pearson and Kennedy talked easily and at length, and the prime minister's encyclopedic knowledge of baseball (Pearson had played semi-professionally in his youth and remained an avid fan) reportedly impressed the president and his staff. The two leaders agreed to resolve the nuclear dispute. Pearson "was sorry that the previous Canadian Government had undertaken nuclear commitments" but, he said, the Liberal minority government would fulfil them and be "prepared to stand or fall in Parliament" on this decision. The House of Commons narrowly concurred on 20 May.

Pearson and Kennedy discussed the thorny subject of American investment in Canada. American corporations and individuals controlled 78 percent of foreign money invested in Canada and whole sectors of the economy were under U.S. control. This had worried Walter Gordon when he headed the Royal Commission on Canada's Economic Prospects in the mid-1950s. He was now Pearson's minister of finance. It had worried John Diefenbaker while he was prime minister, and he was now leader of a touchy and occasionally violently anti-American opposition. And it worried Pearson. As he told Kennedy, his government "did not wish to discourage the inflow of United States capital, but nonetheless it had to be recognized that the effect of United States investment in Canada constituted a political problem." It was, therefore, "the intention of the Government to take steps not to penalize United States interests but to encourage Canadians to invest more in Canadian companies."

The new government's first budget included a takeover tax on sales of shares in Canadian companies to non-residents and an increase in the withholding tax on dividends paid to non-residents if the percentage of Canadian ownership was below 25 percent. These measures created vociferous protest on Wall Street, in Washington, and on the Canadian stock markets, and Gordon had to withdraw or modify them.

The Kennedy administration then decided to teach Ottawa a lesson; in July 1963 it tried to deal with its own economic difficulties by putting measures in place to restrict foreign borrowing. Such a policy had grave implications for Canada, and Gordon had to scramble to strike an accommodation that largely exempted Canada from the measure, demonstrating irrefutably how closely intertwined the two North American economies were. Canada needed the United States, but as a senior finance department official pointed out, Canadians had been "seriously disturbed by this reminder of dependence on U.S.A."

The impact of the Gordon budget fiasco was very sharp. In Canada, it immediately demonstrated that the sure-footedness of the new regime was a myth, and it set the Pearson government off to a rocky start from which it never recovered. Abroad, and most especially in the United States, it persuaded many that Canada's difficulties had not stemmed simply from a Conservative government and a temperamental prime minister, but were in fact more permanent.

Gordon's attitude to the United States was quite different from John Diefenbaker's anti-Americanism, but his belief in the evils of Wall Street and Washington policies had enough in common with the old Chief's to force bureaucrats in the American capital to wonder what had happened in and to Canada. The stable ally of the St Laurent years, the country that generally followed the American lead and welcomed American investment, seemed to have transformed itself into a nationalist troublemaker. John F. Kennedy was concerned enough about the difficulties to direct in the fall of 1963 that all contentious matters concerning Canada were to be brought directly to his and his staff's attention.

Tragically, Kennedy would not survive to see that order implemented. He was killed by an assassin in Dallas in November. His successor, the Texan vice-president Lyndon B. Johnson, knew next to nothing about the country on his northern border, but what little he knew was positive. Canada was an ally, a democracy, a friendly nation.

Perhaps that was behind the Johnson administration's willingness to enter into the Auto Pact with Canada. The automobile industry was the engine of North American industrial production, and the Canadian component of the industry was running on only two cylinders. In 1962, for example, Canada had imported $642 million in autos and auto parts but had exported only $62 million, creating a huge deficit that amounted to more than two-thirds of the nation's total trade imbalance. The Liberals intended to bring the figures more into line by raising exports and creating jobs.

After a long negotiation with Washington, a deal was struck. Canada entered into agreements with its automobile manufacturers to bind them to meet "output targets," and overall free trade was permitted between the two countries in autos and parts. Pearson and Johnson signed the deal in January 1965 at the LBJ Ranch in Texas. At once it eliminated duties on cars, trucks, buses, parts, and accessories flowing in either direction across the border. Only those manufacturers who met specific criteria were allowed to import into Canada duty free. An individual thus could not buy a car south of the border and bring it into Canada at the lower American price without paying duty. The pact increased employment almost immediately, expanded sales to the United States, and met most of the Canadian aims, but it ended forever the possibility of creating a national and diversified automobile industry. To some that was a real detriment.

The Auto Pact reversed the auto trade imbalance. By 1968 Canada had a small surplus; by 1972 it had a very large surplus of $527 million; and by 1993 the Canadian trade surplus in automobiles and parts had reached an incredible $22 billion. So favourable was the accord to Canadian economic interests that Lyndon Johnson came to believe he had been snookered. "You screwed us," the extravagant Texan complained, slightly shocking Canadian ambassador Charles Ritchie even though he had long since become inured to such phrasing from "the leader of the Free World," as LBJ also on occasion referred to himself.

QUIET DIPLOMACY
AND OTHERWISE

Vulgar or not, Johnson's comment was important because it demonstrated his view that Canada was no longer the most loyal of allies. There had been happy moments, to be sure. In March 1964, Greece and Turkey, both of which had troops on the spot, were on the verge of war over the Mediterranean island of Cyprus. The Greek Cypriot leadership of the newly independent nation was at loggerheads with the Turkish minority. A war between Athens and Ankara would have destroyed NATO's position in the Mediterranean and gravely weakened the West, and Canada became involved in efforts to separate the antagonists.

There were suggestions in London, Washington, and Ottawa that either a NATO peacekeeping force or a Commonwealth force should be sent to the area. Canadian troops were scheduled to play a prominent role in any such force. Those plans collapsed and Canada stepped in to create, almost single-handedly, a United Nations peacekeeping force. Foreign minister Paul Martin worked the telephones over a hectic two days and called in past favours to persuade the Nordic countries to contribute troops. The government saw to it that the Canadian battalion of infantry on stand-by for UN service was immediately en route to Cyprus, thus forestalling threatened Turkish intervention, even before Parliament had begun to consider its agreement to participate.

A month before, speaking in the House, Prime Minister Pearson had made clear that Canada had conditions on its participation in any UN force created for Cyprus. The force had to be able to contribute to peace and its mandate had to have a fixed duration. The conditions were good ones. Unfortunately, they would be honoured only in their breach, and Canadian troops in UNFICYP, as the UN force in Cyprus came to be called, remained on the eastern Mediterranean island until 1993. Even so, President Johnson was grateful in 1964, so much so that he asked a slightly bemused Pearson if there was anything he could do for him in return. Not at the moment, was the prime minister's reply.

Peacekeeping really did seem to be becoming the Canadian métier, as the public basked in their country's apparent indispensability. In 1967, however, one indication surfaced that United Nations service carried with it potential embarrassments. In May, Egypt and Israel were moving towards another war, and President Nasser began to make threatening noises about the humiliation his nation had suffered from the presence of the United Nations Emergency Force. Prime Minister Pearson spoke out about the pending conflict and for his trouble was reviled by Nasser as part of a British, French, and Israeli conspiracy against Cairo. Worse, the Egyptians ordered UNEF out of Egypt, singling out the Canadian contingent and demanding that it depart immediately. The UN secretary general, U Thant, weakly agreed that UNEF and especially the Canadians would leave, and the Royal Canadian Air Force moved quickly to fly the troops home. Within hours of their departure, war began with an Israeli attack that led to the deaths of many UN troops from other countries.

These events signalled more than one warning. Peacekeeping that did not press belligerents to accommodate one another was of little use, for one thing. UNEF had after all been in place since late 1956 without Egypt and Israel moving towards peace. Peacekeeping did

President Nasser's display of gratitude (Merle Tingley—
London *Free Press*)

not stop war making, for another thing, and nothing was gained for
the United Nations or for peace in feebly yielding to the demands of
petty dictators.

United Nations peacekeeping, however, was probably more effec-
tive than peacekeeping outside the United Nations. The war in
Vietnam provided ample proof of that. In 1954, a conflict between
France and local nationalists in what was then French Indochina had

ended in defeat for the French. At the Geneva Conference of 1954, the great powers that were party to the peace agreement (not the United Nations) had set up three observer groups, the International Control Commissions (ICC's) as they were called, in Vietnam (divided in two at the conference), Laos, and Cambodia. Each of the ICC's had a team made up of military officers and diplomats provided by India, Poland, and Canada. Ottawa agreed to participate in this operation primarily because it could not find a ready way to refuse the request from the great powers that it join in.

Ever since 1954, the United States had been devoting itself to propping up the government of South Vietnam in its struggle with Communist North Vietnam. American involvement escalated from providing economic and military aid to providing military advisers and, by 1964, growing numbers of combat units. The war continued to expand, nonetheless, as Ho Chi Minh's government in Hanoi maintained its support for Viet Cong communist rebels in South Vietnam with arms, advisers, and funds. Eventually, North Vietnam provided large numbers of well-trained and effective regulars to assist the Viet Cong in its struggle to topple the Saigon regime.

Hard-pressed but still supremely confident of victory, the United States nonetheless began to ask its friends for assistance. Countries such as South Korea and Australia responded by sending troops, but Canada hung back. Its ostensible reason was that military commitments would conflict with Canadian membership on the International Control Commission.

The commission had been created to police the "peace" in Vietnam but there was no peace and scarcely ever had been peace since the Geneva Conference, and the ICC commitment was onerous and discouraging in the extreme to those detailed for duty in the midst of an expanding war. Most of the Canadian service members and diplomats in Vietnam were driven to frustration by the blatant partisanship of the Poles towards the North and the overzealous "fairness" of the Indians, which also usually translated into decisions favourable to communists. The majority became exaggeratedly pro-South Vietnamese long before the end of their tours.

In 1964, Ottawa agreed to let its senior diplomat on the ICC, Blair Seaborn, serve as a conduit between Washington and Hanoi, passing on American warnings to North Vietnam about its "present course and hints of possible rewards in return for a change." The North Vietnam leaders listened carefully but offered nothing, so convinced were they that their cause would prevail. Canadians serving at lower levels on the ICC reacted against that certitude. For some, this took the form of passing information gathered in North Vietnam on to the Americans, an activity that caused great embarrassment in Ottawa when returning officers talked to the press. As far as the Canadians on the ICC were concerned, the South Vietnamese and the Americans were on the right side.

Yet this attitude was not shared by all of the Canadian public. The Vietnam War from the mid-1960s on came to absorb American opinion as the draft rounded up young men and sent them to Southeast Asia, where they were killed or maimed in large numbers. Deserters and draft dodgers began to flee to Canada, perhaps as many as a hundred thousand in all, much to the fury of the American government. Public opinion in Canada started to split on the issue of the war. Although majorities in the opinion polls continuously supported the American position and involvement, large and vocal minorities did not, their strength especially concentrated in academe, the media, and on the left. Canadian students and their professors, many recently arrived from the United States, were as ready as ever to believe the worst about their neighbour and to demonstrate in support of causes popular on American university campuses.

The Pearson government heard the protests, and the clamour reinforced its doubts about the wisdom of the American policy of bombing North Vietnam "back to the stone age," as one prominent U.S. Air Force general delicately phrased it. At the Department of External Affairs, Paul Martin generally supported the United States. The prime minister, however, believed that the Vietnam War was the wrong war in the wrong part of the world, that Americans could not win it.

In April 1965, Pearson journeyed to Temple University in Philadelphia to deliver a speech. Over the very strong protests of Martin, who feared that it could destroy Seaborn's credibility in Hanoi by persuading the leadership there that Canada had lost its

Stop the war

usefulness in Washington, Pearson used the opportunity to urge very gently that the United States consider suspending air strikes against the North to encourage Hanoi to move towards negotiation. "There are many factors which I am not in a position to weigh," Pearson said. "But there does appear to be at least a possibility that a suspension of such air strikes against North Vietnam, at the right time, might provide the Hanoi authorities with the opportunity, if they wish to take it, to inject some flexibility into their policy without appearing to do so as the direct result of military pressure."

The prime minister had known that President Johnson would not be pleased with his remarks, but he had undoubtedly underestimated LBJ's awesome wrath. The two met the next day at Camp David, Maryland, Johnson's retreat. The president called the address "bad," "awful," and asserted that it lent foreign support to his numerous domestic enemies. So heated did the discussion get that the president apparently shook Pearson by his jacket lapels. "The President is tired," a slightly rattled Pearson wrote in his diary, "under great and continuous pressure, and . . . is beginning to show it." In truth, Johnson's irate reaction was almost wholly understandable. His country, his troops, were fighting a war, and the Canadians were profiting from selling war supplies in large and growing quantities to the United States while risking nothing. Then Pearson came to the United States to attack American policy.

Pearson's Temple University speech started Canadians thinking again about how best to deal with the United States. Had his address been counter-effective? Could more be gained by talking discreetly to the administration in Washington and mobilizing America's allies to urge the proper policy on the president? Many in Canada and the United States preferred the strategy of "quiet diplomacy," the idea that Canada would not disagree in public with the United States but would, instead, raise its complaints and seek solutions in private.

Quiet diplomacy had worked reasonably well for years, but it scarcely gratified the widespread desire in Canada for the country to take the lead in speaking out for peace, disarmament, and other good things. Canadians' level of displeasure with the old practice became apparent when Arnold Heeney, an experienced public servant and diplomat, and Livingston Merchant, who had represented his country well in Ottawa, released a report entitled "Principles for Partnership." The report had been commissioned by Prime Minister Pearson and President Johnson in January 1964. Its slightly anodyne conclusions reiterated support for quiet diplomacy: "It is in the abiding interest of both countries that, wherever possible, divergent views between two governments should be expressed and if possible resolved in private, through diplomatic channels." This was met with a chorus of derisive complaint across the country from politicians, journalists, academics, and, so far as could be determined, from ordinary citizens. The impact of Vietnam on the public consciousness meant that the old ways of diplomacy did not seem to satisfy Canadians any more, and certainly not methods that seemed, to some, designed to keep Canada permanently in its place as a lap dog of the Americans.

Walter Gordon, who had resigned from the Cabinet in 1965, was among those who fretted over the appearance of Canadian docility. In January 1967, he returned to the government as president of the Privy Council after a period on the Liberal backbenches. Questions of foreign investment continued to be his main preoccupation, but Gordon was not one-dimensional in his thinking. Soon after his return, he delivered a speech in which he called for the Americans to end their bombing of North Vietnam, to halt offensive operations in the South, and to look for negotiations with the Viet Cong that could lead to a cease-fire and the withdrawal of all foreign troops. If Canada failed to push the United States in this direction, the minister said, "we must be prepared to share the responsibility of those whose policies and actions are destroying a poor but determined people. We must share the responsibility of those whose policies involve the greatest risks for all mankind."

Some of Gordon's colleagues considered his speech a breach of Cabinet solidarity. The killing in Vietnam continued day in and day out, however, and American protests against the war were growing more intense. Pearson merely chastised Gordon, rather than demanding his resignation. The change in opinion that by 1973 would see Parliament pass a resolution condemning American bombing was in train.

In truth, Ottawa's approach to foreign policy in general and Vietnam in particular exuded a slightly stuffy moralism that did not sit well with many Americans. In that telling phrase of Dean Acheson's, "the stern daughter of the Voice of God" was still present all too often, and President Johnson would have little more to do with Canada for the remainder of his term. Somehow the smooth hand of Mike Pearson, the sure touch that was to be in such sharp contrast to John Diefenbaker's, had not prevented serious moments of discord.

THREE INTO ONE

The experienced governmental touch had also been noticeably lacking in defence. Defence minister Paul Hellyer was young and bright, but he had a certain rigidity in his personality. During World War II he had been demobilized from the Royal Canadian Air Force, which was blessed with a surplus of recruits, and re-assigned to the army. There, to his disgust, he went through the rigours of basic training again. The experience persuaded him that the military was rule-bound and inflexible, a view that a brief period as associate minister of national defence in the last months of the St Laurent government did nothing to dispel.

He came into office in 1963 determined to get the armed forces out of their comfortable ruts and to find more money for equipment. To accomplish both these ends, he became convinced, the first steps were integration—melding easily combined recruiting organizations, for example—and simplification of the unwieldy National Defence Headquarters organization. That done, his next goal was unification: the creation of a single service wearing the same uniform.

Hellyer began by issuing a white paper in 1964 that laid out his direction and proposed the establishment of an "intervention force" capable of operating anywhere. In effect, the minister was turning the military away from its fixation on fighting a major war against the Soviets in Central Europe and towards a new concentration on flexibility, mobility, and firepower. Peacekeeping was pronounced a major priority, but not peacekeeping as it had thus far been practised by lightly armed troops. Instead, a hard-hitting force that could travel by air, sea, or land and have air support at its beck and call was to be created to serve the government's ends, ready to move at once to serve UN or NATO purposes.

Refashioning the military (Reprinted with permission—The Toronto
Star Syndicate)

For the next three years Hellyer pushed his proposals through a
sometimes resisting defence headquarters. A chief of defence staff
headed the new organization with functional chiefs under him,
replacing the structure of a chairman of the chiefs of staff and three
service heads. The newly integrated military had a single recruiting
organization, a single training system, a single basic-trades training
organization, and an integrated command structure. To find money
for equipment, ten thousand service members would receive the
"golden bowler" of early retirement. And new equipment was
promised: armoured personnel carriers, self-propelled artillery,
destroyer escorts, and transport aircraft. No one objected to new
equipment, but everything else caused controversy. The next stage
was to cause uproar.

Unification, Hellyer explained, "essentially is a single force, with one name, one uniform, one set of rank designations and one career management policy." This upset senior officers, mainly but not exclusively in the Royal Canadian Navy, many of whom resigned their commissions in protest. Not dissuaded, Hellyer proceeded with his plans. In the process he stirred up a near mutiny; Rear Admiral W.M. Landymore, commanding the navy on the Atlantic Coast, made his objections public. To Landymore, unification destroyed tradition and demoralized officers and men. Hellyer was furious but unmoved. As he pointed out, the military is "under civilian control and this is the way it's going to be run for a change."

With only lukewarm support from his prime minister and his policy under massive public attack, Hellyer might have been expected to relent. Instead he held the course, put his unification legislation to Parliament, and pushed it into law early in 1967. Unification of the armed forces came into effect on 1 April 1968. It was, despite the unfortunate date, a major triumph for a determined minister. The tragedy for Hellyer, a man who wanted to be prime minister, was that his single-minded devotion to his goal had made his rigid personality all too obvious, and his ambitions would be denied.

LE GRAND CHARLES

If there was one additional area in which the Pearsonian deft hand had been expected to repair wounds in the nation's fabric, it was Quebec. Diefenbaker's almost calculated indifference to French Canada and the beginning of the Quiet Revolution in the province had coincided. The Union Nationale government, led for so long by Maurice Duplessis, was driven from power after his death. In its place from July 1960 was a reformist Liberal government led by Jean Lesage, a former federal Cabinet minister and a close friend of Pearson. Lesage's regime moved to modernize the province, updating the education system, cleaning up the conduct of politics, and taking control of major public utilities.

Such changes were viewed as heartening all across Canada, but the mood among newly confident French Canadians extended into a growing sense that Quebec ought to be independent. This attitude soon came to impinge on areas of foreign relations that had hitherto been indisputably those of the federal government. President Charles de Gaulle's France began to take an interest in Quebec and its future, causing the increasing problems between Ottawa and Quebec City to take on an international dimension.

Pearson was well aware of the potential difficulties with Quebec and France when he took power. One of his government's first domestic acts of consequence was to name a royal commission on bilingualism and biculturalism to examine relations between French and English Canadians. Abroad, he and Paul Martin visited Paris to see de Gaulle in January 1964, and the two leaders discussed the Quebec situation. Amidst compliments and all the trappings of a gala welcome laid on as only Paris could do it, the president of France made clear that he had a special interest in Quebec, but he also affirmed that he had no intention of causing difficulties and wanted Canada to remain united and independent. De Gaulle wished to maintain what he called the "happy relations between the French Republic and your federal state." To that end, France and Canada pledged to engage in "regular consultations" and enhanced exchanges in culture and the arts. If that was reassuring, less so was de Gaulle's greeting to Jean Lesage. Receiving the premier as if he were a head of state, the president said that Quebec was on the way to "*autodétermination*," an irreversible process in which France would be pleased to assist.

De Gaulle was moved by the idea of a French nation on the North American continent. Perhaps the president had also been upset by the reluctance of the Canadian government to sell uranium to France without assurances on the use of the metal; perhaps he was unhappy with the short shrift Ottawa gave to the idea of acquiring French-made Caravelle aircraft for Air Canada; perhaps he was simply unhappy with Canadian membership in NATO, France having already withdrawn from the military side of the organization. Whatever the reasons, his views on Quebec had begun to harden. Increasingly, it appeared to de Gaulle as if Canada were an Anglo-

Saxon nation in thrall to the United States and of little use to France. Quebec, however, and especially an independent Quebec, might be salvaged.

The new Canadian ambassador in Paris, Jules Léger, warned of a certain hauteur in de Gaulle's conception of the world and the place of France in it. Quebec was now firmly centred in de Gaulle's view; Léger, however, was not. His address when he presented his credentials to the president had offended the old general, and Léger was snubbed by the arrogant de Gaulle and his hangers-on.

Of course, critics sometimes charged that Canada's Department of External Affairs had a certain arrogance about itself too. And with justice. Although almost one-third of the Canadian population was French-speaking, the department effectively operated in English only. The undersecretary after 1964, the cerebral and legalistic Marcel Cadieux, was a francophone but relatively few of the officers were bilingual, and much more attention was paid to the British Commonwealth than to the French-speaking nations of Africa and Asia. Aid was given in substantial sums to Nigeria and Ghana, to cite examples, but not to Mali or the Congo-Brazzaville. In 1961, as critics in Quebec City did not hesitate to point out, French Africa in all had received a munificent $300 from Canada. Thus there was ample room for Pearson's government to take steps to demonstrate the bicultural nature of Canada abroad.

For the moment, however, it was Quebec that was making the running. For a start, the province opened a *délégation-général* in Paris in 1961 and signed an *entente culturel* in February 1965. This appearance on the international stage troubled External Affairs. Nevertheless, Ottawa had no wish to seek a confrontation with Lesage's government. Paul Martin in fact evinced every desire, as he wrote to the prime minister early in 1965, "to work out a programme of methods and procedures by which Quebec could develop its relations with the French Community. . . in fields of education, culture, aid and any other spheres falling wholly or partly within the area of provincial competence." What Martin feared was an attempt by Quebec to acquire "federal monies now used for these purposes . . . so as to enable the province to undertake international tasks in fields where it will have successfully asserted jurisdiction both internally and externally." So long as Lesage's government recognized the paramount position of the federal government in foreign policy, Ottawa was willing to co-operate.

Even so, federal bureaucrats and politicians felt a growing anxiety that Quebec was emulating the policy followed by Mackenzie King's government in the 1920s: moving step by step towards independence. The Halibut Treaty was much in their minds during the 1960s. It was in the minds of Quebec officials too. Claude Morin, the brain behind Quebec "foreign policy," brazenly told a Liberal politician, "We'll separate from Canada the same way that Canada separated from England: we'll cut the links one at a time, a concession here and a concession there, and eventually there'll be nothing left."

The wholly unexpected defeat of Lesage's regime in 1966 brought no change in the attitude of Quebec City. The Union Nationale under Daniel Johnson continued to play the autonomist game, but de Gaulle threw a new twist in it by turning to overt mischief making. Officials at the Quai d'Orsay and the Elysée Palace went out of their way to encourage Quebec to take a more independent stance. Visiting federal ministers were turned away by presidential aides while Quebec ministers had the red carpet unrolled and the champagne uncorked for them. The French embassy in Ottawa arranged visits for Paris ministers but pointedly excluded Ottawa from their itineraries. A visit to France by the governor general, de Gaulle's old wartime friend General Georges Vanier, was squelched. The governor general was not a head of state, the Paris government said. When General Vanier died in office, France sent a third-rank representative to his funeral. An outraged Mme. Vanier summoned the French ambassador to see her as her last official act and gave him a one-word message for de Gaulle: "1940." Vanier's attachment to France in the darkest days of World War II had been forgotten. Then in April 1967 Paris refused to send a high-level representative to ceremonies marking the fiftieth anniversary of the battle of Vimy Ridge. These carefully calculated insults disturbed Ottawa; so too did secret reports that Paris was funding separatist groups.

The federal government tried to remain calm in the face of such provocations. But when de Gaulle came to Canada in 1967 as part of the country's centennial celebrations, patience reached the breaking point. The Department of External Affairs had agreed that de Gaulle could visit Quebec City before coming to Ottawa, and tedious negotiations ensued with the French embassy on the protocol to govern the ceremonies when the French president disembarked from his cruiser *Colbert* at the quay.

De Gaulle's first Canadian speeches seemed harmless, but after a long and tumultuous drive with cheering crowds from Quebec to Montreal—it seemed like the liberation of France, de Gaulle said—the president broke loose. To the cheers of separatists standing beneath the balcony of Montreal's *hôtel de ville*, the general ended his address with the words "Vive Montréal! Vive le Québec! Vive le Québec libre!" The finale exhortation, an apparent endorsement of separatism, drew cheers from the placard wavers and stunned gasps from federal officials. The public in English Canada, remembering the tens of thousands of Canadians who had died to free France in two world wars, was outraged. Pearson himself wrote, "I could hardly believe my ears," and his Cabinet decided to send an admonitory telegram to de Gaulle. "The people of Canada are free," Pearson said in a public statement, his words white hot. "Every province of Canada is free. Canadians do not need to be liberated." Not at all worried by this, de Gaulle decided not to go to Ottawa and flew home leaving a political crisis in his wake and seriously strained relations between Canada and France. He made matters worse in the next few months by referring to the "so-called" federal government and by claiming that the issue was that "Quebec be free."

"Le grand Charles" had only a short time in power remaining to him; student riots in Paris in May 1968 led to his resignation. His successors, while maintaining their sympathy for Quebec and continuing to assist the efforts of the province to enhance its place abroad, were never willing to go quite so far as de Gaulle in causing trouble. The problems that he had exacerbated were more long lived.

If de Gaulle's time in office was limited, so too was Pearson's. By the end of 1967, after two successive minority governments, dispiriting scandals, and discouraging conflicts with Quebec and other provinces, Pearson was more than ready to leave political life. His government had some substantial accomplishments in domestic politics, but its achievements in foreign policy were limited. An inability to contain Quebec's aspirations abroad was one obvious failure,

De Gaulle in Montreal (Canapress)

just as the speedy decision to send peacekeeping troops to Cyprus was clearly a success. Canadian expulsion from UNEF may not have been a failure of policy, but it did have the effect of chilling public and governmental enthusiasm for peacekeeping for several years.

Over all hung the shadow of Vietnam and its searing impact on relations with Washington. Pearson had spoken out about the war but many Canadians, their nationalism stirred by the centennial and by a growing perception that their country was very different from the one to the south, still considered his government too close to the United States. In the context of the dreadful struggle in Southeast Asia, proximity in policy was no benefit. Scholars looked at Canada–United States relations, at NATO, NORAD, and at the Cold War generally, and concluded—perhaps biased by personal convictions—that quiet diplomacy had constrained the country's freedom of action while providing few benefits. One collection of academic papers, published at the end of Pearson's time in office, was titled *An Independent Foreign Policy for Canada?* The question mark said it all, and that was a telling commentary on Mike Pearson, the Canadian diplomat *par excellence.*

CHAPTER TEN

The Trudeau Pirouette, 1968–1984

PIERRE ELLIOTT TRUDEAU, chosen Liberal leader and prime minister at a party convention in April 1968, was very different in formation and style than the man he succeeded. A bilingual francophone from Montreal, Trudeau had been well educated in Quebec, London, Paris, and Boston. A lawyer, he had practised and taught in Quebec in between extended bouts of world travel. His primary interest was in constitutional questions, where he had made his mark as a writer and as justice minister under Pearson, but he had no formal training in or deep understanding of foreign policy or, more particularly, of defence questions. He had ideas, nonetheless.

SIXPACK DIPLOMACY

Trudeau ordered a complete review of defence policy to make sure that national interests, not NATO interests, determined the approach. For twenty years, he told a British interviewer, "Canada's foreign policy was largely its policy in NATO, through NATO." This would not do any more. Trudeau also desired a "thorough and comprehensive review of our foreign policy" to get away from the "helpful fixer" image that Pearsonian diplomacy had established: the idea that a well-meaning Canada would always be willing to sacrifice its interests for the greater good. He believed, for example, that Canada should recognize China, something put off since 1950 for fear of Washington's response. For Trudeau, Canadian economic, social, and political interests had to come first. Above all, foreign and defence policy had to help cement Canadian unity.

All this talk, prior to his accession to power and immediately after it, upset the Departments of External Affairs and National Defence. Trudeau had placed Mitchell Sharp, also deputy prime minister, in charge of foreign policy. A former senior public servant on the trade side, Sharp was intelligent, able, and devoted to the outlines of Pearsonian foreign policy. In the Defence Department remained Léo Cadieux, Paul Hellyer's associate minister and successor. Cadieux believed in unification of the forces, in making the military more reflective of Canada's bilingual nature, and in NATO. There was trouble ahead.

NATO was the prime minister's first target. Trudeau made clear to Ottawa officials and to foreign visitors that he was not at all sure that "it was right for us to be thinking so much about the European threat. Perhaps we should be worried much more about civil war in North America." This was not completely far fetched in the fall of 1968. After the murder of Martin Luther King, ghettoes in the big cities of the United States had erupted in violence and arson, and the possibility of unrest spilling over the border—or of separatist violence in Quebec getting out of hand—was very real. Trudeau himself had sat under showers of rocks at the Saint-Jean Baptiste Day celebrations in Montreal in June 1968, a performance that helped guarantee him a smashing victory in the general election that followed a few days later. On the other hand, the Soviet threat had not diminished; indeed in 1968 it was very real, and Warsaw Pact nations in August sent tanks into Czechoslovakia to crush the fragile flowering of democracy in Prague. The regime led by Leonid Brezhnev seemed every bit as vicious and aggressive as its predecessors.

Trudeau was undeterred, and he continued to ventilate his ideas, often expressed in Socratic questions, to officials:

Will the US sacrifice Europe and NATO before blowing up the world? . . . What is the point of having large conventional forces if they are going to lose the conventional battle anyway[?] . . . Is NATO the best way to secure peace at the moment? . . . When are we going to arrive at a plan to achieve peace by not getting stronger militarily? . . . Can we assume Russia wants war because it invaded Czechoslovakia? . . . In what way is NATO of value to Canada?

Said at a meeting in December 1968, this shook the diplomats and military staff so much that Marcel Cadieux, the undersecretary in External Affairs, in his diary described it as "*quasi-catastrophique.*" It was still unclear what the prime ministerial questioning of verities set in stone meant for the review of Canada's NATO policy.

The review document reached the Cabinet Committee on External Affairs and Defence at the end of February 1969. Drawn up by officials, it predictably came down on the side of the status quo. Canada should remain in NATO and continue its military contribution to the alliance, though perhaps on a lesser scale. Maintaining peace in Europe, the review argued, was vital for Canada. The ministers on the committee were sharply divided, however, some favouring complete withdrawal from NATO. The prime minister held his counsel, waiting for a meeting of the full Cabinet over the last weekend in March to set government policy.

To counter the officials' report, Trudeau turned to Dr. Ivan Head, a former diplomat and law professor on the staff of the Prime Minister's Office. Quietly drawing together a small team, Head produced a paper, "A Study of Defence Policy," which to the astonishment of most ministers was circulated just hours before the Cabinet meeting. Head projected sharply reduced armed forces, an end to the nuclear-strike role of the air force in NATO, and elimination of the army's Honest John surface-to-surface missiles. The document argued that Canada should not withdraw completely from a military role in NATO but should cut its strength and use its position within the alliance to press for change and the end of the Cold War.

The ministers of external affairs and national defence were appalled by this paper, both for its content and for the way it had appeared in the briefing books for the meeting without any prior notice or, indeed, any indication that it was in preparation.

Cadieux's first instinct was to resign and he had to be persuaded to remain by Mitchell Sharp, who blasted Trudeau for his surprise package. The prime minister agreed to withdraw Head's paper, but the damage was done. Trudeau's preferred course of action had been made clear.

Supporting Trudeau in the Cabinet discussions were many of the younger ministers and close friends such as Jean Marchand and Gérard Pelletier. Among those against him were Paul Martin (still in the Cabinet although he had been elevated to the Senate), an increasingly disgruntled Paul Hellyer, Sharp, and Cadieux. The weight of opinion was against the existing policy, and Sharp and Cadieux soon came to realize that it could not be defended as a whole. The only question was how large to make the cuts in troop strength overseas. For two days the discussion went back and forth, Professor Trudeau leading the seminar; for two days, the fight over the future of Canada in NATO continued in what might well have been an unprecedented debate within a Canadian Cabinet. Extraordinarily, at the end of it all, nothing had been decided. Because the prime minister had chosen to announce a policy on 3 April, there was therefore much scrambling, much last-minute bargaining, and many threats of resignation before matters were settled.

The prime minister's statement defined Canadian defence priorities in the following order: the defence of sovereignty, the defence of North America, NATO, and peacekeeping. Canada was not to be a non-aligned state, a conclusion that produced a loud sigh of relief from the Departments of External Affairs and National Defence. As for troops in Europe, Trudeau made clear that the commitment held good until the end of 1969: "The Canadian force commitment for deployment with NATO in Europe beyond this period will be discussed with our allies at the meeting of the defence planning committee of NATO in May. The Canadian Government intends, in consultation with Canada's allies, to take early steps to bring about a planned and phased reduction of the size of the Canadian forces in Europe."

Still undecided was how much of the ten-thousand-strong air and ground force would stay. Discussions in Ottawa, sometimes vicious in their intensity, pointed to a force of thirty-five hundred; discussions at NATO, marked by more abuse heaped on Canada than anyone had seen before, helped to persuade the government to keep the force to five thousand. At much the same time, the strength of the Canadian Forces was set at eighty thousand, with a defence budget fixed for the next three years at $1.8 billion.

Trudeau thus largely got his way. He had cut the NATO force in half, chopped the size of the forces, and frozen the defence budget. He had also fed fears among diplomats and soldiers that he was completely unaware of the nature of the Soviet threat, even soft on communism himself. The small, pro-military pressure groups in Canada agreed with this assessment but public opinion as a whole did not. The Vietnam War had created the sense in many Canadians that all wars were unjust; that Americans were almost as bad as Soviets; and that the best course for Canada would be to have the minimum military force possible. At the same time, paradoxically, Canadians still tended to believe in the propriety of NATO participation and defence co-operation with the United States. There were elements of both pragmatism and wishful thinking in the public mind—and in the prime minister's.

The same factors were soon evident in the results of the foreign policy review that Trudeau had put in place soon after taking office. Ministerial missions travelled around the globe, the Department of External Affairs organized seminars with academics, and task forces gathered data and formulated concepts. The results, after being subjected to scrutiny in the Prime Minister's Office and the Cabinet, were made public in June 1970.

The format of *Foreign Policy for Canadians*—a slipcase with six brightly coloured booklets—created the illusion of change; the text tried to flesh out that illusion. The helpful fixer image of the past was abandoned for the Canadian national interest: "Canada, like other states, must act according to how it perceives its aims and interests. . . . In essence, foreign policy is the product of the Government's progressive definition and pursuit of national aims and interests in the international environment. It is the extension abroad of national policies." What were those national policies? Social justice. Quality of life. Economic growth.

To critics in the Department of External Affairs and out, the new thrust would diminish Canada's role in the pursuit of world peace, lessen its influence in NATO and on Europe, and emphasize the sale of Canadian products. It was dollar diplomacy. And, the critics asked, where was the United States? Primarily because agreement could not be reached within the department on how to present policy towards the Americans, mention of them was almost entirely left out of *Foreign Policy for Canadians*. So too was discussion of the Commonwealth, Africa, and the Caribbean. For all their emphasis on economic growth, the booklets made no clear statement of Canadian economic policies. Few new initiatives were presented beyond Trudeau's already stated desire to recognize China. The six-pack presented systems analysis in lieu of policy. It raised governmental employment of buzz words to a new level and demonstrated irrevocably that Trudeau had imposed his will on Canadian foreign policy just as much as on defence policy.

GUERRE DES DRAPEAUX

It was harder for Trudeau to impose his will on France, which continued to meddle in Canada. The new prime minister had been intimately involved in the previous government's efforts to deal with France–Quebec questions, both as Pearson's parliamentary secretary and as justice minister, and he had toughened the federal arguments. One sign of his intent appeared in a government pamphlet, *Federalism and International Relations*, distributed at a federal–provincial conference in February 1968. The pamphlet was uncompromising in its defence of federal government prerogatives abroad.

This clear position mattered because, at precisely the same time and with the connivance of the French government, the former French colony of Gabon invited Quebec to attend a conference of French-speaking states on education. Despite Canadian government protests, the provincial representatives duly went. The next month Canada effectively broke relations with Gabon, but it also sent an aid mission out to other states in French Africa. Perhaps support for Canada could be bought with development assistance. Another education conference was soon scheduled, and Quebec's education minister proclaimed that the federal government, under the constitution, had nothing to do with this subject. Nonetheless, Canada asked to be invited and protested to Paris—which no one in Ottawa doubted was running the conference and organizing the invitations—that it was not France's right to interpret the British North America Act.

Further French initiatives included having semi-official emissaries meet francophone minorities in New Brunswick and Manitoba to discuss their plight and hold out offers of cash assistance. Trudeau reacted bluntly in September 1968, calling Philippe Rossillon, one of the French government's troublemakers, a "secret agent" and denouncing this "underhanded and surreptitious" way of doing business. That brought more caution into French activities. So too did the sudden death of Premier Daniel Johnson. His successor as premier of Quebec, Jean-Jacques Bertrand, was no separatist, and he was quick to reach a de facto peace treaty with Ottawa: no confrontations for their own sake.

In fact, the clashes continued, peace treaty or not, at conferences of what was now being called the French "commonwealth," or *la francophonie.* Sometimes the battle was over appearances, a figurative and literal *guerre des drapeaux.* If Canada was present, would its flag be larger or flown higher than that of Quebec or of other provincial delegations? How would the conference roster list Quebec: as "Quebec," or as "Canada–Quebec"? Finally, thanks to France's continued although more discreet manipulation, would Canada even be invited to the conference in Niamey, Niger, in February 1970? An invitation was eventually issued, though the conference saw unseemly bidding for public support by both Quebec and Canadian delegations as each strove to top the other's donations to the host country.

Canada won that round. At a second Niamey conference, however, designed to put organizational meat onto the bones of *la francophonie,* Ottawa conceded the right of the Quebec delegation to speak "in the name of Quebec" while provincial subjects were under discussion. When international questions were treated, Quebec was to speak as a member of the Canadian delegation. Nonetheless, Quebec won a substantial victory when governments, not nations, were declared eligible for membership in the new organization. For the first time Quebec had become a member of an international organization.

Yet the tide of Quebec's nationalism ebbed, for the time being. The victory of the Liberals under Robert Bourassa in early 1970 was one sign of the change. Another was the October Crisis later that year, when Trudeau used the War Measures Act to smash extremist organizations in the province. Ottawa and Quebec struck a deal that allowed the province to be a member of *la francophonie* but required it to keep the federal government informed of its activities. At the same time, Quebec agreed to participate within Canadian delegations at conferences of *la francophonie*, with a limited veto over national votes in areas of exclusive provincial jurisdiction.

"STRICTLY OCCIDENTAL"

Trudeau intended to normalize relations with China. Canada had opened a legation there during World War II, but after the victory of Mao Zedong's forces in 1949 and the outbreak of the Korean War, relations between China and the West remained in hostile stasis. The United States under Eisenhower, Kennedy, and Johnson viewed the Beijing regime with unlimited animosity, notwithstanding China's huge population and enormous importance in Asia. Trudeau had visited China in 1960, and he considered, quite properly, that it was absurd to pretend it did not exist. During his campaign for the Liberal leadership in early 1968 he stated, "Our aim will be to recognize the People's Republic of China Government as soon as possible," and he also wanted to see China join the United Nations.

Although some of Trudeau's attitudes disturbed Canadian diplomats, this one did not. The Department of External Affairs had been moving towards recognition for some time, and the views of allies and neutrals were continuously canvassed. Still, there were concerns. What would Washington say? How would recognition of Beijing affect Canada's ties with Chiang Kai-shek's Nationalist government in Formosa, which still claimed to be the government of all China?

The Americans left no doubt of their reaction. Canadian recognition of China might well open the floodgates of world opinion,

Pierre Trudeau in China in 1973 with Deng Xiaoping
(National Archives of Canada, PA 136978)

dammed for so long by Washington, and it could lead to a wholesale abandonment of the Nationalists, who were military clients of the United States. The Nationalists naturally were also very unhappy, but if Canada could continue to recognize them as the government of China at the same time as it recognized Beijing, they might be prepared to live with their anger.

Mao's government, it soon became clear, would have none of this. A long dance ensued involving much international travel to bring the Chinese to the table. Conservative leader Robert Stanfield quipped in Parliament that a trip by Mitchell Sharp to Stockholm to entice the Chinese was a failure: "If he met anyone it was strictly

Occidental." The Communist government seemed unwilling to recognize the great favour that Canada was trying to confer upon it. Taiwan was part of China, and the Chiang Kai-shek regime was a usurper undeserving of recognition by anyone. In other words, Beijing did not want any form of recognition that failed to accept its sovereignty over all Chinese territory, including Taiwan.

The haggling was intense, but the ultimate solution, made public on 10 October 1970, satisfied both parties: "The Chinese Government reaffirms that Taiwan is an inalienable part of the territory of the People's Republic of China. The Canadian Government takes note of this position." Canada's official relations with Taiwan ended, and the Nationalist regime's envoys departed Ottawa. Bringing China into the family of nations was a major achievement for the Trudeau government, and the "takes note of" formula—which did not require acceptance of the claim to Taiwan made by the People's Republic of China—was soon adopted by other Western states. Soon even the American position began to crack as President Richard Nixon agreed to send sports teams to China, leading to the expression "ping-pong diplomacy." This was followed faster than many had predicted by full recognition.

COMMONWEALTH CONUNDRUMS

Trudeau's policy towards the civil war in Nigeria was less successful. A secessionist revolt by Ibo people in the Nigerian province of Biafra had erupted in 1967, and full-scale civil war soon followed. Television screens were full of horrific scenes each day, in particular of starving Biafran children, and the public began to demand loudly that Canada assist the hungry and homeless. Trudeau was largely unmoved by the Biafran propaganda skilfully marshalled by well paid public relations firms in the United States and Europe, even saying to some protesters, "Where's Biafra?"

Trudeau's reluctance had little to do with Nigeria and everything to do with Canada. A federal state and a member of the Commonwealth, Nigeria had fallen into civil war as its federal regime tried to retake the Ibo province. How could Trudeau, Canada's federal prime minister and the leading opponent of secessionist forces in Quebec, deal with a separatist Biafra? His position was perhaps understandable, though not to those who thought starvation transcended federalist dogma. His "Where's Biafra?" comment was so arrogantly flip, so foolish, however, that he grievously offended the liberal elements in Canada from which his support was drawn. The Nigerian war ended in January 1970 in a complete federal victory.

Other Commonwealth issues troubled Canada in the Trudeau era. At the beginning of his time in power Trudeau was almost completely indifferent to the organization; in this respect he was a very typical French-speaking Canadian. After attending his first Prime Ministers' Meeting in London in 1969, however, Trudeau began to be a believer. It was pleasant to be able to talk informally with First and Third World leaders, and the Commonwealth was the one world arena in which Canada played a central part, especially now that Britain was trying to distance itself from the organization. The position would flatter any Canadian leader, and Trudeau did not prove immune.

He tried to improve discussion at Commonwealth Heads of Governments meetings by attempting to bar set-piece speeches. He also moved to eliminate officials from the conference room so that the leaders could genuinely discuss issues. Above all, he found himself playing the very helpful fixer role he had so scorned in Pearson, as he and his Commonwealth colleagues strove to tidy up the sometimes messy legacy of empire.

Numerous thorny questions remained. Biafra was one; South Africa was another, even though it was no longer a member. The South African question still exercised the Commonwealth because of Pretoria's brutally racist policies, and there were pressures from Africa and Asia to cut all links. Canada declared an arms embargo in 1970; in 1977 it withdrew from all trade assistance programs; and in 1979 it terminated its own trade agreement, ending the imperial "preferential tariff" that South African goods had enjoyed in Canada since the 1932 Ottawa Conference. These measures did not satisfy anti-South African lobby groups in Canada but they cut more ice with Third World leaders, who clearly appreciated Trudeau's well-meaning role in conference discussions.

The issue of Rhodesia was more difficult still. The white settler government had declared independence unilaterally, and the non-white Commonwealth was outraged. The British government, partly motivated by lobby groups within Britain, urged other Commonwealth members to make peace with the Rhodesian government of Ian Smith. The notion was anathema to the African nations, and the Commonwealth pressed its members and the United Nations for ever tighter sanctions, which were then promptly violated by both companies and countries. Ottawa was generally co-operative, pressing London to make no moves to encourage the Rhodesians and thus disrupt the Commonwealth, and supporting the sanctions. By 1977, as a black rebellion underwritten by neighbouring states made headway while costing lives and treasure, the Smith regime found itself in difficulty. In 1979 it was forced to bring majority rule into effect. The next year the renamed Zimbabwe was admitted to the Commonwealth.

MR. TRUDEAU GOES TO WASHINGTON

However titillating Commonwealth questions were for the prime minister, they were essentially a side issue compared to Canada's permanent and most pressing problem. In 1970, *Foreign Policy for Canadians* had said almost nothing about relations with the Americans, which were so all-pervasive that they could not conveniently be wrapped within the covers of a brief booklet. The United States was always there, ten times the population of Canada, fifteen times richer, and immeasurably more powerful. How would Canada under Trudeau deal with the United States and with Richard Nixon, who took office in January 1969? How did the prime minister's compatriots across Canada wish him to approach the Americans?

It was easier to determine the popular mood. As always, most—though by no means all—Canadians looked on Americans as their best friends in the world, the people to whom they felt closest and to whose wealth and comforts they aspired. But the Vietnam War had been tearing apart American society for four or five years by the time

Trudeau came to office, racial strains were severe, and the machinations of the imperialist "Amerika" were a staple of liberal American films, books, and magazines. To many Canadians, as well, the United States was a danger to the world and, just as important, to Canada. The title of one popular book, *Close the 49th Parallel,* seemed all too appropriate.

Trudeau knew the United States less, perhaps, than any previous modern Canadian leader despite his brief schooling at Harvard. His leanings were pacifist and his attitudes on world issues leftist, so much so that to many Americans (and some Canadians) he was as good as a card-carrying communist. The position he had taken during the debates on Canadian NATO policy had done nothing to reassure his critics.

Nixon was a powerful president, alert and intelligent; his key adviser on foreign policy, Henry Kissinger, was shrewd and cunning. Neither ranked Canada very high on their list of threats or allies. Nixon's misconception—that Japan was the country with which the United States had its most important trading relationship—reflected the administration's abysmal ignorance of the first-rank importance that trade with Canada had for the United States. The story also circulated widely that when the Canadian ambassador finally got to see Kissinger, the president's national security adviser opened the talk with "I hope you didn't come here to talk to me about the sex life of the salmon," implying that the only thing Canada had to do with the United States was to regulate the fishing industry.

Trudeau's meetings with Nixon were not especially cordial. The two dealt politely with each other and respected each other's intelligence, but they were certainly not warm. Later Nixon would be caught on one of the Watergate tapes referring to "that asshole Trudeau." Trudeau's private views of the president remain unrecorded, but he realized that he had to get on with Nixon and with the United States. On his first visit to the new president in March 1969, he tried his best to define the difficulties Canada faced in sharing the continent with the United States: "Living with you," he told the National Press Club, "is in some ways like sleeping with an elephant: no matter how friendly and even-tempered the beast, one is affected by every twitch and grunt."

Trudeau calls at Nixon's White House (Macpherson, *Toronto Star*,
Reprinted with permission—The Toronto Star Syndicate)

Those twitches and grunts could become threatening. In August
1971, the Nixon administration slapped a whole series of economic
measures into place, including a surcharge on all dutiable imports, in
an attempt to deal with the American balance of payments. The
Auto Pact itself, a cash cow for Canada, escaped cancellation only by
a hair. The "Nixon Shock" hit Ottawa like a thunderclap and caused
near panic at this threat to trade and to American investment in
Canada. Perhaps as many as a hundred thousand jobs might be
affected.

After officials had failed to resolve the problem on their own,
Trudeau went to see the president in December. Had the United
States made a conscious decision that Canada must never be in a
surplus position on trade, investment, and current account? If so,
Canada would have to sell off more and more of its economy in

order to balance the books. Helped by Kissinger, Nixon saw the wisdom of Trudeau's position, and eliminated the punitive measures. Trudeau was delighted when Nixon told the world, "We don't want to gobble you up."

Canadians were thus in a happier frame of mind when Nixon paid his first presidential visit to Ottawa in April 1972. Nevertheless, in a speech he had played an unusually large part in drafting, Nixon called for an end to the "sentimental rhetoric" of the past. "It is time for us to recognize that we have very separate identities; that we have significant differences; and that nobody's interests are furthered when these realities are obscured." In other words, the special position that had long characterized Canada's relations with the United States was over and exemptions made for Canada in December 1971 were unlikely to be repeated. Richard Nixon had made a Declaration of Independence from the incubus to the north.

Still, Canada could be useful to the Nixon government. Having promised to get out of the Vietnam War, the president had to deliver. In January 1973, his envoy Kissinger struck a deal with the North Vietnamese to end the war, or rather, to end the war just long enough for the Americans to withdraw. Nixon had brought Hanoi to serious bargaining by unleashing a massive bombing campaign, greeted in the Canadian Parliament with shock and inducing a government motion to denounce the prolongation of the war. Perhaps that response helped make Canada acceptable to the North Vietnamese; Washington and Hanoi both wanted Canada to take part in a new International Commission of Control and Supervision to watch over the truce. In 1954, Canada had participated in a three-nation commission. This time it formed part of a foursome: Canada and Indonesia represented the West and Hungary and Poland the Communist East.

There was little enthusiasm in Ottawa for this thankless peace-keeping task, but the request could not be evaded. Canada agreed to provide 290 service members and civilians for a short period but only if the ICC could actually be made to function effectively. Moreover, Canada pledged to follow an "open mouth" policy, telling the truth about violations and speaking out about its commission partners' cover-ups. The new ICC proved to be very like the old.

Loud protests by the Canadian commissioner did little to change matters, and at the end of July 1973 Canada escaped from the commitment. Nonetheless, the United States was grateful for the assistance in extricating itself from the Vietnam morass. The South Vietnamese were soon to be conquered by the armies of the North.

THE THIRD OPTION

The new Nixon doctrine towards Canada shook Ottawa. If Canada no longer enjoyed a special relationship with the United States, perhaps it was time to look elsewhere. Some signs that the government was prepared to do so had already appeared. In May 1971, Trudeau had visited the Soviet Union and stunned his Cabinet by signing a Protocol on Consultations with Chairman Brezhnev to establish regular meetings between the two nations. The prime minister told a press conference in Moscow that the "overpowering presence" of the United States had created "a danger to our national identity from a cultural, economic and perhaps even military point of view."

The Americans were unhappy with Trudeau's manoeuvring, and some actually feared that it represented a move out of the American and Western orbit. In fact, Trudeau had been simply foolish to speak as he had, though Premier Alexei Kosygin promptly paid a return visit to Ottawa, presumably with the hope of bolstering the new relationship. The visit did not go well, not least because lax security let a man shouting "free Hungary" physically attack the Soviet leader.

Few genuinely believed that Trudeau would take Canada into closer ties with Moscow. Yet he was looking around and so was Mitchell Sharp. In 1972, just before a federal election in which polls promised a tight race, the secretary of state for external affairs released a document that quickly became known as the "third option" paper. The thrust was clear. Canada had three choices before it: to "seek to maintain more or less its present relationship with the United States," which almost no one any longer believed possible; to move towards closer integration with the United States, which few in 1972 thought desirable; or to "pursue a comprehensive long-term strategy to develop and strengthen the Canadian economy and other aspects of its national life and . . . [thus] reduce the present Canadian vulnerability." The government preferred the third option, which implied a drive to expand and enhance links with the European Community (EC) and Japan. It may also have sounded good to Canadian voters, though Trudeau's government was reduced to minority status.

The country had to go some distance to increase trade with Europe and Asia. Canadian trade with EC nations had actually been declining in percentage since 1958. Trade with Japan was good but the Japanese, their market protected by a maze of regulations, rules, and quality standards, wanted only Canadian raw materials. Still, it was worth a try. From late 1973 on, Canada made a real push towards Europe and Japan. Trudeau himself played a major role, visiting the key European capitals and lobbying heads of governments intensively. In talks with one key leader, Chancellor Helmut Schmidt of Germany, Trudeau even agreed to secure German Leopard tanks for the Canadian force in NATO, an astonishing indicator of just how committed the erstwhile peacemonger of 1969–1970 was to the new economic initiative.

It worked. Despite anxieties in the EC that Canada was pressing it to make moves in a direction in which it was not yet prepared to go, a contractual link was struck in 1976. The EC and Canada gave each other most-favoured-nation status in trade, undertook a program of commercial co-operation, and called for joint ventures, scientific exchanges, and the like.

The same pressures were applied to Japan. They stirred similar concerns, but thanks to the Japanese ambassador in Ottawa, Yasuhiko Nara, the difficulties were overcome. (In the process, the ambassador became close to Trudeau, and his wife taught Margaret Trudeau, the prime minister's young spouse, how to prepare sushi.) In October 1976, a "Framework for Economic Cooperation" was duly initialled. The countries agreed to expand trade, increase investment, and exchange expertise.

The contractual links with the EC and Japan were a notable success for Trudeau, and it was pleasant to pronounce them so. Unfortunately, they did not alter Canadian dependence on the United States. The government's trade bureaucracy considered the links a daydream, flying in the face of geographical reality. Almost no one at the Department of Trade and Commerce took them seriously and neither did their business clients. Deterred by the difficulties of fighting for business in multilingual Europe, Canadian companies hung back, and the intricacies of Japanese culture simply baffled them. Trade figures with Japan increased to $5.3 billion in exports and imports combined, but the grand words about co-operation proved meaningless. It was the same with Europe. Just as Canadian exporters instinctively looked south, European exporters were simply not especially interested in Canada. It was very hard to reverse established patterns. Trudeau had tried, but ultimately he, or rather his bureaucracy and Canadian business, had failed.

Richard Nixon was defeated not by the electorate but by his own paranoia and stupidity in the Watergate affair of 1973–1974. To replace him came Gerald Ford, an athletic and not overly bright politician from Michigan, who looked on Pierre Trudeau and Canada in a kindly way. He invited Canada to attend the 1975 summit of key Western nations, a group that became known as the G-7 once Canada and Italy joined. The summits have never been crucial events; they mostly provide photo opportunities and occasions for high-powered schmoozing. Membership mattered to Canada, however, because it demonstrated (if only to the credulous) that the nation was almost a great power.

The Canadian leader was not so grateful, however, as to accept American demands that Taiwan have its athletes at the 1976 Montreal Olympics parade under the name of the Republic of China. The president was furious at the Canadian refusal, but neither his anger nor his presidency lasted very much longer. Ford's defeat in the election of 1976 put Georgia's former governor, Jimmy Carter, into the White House.

A Democrat, his party historically attuned with Canadian Liberals, Carter got on well with Trudeau, though he knew very little about Canada. His national security adviser, Zbigniew Brzezinski, however, did. The son of the Polish consul, he had grown up in Montreal and been educated at McGill University, and he had views about the place of Quebec in Canada.

His familiarity with the issue was significant, for in 1976 René Lévesque led the Parti Québécois to power in Quebec City. The separatists were in office, to everyone's astonishment, and new questions were at the forefront of Canadian–American relations. How would Washington react to the possible break-up of Canada? What would the Carter administration do if Quebec sought a relationship with the United States? Brzezinski was said to favour a gentle response, if not an openly welcoming one, to separatism. But Vice President Walter Mondale, Secretary of State Cyrus Vance, and the able and tough ambassador to Canada, Thomas Enders, disagreed. They persuaded Carter, who in truth needed little persuasion, that Ottawa should be backed just as much as was diplomatically possible. The United States would favour a strong and united Canada, and Ottawa breathed a sigh of relief and began to retreat from the "third option."

René Lévesque therefore made little headway in his efforts to muster support south of the border. Business groups were markedly cool to his speeches, and the American administration discouraged Quebec from opening a permanent mission in Washington; instead Lévesque created an expensive operation in New York. Quebec City had better luck in American academia, distributing grants and research funds to create a minor principality in Quebec Studies that in some parts of the United States rivalled the Canadian Studies empire established by Ottawa. The chilly official u.s. attitude also led the Parti Québécois to drop its earlier policy of Cold War neutrality for an independent Quebec. The putative republic promised to join NATO and NORAD and to have a foreign policy much like Canada's, though that thought could not have received instant approbation in the Pentagon.

BRIEFLY TORY

Towards the end of Jimmy Carter's not wholly successful presidency, Canadians threw out the government of Pierre Trudeau, and the much-admired, much-hated leader announced his retirement from politics as soon as a convention could select his successor. In his place as prime minister came Joe Clark, the young Alberta MP who had unexpectedly captured the Conservative leadership in 1976 and was thus able to capitalize on the unpopularity of Trudeau's regime.

Clark was pea-green on foreign policy questions, as at once became obvious when he tried to implement his Toronto campaign promise to move the Canadian embassy in Israel from Tel Aviv to Jerusalem, the city claimed by Israel as its true capital. Arab states were outraged. Faced with a boycott of Canadian firms, Clark had to appoint Robert Stanfield, his predecessor as Conservative leader, as a one-man fact-finding mission to get him off the hook.

His choice for secretary of state for external affairs, Flora MacDonald, was just as much a novice in diplomacy. Flora, as everyone called her, blew through the stuffy corridors of the Department of External Affairs headquarters as a new wind. She talked to secretaries (she had been one at Tory party headquarters in the early Diefenbaker years) and desk officers at will, and she fought bitterly and at length with Allan Gotlieb, the undersecretary whom she had inherited from the outgoing administration.

Brilliant, intellectual, a long-time and close adviser to Trudeau, Gotlieb balked at his new minister's populist approach. He believed that diplomacy should be arrived at through a bureaucratic process of countless committee meetings, that it should be conducted in private, and that ministers should consult their senior officials closely and follow their advice. He saw the Department of External Affairs as a central agency of government, exercising control and co-ordination over all governmental operations abroad.

Very little of this sat well with MacDonald, who like all Clark ministers intended to see that bureaucrats did what politicians wanted. Mirror committees of deputy ministers, making decisions that were then fed to the ministers for ratification, were not what she wanted. MacDonald was a trial, and for a department that had been badly battered by Trudeau's indifference to diplomats, for a once-proud bureaucracy that had seen itself as the élite of the public service and been forced to watch helplessly while the Prime Minister's Office snatched away many of its prerogatives, the Conservative regime was yet another heavy cross to bear. Conflict was inevitable, and an explosion would certainly have resulted had the government lasted for more than its six months in office.

Thus MacDonald was to be remembered for only two things in addition to her style: accepting refugees from Vietnam, and authorizing the rescue of American hostages in Iran. She proved receptive to the pleas for help uttered by thousands of Vietnamese refugees who were fleeing their homeland in search of freedom and opportunity. Under her lead, Canada agreed to accept up to fifty thousand boat people, the government pledging to sponsor one refugee for every one privately sponsored. This was much the most generous program in the world.

MacDonald also showed well in the Iranian hostage-taking incident. After the Iranian revolution toppled the Shah in 1979, the American embassy in Tehran was stormed and captured by militants in November. A few of the embassy staff made it to the home of the Canadian ambassador, Kenneth Taylor and, with full authority promptly given from Ottawa, they were taken in and hidden. Late in January 1980, the Americans were smuggled out with the aid of Canadian passports. The remainder of the hostages, an American rescue attempt having resulted in utter disaster in the Iranian desert, would not be released until November 1980. Their captivity contributed mightily to the destruction of Jimmy Carter's presidency.

The story of Ambassador Taylor's role broke in the Canadian media in the midst of the 1980 election campaign, as Joe Clark, his government's budget rejected in Parliament in December 1979, struggled to hold on to power. It led to an outpouring of unprecedented American gratitude. Canada had never stood higher in American estimation, for an act that was, after all, nothing more than should have been expected of friends and neighbours. The Iranian rescue did not change political minds in Canada, however; the people tossed out Clark's government and re-installed the Liberals, led once again by the resurrected Trudeau, who had decided not to resign after all. "Welcome to the 1980s," the smug prime minister told the nation that election eve.

"EQUIDISTANCE"

Pierre Trudeau's astonishing return to power gave him another chance to achieve one of his great goals: the return of the constitution from Westminster to Canada. The British North America Act of 1867 was a British document and, for lack of agreement between the federal and provincial governments on an amending process, Canada had been unable to "patriate" it. In a long, wearing negotiation culminating in 1981, Trudeau achieved his agreement, though without the acquiescence of the Parti Québécois government of Quebec. Moreover, he succeeded in embedding the Canadian Charter of Rights and Freedoms within the constitution. The Queen presided at the ceremony on Parliament Hill the next year to mark the formal coming into force of the new constitution. Amid the celebrations it was almost forgotten that another of the threads tying Britain and Canada together had been severed. By 1982, in fact, the monarchy was one of the very few that remained.

Britain had long since taken second place to the United States in Canadian eyes, especially after Jimmy Carter was succeeded by Ronald Reagan, the B-movie actor and former governor of California. Reagan was no intellectual, and his simplistic views were unlikely to meet much admiration from Pierre Trudeau. Still, Reagan liked Canada even if he knew nothing more about it than he had learned in movies featuring the Mounties. Canada's calm presence—Reagan did know that Canada was calm—meant that the United States need have no anxiety about its northern border.

Canada could nonetheless cause difficulties. Even before Reagan's team took over the White House, the Trudeau government had brought its National Energy Program into place, and the NEP violently roiled the waters of federal–provincial and Canadian–American relations. The details were complex, but in essence the program meshed two issues crucial to the United States. Washington was outraged first by the intention stated in the program to buy back foreign-owned, and especially American-owned, energy-producing firms in Canada. Foreign investment had been a bone of contention between the two countries for years, especially since the Trudeau government created the Foreign Investment Review Agency in 1973 in the full flush of enthusiasm for the "third option." Second, energy in particular was essential to Washington, and powerful U.S. multinational energy companies always had the administration's ear.

The NEP led some Americans to suggest darkly that Canada was a First World country with Third World economic policies. The State

Department protested against the NEP as "unnecessarily discrimina-
tory." There was little inclination to change the policy in Ottawa,
but world oil prices slipped back from their peaks in 1981, and the
next year prices began to fall. One of the major assumptions of the
NEP—that prices would continue to skyrocket—had failed to ma-
terialize and this left the policy in tatters. The Conservatives would
do away with the NEP shortly after they came into office in 1984.

The National Energy Program distressed the United States but
not so much as Trudeau's attitude towards the Cold War. The
Soviets had sent their army into Afghanistan in December 1979,
causing East–West tensions to skyrocket. The hawkish Reagan
wanted to confront the Soviet Union there and wherever else possible. When, for example, Soviet fighters shot down an errant Korean
Airlines B-747 jet in August 1983 near Sakhalin Island with huge loss
of life, the American response was fierce. Embarrassed, the Soviet
Union replied that the passenger jet was spying, and for a time tensions were high enough to threaten to explode into war. Apprised of
the intelligence data, Trudeau evidently believed that the United
States had purposely exploited the inexcusable Soviet error as a
deliberate slaughter of innocent travellers. American officials, he
said, "were trying to create another bone of contention with the
Soviets when they didn't have a leg to stand on."

The prime minister's attitude to the Soviet Union genuinely
angered those in the White House. Trudeau's speech in Moscow in 1971
had not been forgotten nor had his cozying up to Cuba's Fidel Castro
on a 1976 visit to Havana. His address at Notre Dame University in
South Bend, Indiana, in May 1982 also offended Washington mightily.
In it, he had suggested that Canada was edging towards "equidistance"
between the two superpowers. The prime minister was frustrated with
the Cold War and disillusioned with American and NATO intransigence,
which matched that of the Warsaw Pact. At the 1983 G-7 summit at
Williamsburg, Virginia, Trudeau pressed Reagan and the president's
British soulmate, Prime Minister Margaret Thatcher, so hard towards
accommodation with Moscow that they accused him of giving comfort
to the Russians.

Thatcher did not forget. In her memoirs, she remarked that
"Liberal leftists" such as Trudeau "seemed unable to grasp . . . that

Castro and Trudeau in Havana, 1976 (National Archives
of Canada, PA 136976)

such acts of brutality as the shooting down of a civilian aircraft were
by no means uncharacteristic of the Communist system itself." As so
often since the end of World War II, friends of Canada were beginning to find its rhetoric about peace insufferable.

"LET'S LOVE ONE ANOTHER"

Trudeau was, he realized by late 1983, very near the end of his political life. His party was low in the opinion polls, and he wanted the
retirement that he had chosen to abandon in early 1980. As he said
to some of his officials, "It is irresponsible for me to wait until I'm
out of power to do something," a comment provoked by watching
politicians such as former German chancellor Willy Brandt and u.s.
defense secretary Robert McNamara speak out for peace after their
influence had ended. In his view, Canada had to try to lower tensions, civilize the East–West dialogue, and help the world escape
from the Cold War.

The prime minister had a working group of bureaucrats prepare a list of possible actions, from which came the decision to advance a number of major proposals: a conference on nuclear arms control; a ban on testing and deployment of high-altitude weapons; acceleration of the pace of disarmament negotiations; and conversion of the Stockholm Conference on Security and Cooperation in Europe into a foreign ministers' meeting. The "Peace Initiative," as it was already being called, was to be aimed at the leaders, not at the people, and therefore involved a substantial program of travel in the last few months of 1983, to Europe, Asia, and the United States.

The initiative was launched in a major public address in Canada on 27 October. Ottawa had not consulted either its allies or its foes, as the prime minister worried that American approval might destroy the credibility of the initiative with the u.s.s.r. before it had a chance to get off the ground. Indeed, considering the truism that Canada–u.s.s.r. relations improved whenever Canada–u.s. relations were bad, the best chance for success with the Russians probably lay in a hostile response from Reagan. No one expected miracles, but Trudeau believed that the perils of continued hostility between the superpowers were such that chances had to be taken.

The prime minister's travels began in November; Western Europe was first on the agenda. None of the NATO leaders expressed overt enthusiasm. At the Commonwealth Prime Ministers' Conference in New Delhi and in a subsequent trip to Beijing, the auguries were marginally more hopeful. In December, the proposed visit to Moscow was postponed and eventually eliminated by the illness of General Secretary Yuri Andropov, Brezhnev's successor. Washington was next. The administration was busily touting the virtues of the Strategic Defense Initiative (Star Wars), and Reagan's White House was not much amused by the Canadian visitor. "Oh God," one official said, "Trudeau's at it again." Another senior State Department official sneeringly called the prime minister a leftist high on pot.

With Reagan, surprisingly, Trudeau had a measure of success. Cleverly he took the softest of soft lines. "Mr. President," he is reputed to have said, "your intentions are good and I agree with them wholly. You are a man of peace. You want peace through strength. Because of your policies the u.s. has regained its strength and self-confidence. But, Mr. President, your message is not getting through. The people think you want strength for its own sake, and that you are ready to accept the risks of war. You must communicate what you truly believe in." Some American observers believed that Trudeau treated Reagan as a simpleton. Perhaps this was so, but Canadian diplomats thought they detected some subsequent cooling in the president's belligerence.

After a final series of visits to East European capitals in January 1984, Trudeau shut down his initiative and declared victory. A brief visit to Moscow for Andropov's funeral won him a half-hour with Konstantin Chernenko, the already-ill successor, but there was no evident movement from a comatose Soviet leadership. In February, after "a walk in the snow," Trudeau announced his decision to leave politics as soon as a successor was chosen.

The Peace Initiative had accomplished little. Somehow, after sixteen years in power, after countless NATO meetings, G-7 summits, Commonwealth meetings, and UN sessions, Trudeau really did not seem to understand how great-power relations worked. He simply could not understand that the United States and the U.S.S.R. did not want the smaller states interfering in what they considered to be their affairs. Nor did he appear to realize that Canada, a small power without much clout, had little influence on the course of events.

In part, Canada's lack of weight could perhaps be attributed to Trudeau himself, who appeared to be more than a little quixotic to some of the leaders who had dealt with him over the years. The Peace Initiative might have had some impact if the groundwork had been properly laid in the usual intensive diplomatic negotiations stretching over months. That was not Trudeau's way, and neither the world situation nor his personal plans permitted it at any rate. Trudeau's message—characterized by a senior Canadian official as "Let's love one another"—fell largely on deaf ears.

Trudeau had nevertheless been right to try. Global tensions were serious enough to make war a real possibility. Something had to be done to halt the slide to conflict, and the Canadian leader's analysis of the global crisis was the right one. In fact, though probably not because of his efforts, the upward spiral of tension did ease. Kohl in West Germany, Craxi in Italy, and others began to urge accommodation, and both Thatcher and Reagan seemed to become more interested in talking with Moscow than in painting the u.s.s.r. as the "evil empire." Trudeau had taken risks for peace, and he deserved some of the credit when the world situation improved. When he was asked to assess the results of the Peace Initiative, he put the answer in his laconic way, complete with patented shrug, "Well, there was no war."

At the end of his career, then, Trudeau had become a committed "helpful fixer," a Canadian leader much like his predecessor. For a politician of such fixed principles on, for example, the constitution and nationalism, Trudeau had unexpectedly proved to be remarkably flexible in foreign policy. He had in fact turned full circle, from near indifference to the Soviets and boredom with the Cold War and NATO to the realization that Canada had to be concerned about the East–West struggle. If no effort were made to reduce tensions, then Canada could be destroyed along with the rest of the globe.

He made no similar pirouette in his attitude to the United States. His misunderstanding of the American giant remained unaltered, and despite his undoubted intelligence, Trudeau never seemed able to learn how to deal with the American eagle without provoking it.

Above all, perhaps, what mattered about Trudeau for the Canadian people was the notice he drew wherever he went. Often, it was because of his dating habits; too often, it was his outrageous behaviour abroad. Most frequently, however, world leaders and the global media viewed Trudeau as a sensible advocate of important ideas. His peace initiative may have been as naïve as some said, but the idea that the race to war had to be checked was correct. His belief that the developed world had to do more for the less developed nations was similarly right, and Trudeau won and kept the respect and affection of Third World leaders. Very simply, he mattered in a way that few Canadian leaders had mattered, and this flattered Canadians. Even those who detested the man had to recognize that he cut a figure in world affairs. Trudeau mattered and so, therefore, did Canada and Canadians.

CHAPTER ELEVEN

A Shrinking Global Precinct, 1984–1993

IERRE TRUDEAU had had his difficulties with the United States. His attitudes to NATO, recognition of China, the Soviet Union, and how best to react to the threat of nuclear war had put him in constant confrontation with presidents from Nixon to Reagan, and there is no doubt that his years in office had troubled the ordinarily calm waters of Canadian–American relations.

Canadians jealously guarded their independence from the United States, and they rather liked the idea of a prime minister who had no hesitation in plucking tail feathers from the American eagle. It suggested strength of mind and spirit. Paradoxically, they also wanted their leaders to get on with their American counterparts, to be seen to be good and loyal allies in the Cold War. The love–hate relationship that so characterized Canadian views of the United States clearly also affected the public's estimation of links between president and prime minister.

Trudeau was succeeded briefly by John Turner as prime minister, but Turner, ill advised and out of practice in the political game since his resignation from Cabinet in 1976, promptly put the country into an election and lost decisively as Brian Mulroney and the Progressive Conservative Party rolled to a huge majority. Mulroney was a bilingual Quebecer of wholly Irish extraction and he had never been a student of foreign policy. His youth had been spent in a company town that had headquarters in the United States, however, and his last employment before entering politics was as head of a branch-plant corporation. He understood Americans better than Trudeau ever had. The new leader admired the energy, drive, and power of the United States, and he lost no time in proclaiming his goal of "good relations, super relations" with the United States. This was one promise that Prime Minister Mulroney would not fail to carry out.

COLD WARRING

One of the issues at the forefront of Mulroney's tenure, defence, was of crucial importance to Canada–United States relations. The armed forces by the end of the Liberal mandate in 1984 were in parlous condition. The long Liberal regime had seen unification and its wrenching effects. This had been followed, late in the 1960s, by the creation of French-language units and a drive to make as many officers as possible bilingual. Complaints within the military grew loud that incompetents were being promoted on the strength of their linguistic fluency. As the 1980s got underway, public pressure grew to open the military up to women. The Royal Military College took in women as cadets, female recruits in the services did basic training almost as rigorous as that given men, and over the decade the list of specialties open only to males shrank. By the end of the 1980s, homosexuality ceased being a bar to military service. Such changes reflected the realities of Canadian life in the late twentieth century, but there was no hiding that all placed a strain on the armed forces.

However serious these social issues were to the Canadian Forces, they paled beside the problems of equipment and personnel strength. The eighty-two thousand personnel in the unified forces had out-of-date equipment. The problem was most severe in the navy, whose twenty-three ships seemed held together mostly by rust. Electronic equipment on some ships was so old that vacuum tubes had to be purchased in Eastern Europe, the only place where they were still manufactured. The Liberals had launched a six-frigate building program in 1977, but it would be years before they were ready. The air force, with CF-18 aircraft coming into service, was in slightly better condition, though transport capabilities were woefully weak and the condition of the radar warning lines in northern Canada was deficient enough to irritate the Pentagon, still fearful of a Soviet attack across the pole. The army was also suffering equipment problems, its tanks outdated, its armoured personnel carriers and trucks approaching obsolescence, and its defences against attacking aircraft still based on World War II technology. Late in the 1970s, the Liberals had pledged to NATO that Canada would increase spending by 3 percent a year, a promise faithfully carried out, but fifteen years of neglect still had to be overcome.

The Mulroney government initially seemed serious about making the necessary renovations, much to the delight of the Reagan administration, the Pentagon, and the hawkish U.S. ambassador to Canada. Campaign promises had been fulsome and the new defence minister, Nova Scotia MP Robert Coates, intended to undo unification. Almost his first act was to direct that new uniforms be prepared for each of the services ("Coates of many colours," critics jeered), an expensive use of scarce dollars that upset the military chiefs. Coates also pledged to increase the size of the forces and to add six more frigates to the 1977 construction program, but financial realities and budget deficits soon intervened. Instead of being increased, the defence budget was cut by $154 million to $9.37 billion in the first Tory financial statement. This was only the first shock for the armed forces and for the Reagan administration. Certainly, Coates's embarrassment was severe; it became even more so when a personal indiscretion led to his ouster from the Cabinet.

His successor, Yukon MP Erik Nielsen, was one of the most influential figures in the government as a tough party loyalist, a member of all key Cabinet committees, and the minister in charge of a powerful task force looking at ways to save money. Within days of taking office, Nielsen announced an increase of twelve hundred troops to serve with the brigade in NATO.

The next item on the agenda was an overhaul of continental radar defences. The Distant Early Warning Line, completed in the late 1950s, was outmoded, destined to be shut down in July 1993— and to leave behind a massive environmental clean-up job. Its replacement, the North Warning System (NWS), was designed to protect against the possibility of attack from Soviet air-launched

Cruise missiles. The project was scheduled to cost $7–8 billion, of which Canada's share would be approximately $1.2 billion; operating costs were expected to run to $130 millon a year. Marked for completion in 1994, the NWS was to include a mix of fifty-four long- and short-range radar sites, some staffed, some not, along the 70th parallel, and four forward bases in the high Arctic for CF-18 jet fighters. There was one substantial gain for Canada in this expensive system: unlike the DEW line, whose operators were wholly American, the NWS bases in Canada were under Canadian control.*

The first days of Nielsen's tenure were, therefore, as one book on the Mulroney government observed, "seventh heaven at National Defence Headquarters." At the Pentagon, too. The illusion was brief. Nielsen turned out to be as politically trouble prone as his predecessor, and the budget for 1986–1987 was increased by only 2.75 percent, less than inflation and less than the Liberals' 3 percent.

Nielsen soon was gone and his replacement, the young Perrin Beatty, had to preside over a military once again restive and discouraged. Beatty did issue a white paper in 1987, the first in almost two decades, but the extreme anti-Soviet language of its paragraphs on the Cold War did not sit well with a public that could see, even if the government could not, that the regime of Soviet leader Mikhail Gorbachev was different from its rigid, gerontocratic predecessors.

Beatty's announcement that Canada was to acquire nuclear submarines to enforce Canadian sovereignty in the Arctic was similarly ill received. The rationale gave critics a field day. Had Beatty and his advisers made the case that nuclear submarines were the best defence against Soviet underwater craft, public debate might at least have been conducted on rational terms. By hinting that a Canadian undersea fleet could somehow stop the United States Navy from using the Arctic, Beatty fell into something close to ridicule. What would happen, editorialists and others asked, if a Canadian boat encountered a USN submarine in Canadian water or ice? Would it

---

*The collapse of the Soviet Union, however, led the Pentagon to cancel or delay several components of the NWS and to refuse to pick up the American share of construction costs for the forward air bases.

sink it? There was, of course, no answer. Nuclear submarines, much desired by the navy and by defence contractors, were never acquired, becoming yet another victim of budget cuts.

"AN UNEASY CHAOS"

The Soviet Union itself soon disappeared. Gorbachev had come to power in 1984, and he could not hold the economically crippled giant together. The u.s.s.r. turned out to be a military superpower supported by a Third World economy. The irony of Gorbachev's position was to have the nominal power to repair the financial and supply problems of his country while knowing that they were essentially unresolvable under an economy hopelessly inefficient from the top down.

All at once, in the most startling events since 1945, the Berlin Wall tumbled down and Germany re-united, the Warsaw Pact dissolved as the Eastern European satellites seized their independence, and the Soviet Union collapsed into a collection of fractious, squabbling states. The years from 1989 to 1991 moved at blurring speed as history accelerated; the Cold War was in place at the beginning of this short period and gone by the end.

Canada was quick to recognize the new nations that emerged from the fractured u.s.s.r. Indeed, Mulroney broke the Western consensus against hurried recognition when, in a politically inspired gesture that won plaudits from Ukrainian Canadians, Canada became the first nation to recognize the independent Ukraine in December 1991. The post–World War II era was over, and Western nations soon began to provide very large sums in aid to their former adversary to prevent total breakdown. (Canada promised $2.6 billion in aid and credits to Russia.) The West was the undoubted victor in the Cold War.

The end of the "terrifying stability" of the Cold War with the Soviet Union was replaced, as one diplomat said, with "an uneasy chaos." Although substantial progress had been made on nuclear disarmament as a result of complex superpower negotiations over many years, for example, Soviet disintegration did not terminate the nuclear threat. Stockpiles more than large enough to incinerate the globe remained. Nuclear powers such as China and France were not party to the superpower arrangements, and nations such as Israel, South Africa, and India probably had nuclear weapons at the ready. Other states—Pakistan, Iran, Iraq, and North Korea among them—sought to develop nuclear capability. Moreover, new nations emerging out of the old u.s.s.r., such as Ukraine and Kazakhstan had suddenly become independent nuclear powers and claimed not to be bound by old pacts reached between the u.s.s.r. and the United States.

The changed world situation did not stop international trade in conventional arms. The Middle East, Southeast Asia, and Africa all continued to absorb billions of dollars in advanced weapons as old rivals sensed an opportunity and newly freed peoples sought to settle old scores. Competing with nations from both the old Warsaw Pact and the West, and despite repeated internal and international protestations of virtue, Canada did its best to capture as much of this business as possible. Two-thirds of Canadian sales of military equipment went to the Middle East in 1992; Saudi Arabia purchased $227 million worth, mostly in armoured vehicles. Arms sales to European nations fell by 30 percent in the same year, however, while such trade to the United States amounted to approximately $700 million.

Canadian opponents of arms sales argued that they simply fuelled global tensions. As even the Czech Republic under humanist writer President Vaclav Havel discovered, however, pledging to halt arms sales abroad was "naïve." "Other countries are trying to fill our former markets," one senior Czech official said, "and we have factory capacity that is not being fully used." Ottawa could have said the same thing. The only way to tackle the problem of the global arms trade was with concerted global action. To their credit, Canadian officials tried to press for this, but predictably without success. Some problems appeared insoluble.

What now for NORAD, NATO, and Canada's contribution to the military arms of the Western alliance? NORAD was renewed after the Soviet collapse, and work on the suddenly irrelevant North Warning System went on slowly. The "war on drugs," declared by the United States administration and also pursued in Canada, gave the air defence system a kind of half-life, as interceptors attempted to apprehend airborne cocaine smugglers. Forty-four aircraft (four in Canada) stood on alert in mid-1993, ready for takeoff on five minutes' notice. Even if a smuggler were detected, the supersonic jets flew much too fast to get tail numbers from suspicious aircraft. Still, NORAD had a role of sorts.

When the Mulroney government reconsidered its troop commitments to NATO in Europe, however, it did not take long to announce major reductions. Without consulting its NATO allies, the Conservatives in 1992 announced a total withdrawal of Canadian forces from Europe, a process completed in July 1993 at a projected budgetary saving of $2.2 billion. Canada was now "committed but not present" insofar as NATO was concerned. The Germans strongly protested the Canadian withdrawal, however, and Chancellor Helmut Kohl personally appealed to Mulroney to keep at least some troops in the alliance for fear that the Americans might seize on Canadian cutbacks as an excuse for speeding their own.

There is no doubt that the public supported these defence cuts. Much less support could be found for two billion-dollar helicopter acquisition contracts that followed the end of the Cold War. A strong case could have been made—though almost no one made it—that Canada had a continuing stake in a stable Europe. The frozen stability of the Cold War had suddenly been replaced by nationalism and spreading civil wars, and this was the moment at which Canada chose to retreat to North America. NATO had begun to consider admitting former Warsaw Pact adversaries and was groping for a constructive role. A small military contribution was both necessary and justifiable.

WARMAKING AND PEACEKEEPING

The Canadian Forces were without an enemy. Their strength of just over eighty thousand was approximately the same as it had been when Mulroney first came to power, and their equipment was still obsolescent, but paradoxically they had their highest public profile in decades. The reasons were twofold: war against Iraq in 1990–1991 and United Nations peacekeeping.

When Iraq invaded Kuwait in the summer of 1990 in as clear an act of undoubted aggression as the world had witnessed since 1945, Canadian public opinion was sorely divided. The Middle East was an area of interest and concern to countless Canadians, but the Kuwaitis, oil-rich and feudal, were no one's favourites. The Iraqis, moreover, had until 1988 been thought to be doing the work of the West, thanks to their eight-year long and extremely costly war against fundamentalist and anti-Western Iran. Besides, some commentators said, the invasion was just about oil, and oil was almost by definition evil, especially when Canada did not import petroleum from Kuwait.

President George Bush did not see it this way. Calling for a "new world order," which under the tutelage of the one remaining superpower would hit out at aggressor nations, the president stage-managed a multinational response. His actions eventually brought the UN Security Council, at last liberated from the paralysis caused by the Cold War, to agree with the United States. Tough economic sanctions were imposed on Iraq with the support of Russia and the acquiescence of China. Soon a great military coalition was in the field, massing its strength in Saudi Arabia under American leadership and with the authority of a United Nations mandate.

Bush asked Canada to contribute to the military force, and on 10 August the prime minister denounced Iraq's flagrant "violation of international law." Canada's reputation in the world was based on its expertise in peacekeeping, Mulroney said, but this "does not remove from us the responsibility" to respond to threats and attacks on other nations. To that end, Canada would send two destroyers and a supply ship to the Persian Gulf. The vessels were outdated and poorly armed, but they demonstrated a degree of commitment to the UN and U.S. effort. They were soon followed by a squadron of CF-18s, ground troops to protect it, and a field hospital.

Liberals and New Democrats turned themselves inside out trying to endorse sanctions but to oppose both a resort to force and any Canadian commitment. After the government had dispatched ships and aircraft and had supported the American resolution at the Security Council to authorize the use of arms to drive Iraq out of Kuwait, the opposition inconsistently continued to argue against force while professing to back the service members in the Gulf region. "To oppose this war," NDP leader Audrey McLaughlin said, "is not to oppose the United Nations; it is to oppose a militaristic vision of the United Nations." Charlotte Gray wrote in *Saturday Night* magazine that the anti-participationist position contained a mixture of "idealism, legalism, internationalism, and kneejerk anti-Americanism," though the last was probably the predominant attitude. To many Canadians, anything the United States did was bound to be wrong.

The war in January and February 1991 was short and brutal. A massive air campaign knocked out Iraqi command-and-control installations and cowed the enemy troops, and a short, sharp ground attack liberated Kuwait and destroyed most of the Iraqi military. The Canadian navy and air force played their small parts very creditably, and the public basked in the virtually bloodless victory. Only the Iraqis suffered terrible casualties.

By participating in a war, even a semi-United Nations war, Canada was perhaps in danger of destroying its reputation and value as a "disinterested" peacekeeper. Peacekeeping had initially been a minor and subsidiary role for the Canadian Forces. In the early 1950s, it ordinarily required only a few officers; by the time of the Suez Crisis, it absorbed larger numbers; and Cyprus required an infantry battalion that the army believed it could ill afford. Peacekeeping commitments also dragged on—Canada's role in Cyprus lasted from 1964 to 1993—and multiplied. In 1993, Canada had observers or units on UN service in Angola, Iraq–Kuwait, El Salvador, Mozambique, Cambodia, Somalia, the former Yugoslavia, Rwanda–Uganda, Cyprus, the Sahara, and on Israeli–Arab borders. At its peak, the total was some forty-five hundred personnel: 10 percent of all the world's troops on UN service and almost 5 percent of the Canadian military's strength.

Participation in the war against Iraq, it turned out, did not interfere with this proud tradition of UN service. The United Nations had always been glad to use Canadian personnel on peacekeeping. As a Western power and a NATO member that had always thought in terms of fighting wars overseas, Canada had capacities in logistics, communications, and air transport that other small nations did not, and its personnel were well-trained professionals. Those qualities remained even if Canada had been unmasked as a "warmonger" by the Gulf War. Within weeks of the end of the Gulf War, Canada was asked to send an engineer unit to clear mines along the Iraq–Kuwait border as part of a United Nations peacekeeping force. Other invitations followed for troops in the Western Sahara, in Cambodia, in Rwanda–Uganda, and in the former Yugoslavia. United Nations needs seemed endless and demands for Canadian participation in peacekeeping equally so. It was even possible that the wartime military efficiency demonstrated by the Canadians in the Gulf increased UN interest in using the country's armed forces as peacekeepers.

The Canadian Forces were delighted with these calls for troops. With no enemy to prepare against after the demise of the U.S.S.R., peacekeeping provided a credible, necessary justification for the continuation of respectable armed forces despite budget deficits. Moreover, the Canadian public greatly admired peacekeeping and the blue berets, so much so that the federal government used peacekeeping as a major part of its unsuccessful "feel good" campaign during the October 1992 constitutional referendum, dedicating a massive monument in Ottawa to commemorate Canadian peacekeepers.

The risks in peacekeeping became clear in 1992, when Canada dispatched peacekeepers to the former Yugoslavia, a country that had fractionalized at the end of the Cold War and fallen into a vicious, internecine civil war. The rights and wrongs of the issues were complex but the UN presence seemed to provide a cover for genocide, euphemistically referred to as "ethnic cleansing," as Croats, Serbs, and Moslems tried to set up their own states and drive one another out of territory they claimed as their own. The UN presence, most notably in Bosnia, failed to provide sufficient reason for antagonists not to fire. Some came to believe that the UN flag even provided an incentive by giving enhanced television coverage to one side or another. Canadians suffered casualties because their equipment, not least their almost thirty-year-old armoured personnel carriers, was unable to withstand the modern armaments in the hands of a polyglot militia.

The Somali experience reinforced the lesson. There was for all practical purposes no Somalian government, at least none that controlled any territory, and the United Nations was trying to impose law and administration, to create the infrastructure of a modern state

Peacekeeper: Major General Lewis MacKenzie, chief of staff
of the UN force in the former Yugoslavia, 1992 (Canapress Photo
Service—Morten Hvaal)

where none existed. For one of the few times in its history, the United
States sent troops on a UN mission, and the Americans dominated the
scene—and the media coverage. They called it peacekeeping, but it
was not. The task quickly bogged down, first into clan warfare and
then into a small war between UN forces and local warlords. The
Canadian unit in northern Somali was out of the line of fire, happily,
but it quickly found itself in hot water nonetheless, its good work forgotten as cases of murder, torture, and racial incidents erupted. The
Canadians soon left, but the court-martials for these offences continued, reminding the public that peacekeeping could have a dark side.

The new post-Cold War order had dangers, in other words. It
was also extremely costly. The Canadian government expended $226
million in direct costs in 1993–1994, but the total bill to keep more
than two thousand men and women in the former Yugoslavia alone
was more than $1 billion when pay and other costs were factored in.
What is more, the United Nations proved hopelessly inefficient in
organizing and administering peacekeeping.

Peacekeeping also raised problems for the country's small army, and especially its hard-pressed infantry. They numbered no more than five thousand soldiers all told, and had difficulty providing enough troops for simultaneous peacekeeping operations in Cyprus, Somalia, and Yugoslavia while following the usual six-month rotation policy. Reservists were pressed into use but this source, given its tiny size and generally inadequate training, was strictly limited. The demands of peacekeeping had begun to outstrip personnel and budgetary limitations.

The simple truth was that Canada had taken on too much, and the government soon would be obliged to tell the United Nations that it could not accept another request, however much this might distress public opinion. In fact, to refuse a request might even be a good thing, for it would liberate Ottawa from the pressure to maintain Canada's perfect record of having served in every UN (and non-UN) peacekeeping operation. Governments are supposed to be capable of rational decision making, and the Canadian automatic response of sending in the peacekeepers was no longer adequate as a substitute for a clearly thought out policy, especially when peacekeeping had taken on a wholly new meaning.

"FROM GLOBALISM TO CONTINENTALISM"

Prime Minister Mulroney proved to be as active as any of his predecessors in playing global diplomacy. Indeed, because his political rival, former party leader and prime minister Joe Clark, was secretary of state for external affairs, elements of tension existed between the Prime Minister's Office and the Department of External Affairs. Part of the difficulty came from Clark's less-than-surefooted early handling of the portfolio. The minister initially tended to be secretive and to mistrust diplomats, whom he believed had caused his government problems in 1979–1980. The ministerial staff was therefore larger than usual and far more powerful, and communication between the minister and his chief civil servant was less frequent than in the past. The undersecretary, Marcel Massé, had worked closely with Clark when he was prime minister but their relationship five years later simply did not work well.

The department was also experiencing organizational problems of a serious kind, much exacerbated by financial cutbacks. Trudeau's government in 1982 had combined the trade policy and promotion activities of the Department of Industry, Trade, and Commerce and the responsibility for immigration under an expanded Department of External Affairs with three ministers. The Pearson Building, headquarters of the Department of External Affairs, therefore experienced terrific space problems. It was also difficult to work out pecking orders at home and abroad. Soon some within the department began to complain loudly that former trade commissioners were getting too many ambassadorial appointments, only lightly masking their concern that commerce was coming to outweigh diplomacy abroad.

At the same time, the Mulroney government greatly exceeded every previous administration, even Trudeau's much longer one, in its appointment of non-professionals to diplomatic posts. To Paris went Lucien Bouchard, a Mulroney crony from his days at Université Laval; to London went Fredrik Eaton, the department-store magnate; and so on down to minor posts and consulates. Even the 1984 appointment of former Ontario NDP leader Stephen Lewis as ambassador to the United Nations was in this political category; surprise and praise at the nomination of the social-democratic Lewis was so pronounced that it helped camouflage a flood of other patronage postings. Lewis at least carved out a reputation for himself, something that could not be said of most other non-professional appointments.

Making matters worse for external affairs officers were cutbacks in Canadian representation abroad. In the early 1980s, the country had 124 embassies and consulates, located in 85 nations. After repeated cuts in expenditures, this had been reduced to 106 posts in 77 countries by 1993, and before the end of the year Canada and Australia announced plans to share consular and other services around the world. In London's Trafalgar Square, Canada House closed its library, and the high commission began to move all government operations

to Macdonald House, an undistinguished building located with preg-
nant symbolism directly across Grosvenor Square from the United
States embassy. The press office in Bonn shut down, as did Canada's
tourist office in Germany. Radio Canada International was savaged
by repeated budget cuts, eliminating programming in German,
Japanese, Hungarian, Polish, Czech, and Portuguese. Joe Clark,
despite his increasingly favourable press coverage, was presiding over
a rapidly shrinking global precinct in a meaner world.

The prime minister was not averse to twisting the knife on occasion. In 1985, Clark publicly expressed concern that President
Ronald Reagan had imposed a ban on trade with Nicaragua and its
leftist Sandinista government. With a red-faced Clark made to stand
silently at his side, Mulroney promptly declared that he was not
unhappy over the failure to advise Canada of the u.s. move: "Why
would they call us up to tell us something or ask our advice when
they knew our answer in advance?"

To his credit, Clark gradually mastered his portfolio, and tried
hard to make his relationship with Mulroney work. The clumsiness
that had characterized his first years in external affairs disappeared,
while that of ministers closer to the prime minster appeared to
increase. Joe Clark became one of the administration's most competent members. As a tribute to Clark's skills Mulroney pulled him
from the portfolio and put him in charge of the even more delicate
constitutional questions that followed the failure of the Meech Lake
Accord. His replacement was Barbara McDougall, a Toronto MP
often considered a potential successor to Mulroney. Her performance as secretary of state for external affairs, however, quickly
demonstrated that this portfolio required a cool head and global
experience. McDougall's suggestion that Canada might recognize
Soviet plotters who tried—and quickly failed—to oust Gorbachev
was a gaffe of major proportions.

Mulroney himself acquired international experience and standing. He travelled annually to the G-7 summits of leaders of the seven
major industrial economies (not the seven *largest* GNPs, as many mis-
takenly believed, for countries such as China, Russia, India, and
Brazil had larger total domestic production than Canada by the early
1990s). Scarcely a meeting passed at which the prime minister's aides

did not claim for him an important—no, vital—role. At his first summit in 1985, Mulroney was touted as having helped resolve a dispute between Reagan and French president François Mitterand, which played well in Canada until the French brutally remarked that the bilingual Canadian leader had done nothing more than translate for the unilingual presidents. Years later, Mulroney's officials suggested that his understanding of Mitterand's psychology and political problems helped greatly in bringing the French leader into line with President George Bush over policy during the crisis that preceded the Gulf War.

Mulroney also established close friendships with the German and French leaders; Chancellor Kohl of Germany publicly referred to "my friend Brian," and the warmth of some other leaders was evidently genuine. It is nonetheless unclear what benefits this brought for Canada, as fellow feeling for the prime minister was far from universal. Britain's Margaret Thatcher, as her acerbic memoirs demonstrated, was no fan. She deeply resented Mulroney's efforts to press her to support Commonwealth sanctions against South Africa in 1985.

Mulroney was not deterred, to his credit, and Canada maintained its vigorous pressure on South Africa. Speaking at the United Nations in 1985, the prime minister said, "Only one country has established colour as the hallmark of systematic inequality and oppression," and he backed his words with deeds. Even Stephen Lewis, Mulroney's choice for UN ambassador but not an admirer of his, remarked, "I must give him credit for his singlemindedness." That trait led Mulroney to invite the recently freed leader of the African National Congress, Nelson Mandela, to address Parliament in 1990. Shortly after Mulroney's resignation as prime minister, sanctions on trade with South Africa were finally lifted, a tribute in part to the genuine efforts of the de Klerk government to move the country towards democracy.

The prime minister also participated actively in meetings of *la francophonie*. Quebec continued to play a major part in the organization of French-speaking nations, and although Premier Robert Bourassa and Mulroney were friends and political allies, the premier's government made occasional efforts to score political points at the expense of Ottawa. In 1985, Ottawa and Quebec City had agreed that

Quebec could have a special but not independent status within the Canadian delegation to *la francophonie*. Quebec City would be able to participate directly in discussions on culture and education but not on matters under exclusive federal jurisdiction, such as global economic questions and international affairs. As an "interested observer," however, Quebec could help to shape the Canadian position on these areas prior to speeches or interventions at the conference. At the Paris meetings in February 1986, Bourassa promptly violated the understanding by calling for "a new Marshall Plan" to distribute surplus foodstuffs from the European Community to Africa. An angry Mulroney complained about being "blindsided," but the "diplomatic triumph" was, as Bourassa declared, Quebec's. The old game went on regardless of which party was in power in Quebec City.

It was business as usual in federal government handling of foreign aid, too. A large bureaucracy had grown up in Ottawa to direct official development assistance. It centred on two organizations: the Canadian International Development Agency, created in 1968 to administer projects; and the International Development Research Centre, instituted in 1978 by Trudeau to foster research on the subject (and to provide a job for his former aide, Ivan Head). The United Nations target for aid from First World nations was .7 percent of GNP per year; Pierre Trudeau had pegged that figure as his government's target, and in 1975 Canadian aid amounted to .52 percent, the closest Canada ever came. Under Mulroney, aid decreased substantially, to .43 percent of GNP in 1992. Cuts to the Official Development Assistance sector (the government term for its foreign aid) were to total $4.6 billion over a seven-year period projected to end in 1994–1995. Even the $1 billion in aid that survived, channelled through CIDA, was sure to be reduced further as the federal government scrambled to slash its deficit; additional cuts of 10 percent a year were planned for 1993–1994 and 1994–1995.

Making matters worse was the widespread sense that CIDA was inefficient, wrapped in red tape, and more concerned with protecting its shrinking staff and budget than serving its client states. The auditor general reported in early 1994 that the agency contracted out too much work and that CIDA personnel, rotating from one assignment to another, rarely saw the completion of projects for which they were responsible. Because staff members dealt with unfamiliar subjects in strange cultures, the auditor general said, "they inevitably will be focused on desk administration and buried in paper rather than substantially involved in generating development results." Critiques of that sort did nothing to build support for foreign aid.

More inward-looking than hitherto, Canadians did not seem to care very much that aid was decreasing. Opinion polls demonstrated that 60 percent believed Canada spent either the right amount or not enough on aid, but very few seemed willing to see hard-pressed domestic programs reduced in order to put more towards the intractable problems of the Third World. Nonetheless, whenever television showed starving children in Africa, as it did all too frequently, or the victims of civil war in Bosnia, the Canadian government and citizens remained quick to offer financial and material assistance.

The public also exhibited a natural human desire to help the refugees created by these civil wars and bloody conflicts. The Canadian immigration system, however, had become creaky in administration and more than a little porous. Family reunification policies seemed to some citizens to allow one individual to bring large, extended families to Canada. There were public concerns that immigration was changing the face of the cities and swelling welfare rolls. These claims were denounced as racist by immigration advocates, who revelled in the increase of non-European immigration to Canada to more than 60 percent of the total by the mid-1980s. Exacerbating the issue, several cases in which boatloads of "refugees" claiming to be fleeing persecution literally washed up on Canadian shores were highly publicized. Critics claimed that these people were "economic migrants" seeking a better life in Canada and doing nothing so much as jumping the queue to get ahead of others who had applied for immigration in the normal fashion.

The issue of granting refugee status became a legal and political one, pitting the humanitarian impulse and the Canadian Charter of Rights and Freedoms against concerns both that the system be fair and that Canada could not afford to accept as many immigrants as it did. By 1992, in the midst of a major economic downturn, the government had begun to toughen its regulations, fearful that Canada alone among the industrialized nations would provide a safe haven for refugees at a time when European nations and the United States were erecting barriers.

Under Mulroney, Canada finally moved to join the Organization of American States (OAS). For years, Canadians had turned their backs on the rest of the Americas, which appeared from north of the 49th parallel to be largely a collection of weak countries run by dictatorial militaries. Supporters of the OAS argued that Canada was part of the western hemisphere and had to recognize its responsibility to assist in democratization; opponents suggested that the OAS was an American puppet organization and membership would merely oblige Canada to follow the U.S. lead in yet another international forum. Mulroney decided that the benefits outweighed the risks, and in 1990 Canada finally filled the seat that had remained empty from the time the Pan-American Union was formed.

It did not take long before critics' fears were realized. Later in 1990, United States forces invaded Panama with the aim of capturing the country's president, Manuel Noriega, a reputed drug profiteer. The brief invasion produced many civilian casualties, but it achieved its aim. The prime minister, while expressing regret for the use of force, lent his support to President George Bush's action. Mulroney may well have acted in the same way if Canada had remained outside the Organization of American States, but opponents were quick to draw the connection.

Global foreign policy mattered in the Mulroney years, but to a quite remarkable degree its importance became secondary to relations with the United States. Under the Conservatives, one external affairs official lamented, "there's been a tremendous shift away from globalism to continentalism . . . [and] the end of Pearsonian internationalism." In this interpretation, the years after 1984 marked a decisive shift in Canadian history. For the first time Canada apparently cast its lot wholly with the United States. As we have seen, the government was still interested in the world and its problems, but it was undoubtedly focussed now on Washington first and hemispheric concerns throughout the Americas next, as missions overseas were slashed and troops pulled back to Canada. Under Mulroney, Canada seemed to abandon its traditional search for counterweights to American power and influence.

READY, AYE READY

Mulroney believed that relations with the United States were in a terrible state when he took power in 1984. The chill between the previous Canadian government and successive American administrations probably was and has been exaggerated in accounts then and since, but unquestionably Reagan and his government looked on Canada under Trudeau with a jaundiced eye. Mulroney, a Conservative, believed that he could get on better with like-minded Republicans than the Liberal Trudeau had, and he was right, as was obvious even when he was in opposition. When the United States sent troops into the Caribbean island of Grenada in 1983 to block a bloodbath between Marxist factions, for example, Trudeau's response had been cool, not least because Canada had not even been given the courtesy of advance notice. The Conservative leader's reaction was much warmer: "If our friends need the benefit of the doubt from time to time, so be it." "Ready, aye ready," he seemed to say.

Once in power, Mulroney moved quickly to make a good impression on the White House and corporate America. He told New York business leaders that Canada was open for investment once more, demonstrating his goodwill by gutting the Foreign Investment Review Agency (FIRA) and the National Energy Program. FIRA, created in 1973 to monitor foreign investment in Canada, had the power to block takeovers or to impose conditions upon them. Corporate investors, and not only American ones, deeply resented the delays, although they were almost always the only weapon that FIRA employed. Mulroney transformed the mandate of the agency to encourage investment and altered its name to Investment Canada. Foreign investment continued to climb, reaching $134.7 billion by 1987. Direct investment, rather than simple shareholdings or portfolio investment, rose rapidly. The NEP was similarly dismantled, again a source of gratification in Washington and also in Alberta, the major oil-producing province.

The new mood was much in evidence at President Reagan's first visit to Mulroney's Canada in 1985. When the freshly elected president had come to Ottawa in 1981, jeering protesters had forced Prime Minister Trudeau to ask the crowd to desist so that the visitor could speak. Not in Quebec City in 1985 at the "Shamrock Summit," so called because the prime minister and the president made much of their Irish origins. A carefully stage-managed love fest, the brief session saw the two leaders agree to refurbish the North Warning System at a cost of $7 billion and to begin—too slowly for Mulroney and for Canadian opinion—to tackle the problem of acid rain caused by toxic smokestack emissions drifting north across the boundary. The decisions were important, but most striking was the artificial and deliberately created bonhomie of the meeting.

The contrast with the frigid politeness of the previous regime was sharp, nowhere more so than in the televised gala performance when Mulroney and his wife drew an obviously reluctant Reagan onto the stage to croon a mawkish duo of "When Irish Eyes Are Smiling." To Mulroney, oblivious of the way this scene smacked of undignified abuse of both his visitor and the airwaves, this was the sign that he and his nation had arrived. Afterwards, Canadians viewed their

The Shamrock Summit, 1985, Mulroney and Reagan in the lead
(Canapress Photo Service—Paul Chiasson)

prime minister's efforts to foster relations with the United States with increasing suspicion. For many, the episode forever destroyed Mulroney's credibility. Elected in part to bring order and friendship back into Canada–United States relations, the government now paid a high price for appearing to go too far too fast.

The prime minister nevertheless recognized that the public, while it wanted good relations with the United States, did not wish Canadians to appear supine. Care was therefore needed in deciding how to react to the Strategic Defense Initiative, a grandiose and costly scheme of Reagan's to develop a defence system to protect the United States from missile attack. SDI, or Star Wars as it was popularly known, demanded a massive research effort, and the plan, not to say the prospect of official Canadian participation, stirred a substantial outcry. Discreet inquiries revealed that the Pentagon wanted to go it alone and that the potential benefits to Canadian researchers were very small. Mulroney could decline any government role with good grace, though he was careful not to rule out corporate participation. The decision, announced in September 1985, was praised by peace groups, and even the United States government seemed completely unperturbed.

Another issue, Canadian sovereignty in the North, was harder to massage. The United States had never fully accepted Canada's claim to control the entire Arctic archipelago. Most especially, as a world naval power, the United States refused to recognize the Northwest Passage as Canadian internal waters; to Washington, the passage was an international strait open to all. Conflict over the route had first arisen in 1969 after the SS *Manhattan*, a giant oil tanker, had tested the feasibility of using the passage.

In the summer of 1985, the U.S. Coast Guard proposed to send its vessel, the *Polar Sea*, through the ice. When the story belatedly broke in the Canadian press, both governments hurried to escape from a potential crisis that threatened to unleash an unwanted nationalist uproar in Canada. The Americans agreed that Canadian observers could sail on the *Polar Sea*, and they pledged to abide by the Arctic Waters Pollution Act of 1969 (an important concession, because the Coast Guard ship was an oil-leaking tub). In return, although the United States had studiously refused to ask Canadian permission for the voyage, Canada duly granted it.

Joe Clark's new pet (Edd Uluschak)

In September, the Cabinet passed an order-in-council formally setting out its jurisdiction over the whole of the Arctic. Promises quickly followed that the country would expand its military presence in the Arctic and build a giant icebreaker, which would at last let Canada get into its own waters all year round. The plan for the icebreaker was scrapped sometime later, another victim of the budget deficit, but something useful did emerge more than two years afterwards. In January 1988, after hard bargaining, Canada and the United States signed an agreement on Arctic co-operation, which required Canadian consent prior to any voyage by American vessels.

AFTER FTA, DO WE HAFTA NAFTA?

The squabbling over SDI and the *Polar Sea* demonstrated that Canadians' concerns over their place in North America were once again mounting. Government response to these questions had been calculated to demonstrate that Ottawa was no patsy, a matter of crucial importance because in September 1985, as both issues were at their peak, Prime Minister Mulroney announced his government's intention to enter into negotiations with Washington for a free trade agreement.

No issue was more potent. Free trade had been in place for a decade from the mid-1850s, and the Reciprocity Treaty of 1854 had been viewed as a great success in Canada. Successive efforts to replicate that experience foundered, as we have seen, not simply on American protectionism but on Canadian nationalism. Free trade was seen as a threat of the most serious kind. By focussing on north–south trade, it endangered the fragile east–west links that tied Canada together, appearing to put the whole Canadian experiment in jeopardy. Moreover, free trade roused anti-American sentiments of the crudest kind. The bully in Washington, this time in league with its puppet in Ottawa, imperilled the country's very survival, or so it seemed to many.

Ironically, Mulroney had denounced the idea of free trade when it was raised during the Progressive Conservative leadership race in 1983: "Canadians rejected free trade with the United States in 1911," he told *Maclean's*. "They would do so again." But the view from the seat of power seemed different, and the prime minister was ready to try for free trade once more.

The government's reasons for action were clear. The European Community was moving rapidly towards further economic and even political integration, and trade disputes between the protectionist EC and its trading partners were increasing; Japan's tariff and non-tariff barriers were even higher. Canada had contractual links with both the EC and Japan, but by 1985 neither had produced tangible benefits. Moreover, Canada's mid-1970s attempt to alter traditional trading patterns and reduce dependence on the American market had not succeeded. The percentage of trade with and investment from the United States continued to increase, while trade with Europe declined in percentage terms. The Liberals had tried in a half-hearted way to get sectoral free trade with the United States, to create a common market in certain specified areas such as steel, but these talks had gone nowhere.

Now the time had come, the government decided, to try for something bigger, to recognize that Canada was a North American nation for better or for worse, and to seek complete economic integration with the country's largest economic partner. Thanks to the General Agreement on Tariffs and Trade and to a number of Canadian–American agreements, tariffs had already ceased to matter very much. Almost 85 percent of Canadian goods entered the States free of duty. (Total exports to the United States in 1989 amounted to $89 billion.) Over 60 percent of u.s. manufactures came north without cost. (Total exports to Canada in 1989 were $78.8 billion.) At issue now were fundamental questions of foreign investment, culture, water, services, and the like.

The drums in favour of free trade had been beating in corporate Canada for years. Senate committees had called for it in 1978 and 1982. Economists had always liked the idea, and the Royal Commission on the Economic Union and Development Prospects for Canada, established by Trudeau with former Liberal minister Donald Macdonald at its head, praised the idea in its report in September 1985. "The day of the apologetic Canadian is gone," the commission said, "and there is no reason to suppose that our present confidence will be undermined by an arrangement designed only to secure a continuing exchange of goods and services with the United States." Macdonald agreed that a "leap of faith" was involved in free trade, and he was prepared to jump. The public seemed to agree, polls demonstrating that almost four in five Canadians favoured free trade in 1984.

With royal commission report in hand—one drafted by a political opponent—the prime minister promptly called for negotiations. In Parliament, he firmly pledged that any free trade agreement would not affect political sovereignty, social programs, or special policies aimed at countering regional disparities, culture, or the linguistic character of Canada. It was just as clear what Canada wanted: guaranteed access to the American market; freedom from protectionist measures aimed at reducing imports; and a binding dispute resolution process.

For its part, Reagan's Washington believed in free trade as a key component of the gospel of Republican capitalist ideology. The

United States hoped to secure an agreement that would force Canada to give American goods access once and for all. It wanted some way of limiting the subsidies that Canadian governments offered to a vast array of industries and regions. It wanted to end controls on American investors. It wanted to open Canadian governmental purchases to American bidders. And the United States wanted American trade laws to apply to its own subsidiaries operating north of the border. In effect, the administration aimed for a free trade agreement that would set out the economic, regulatory, legal, and political infrastructure for a new North America: what Reagan called an economic constitution.

Both sides began their preparations. The potential deal, however important to the United States, would have enormous consequences for Canada, and Ottawa gave the matter top priority. To head the bargaining team, Mulroney called on Simon Reisman, a retired senior trade official, the negotiator of the Auto Pact of 1965, and a long-time advocate of free trade. Reisman was tough and blustering, an apparently hard person to withstand. His staff was large, his budget substantial, and research and formulation of tactics began before the end of 1985. The Americans were slower off the mark. Their chief negotiator was Peter Murphy, a relatively junior official with a calm demeanour. In a reversal of national stereotypes, Reisman bellowed while Murphy smiled seraphically.

The negotiations began in May 1986 and lasted until October 1987, reaching the verge of dissolution several times. Part of the difficulty was that American trade laws continued to smack Canadian industries even as the talks proceeded. Soon after the beginning, for example, the United States put a 35 percent tariff on Canadian red cedar shakes and shingles, a major British Columbia export. Canadian retaliation promptly followed, but the government argued that such incidents demonstrated the need for a free trade agreement. There was probably some truth in this, but many Canadians viewed the cedar shakes tariff and a similar dispute about softwood lumber as nothing less than American bad faith. Only 52 percent supported free trade by mid-1986.

The American tariff decisions were undertaken in the face of extraordinary lobbying by the Canadian embassy and industry groups in Washington. Ever since the beginning of Allan Gotlieb's tenure as ambassador in the early 1980s, when Canada had come to realize that Congress was the locus of political action and not, as it had traditionally believed, the Executive Branch, diplomats had lobbied for Canadian causes. Appointments were made with senators and members of congress, aides had their arms twisted, and the dinner table and cocktail party became, as never before, a workplace. In the past, the embassy would have relied on the president's people or on the State Department to bring Congress into line; but ever since the Carter and Reagan administrations had proven unable to persuade the Senate to ratify a treaty settling long-standing Atlantic fishery disputes, the need for a new approach had become clear. Gotlieb was masterful at lobbying. Harassment on shakes and shingles perhaps could not be stopped, but it might be toned down. Gotlieb, a true believer in the free trade agreement, proved to be immensely skilful at building support for it among often sceptical legislators.

In September 1987, the talks were at a critical stage. A frustrated Reisman broke off negotiations because the United States refused to agree to an acceptable binding dispute resolution mechanism. The political leaders stepped in, energizing the negotiators with their high-powered urgency and bringing them back to the table. Finally, on 3 October, enough had been accomplished for the two sides to sign an agreement of intent. The details were fleshed out in the legal text over the next two months and the agreement was declared complete on 7 December. On 2 January 1988, Prime Minister Mulroney and President Reagan put their names to it. By this point, 44 percent of Canadians favoured free trade and 42 percent were opposed.

Under the FTA, as the Free Trade Agreement was universally known, Canada and the United States committed themselves to the total elimination of all tariffs by the end of 1998, some reductions to begin at once and others to be phased in over five to ten years. The FTA also created a bi-national tribunal intended to ensure that each country had secure, guaranteed access for its products into the other's market. The Americans won a guarantee of non-discriminatory access to Canadian natural resources, including oil and gas; if these were ever in short supply, the United States was to receive a proportionate share of Canada's production. American investors could purchase Canadian industries valued at $150 million or less (except in a few specified areas) without any governmental review. Moreover, the FTA committed the two countries to concert their negotiating positions outside North America on issues such as investment, services, and agriculture.

The power of the bi-national tribunal was limited. It was able to examine complaints from one country against the other but could only require each not to violate its own trade laws. In other words, there was no guarantee either of access or against harassment; and harassment duly continued in both countries with a series of dumping cases and tariff hikes. The natural resource clauses effectively removed the Canadian ability to set a made-in-Canada price for petroleum. Canada could never again have a national energy program. FTA clauses on foreign investment eliminated any possibility of a Canadian government ever again trying to control American investment in Canada. Most startling of all, the clauses on concerted international negotiating positions required Canada to accept for the first time that its posture in international affairs was to be decided on the basis of bi-national trade.

The FTA document had further implications. The negotiators had said nothing about preventing an American corporation with a Canadian subsidiary from deciding to serve all North America from its U.S. plants. Unemployment in the manufacturing sector might well increase in consequence. Many Canadians also feared a corporate demand that social services be lowered to the American standard to allow a "level playing field," as Canadian industry struggled to survive in the face of unprotected competition. Medicare would not necessarily end, but its benefits could be watered down. A national day care scheme would not necessarily be prevented, but if one were implemented the government might have to compensate American day care companies for loss of potential profits in Canada. The agreement was, as Mulroney said, "cancellable on six months' notice," but the realities seemed far more permanent.

Over the heated if futile protests of Liberals and New Democrats, the House of Commons approved the legislation on 1 September 1988. The Liberal-dominated Senate blocked the progress of the bill into law, however, and Mulroney dissolved Parliament and went to the people. The resulting election of 21 November 1988 was at once one of the most entertaining and the most important in the country's history.

The Liberals attacked the deal with great vigour; party leader John Turner scored heavily against the prime minister in the televised leaders' debate. Canadians worried, as Turner had told them, that whatever its economic benefits, the FTA would day by day, month by month, erode Canada's distinctiveness as a North American nation unlike the United States. Ultimately the flag would follow trade and political sovereignty would be lost. To critics of the agreement, its psychological impact on the fragile national identity more than outweighed any promised economic gains.

The Progressive Conservatives appeared to be in serious danger of being toppled from power until massive pro-FTA advertising reversed the tide, funded by the seemingly unlimited bankrolls of the Conservatives and business groups favourable to the deal. By election eve, the opinion polls showed that a bare majority favoured

Contents unknown (Malcom Mayes)

the FTA; the prime minister also had strong support in Quebec, where the agreement was not an emotional issue. The Mulroney government retained power with a comfortable majority. Of course, many additional factors played a part in the election outcome, but for the first time when confronted with a choice between continentalism and autonomy, the Canadian people had opted for the former. The ghosts of 1891 and 1911 were laid to rest in November 1988.

The FTA then passed easily through the legislative process and became law. Almost immediately, its critics appeared to see their worst fears realized. As North America slid into a long-lasting recession, job losses mounted. Factories shut down, most especially those in southern Ontario, and many were relocated to the United States or, increasingly, to Mexico. To December 1990, organized labour estimated that 226 000 jobs had been lost, most gone forever. The robust growth promised by FTA supporters simply was not visible in a recession-wracked economy, though total trade figures rose gratifyingly. By 1992, the United States took $98.6 billion in goods from Canada and sent $90.6 billion northwards. Yet Canadian export growth was concentrated in traditional areas—autos, petroleum products, and natural resources—and even those sectors reduced their employment levels. Instead of prosperity, Canadians experienced increased welfare caseloads and higher unemployment.

Just as bad in the eyes of both opponents and supporters, American trade actions against Canadian exports continued. As Jeffrey Simpson later wrote, "Although a majority of binational free trade panels created under the agreement ruled in Canada's favor, it sometimes appeared that Canada's vaunted gains against American protectionism were not worth what had been yielded in the negotiations." Even Simon Reisman, who stoutly denied the charges from critics and academics that he had been out-negotiated by Peter Murphy, was so furious at the continued harassment that he described the Americans as "bastards."

After the election of 1988, the NDP continued to promise to abrogate the FTA, the Liberals to re-negotiate it. As Simpson pointed out, however, "free trade with each passing day became more deeply imbedded in the Canadian economy. Businesses made hundreds, even thousands of decisions based upon it." Canadian corporations, already having spent large sums to take advantage of or to protect themselves against the FTA clauses, would be unlikely to accept calmly another expensive turnaround.

Indeed, the ink was scarcely dry on the FTA before negotiations got underway for the North American Free Trade Agreement (NAFTA), which would include Mexico and its burgeoning population of almost 90 million. Greatly desired by the American administration of George Bush and almost equally so by that of his Democratic successor, Bill Clinton, NAFTA was seen as the first step towards the creation of a hemispheric free trade area. "It's the 1990s version of the Monroe Doctrine," one U.S. lobbyist said, referring to the early nineteenth-century American edict that forbade European nations from expanding their empires within the Americas. The modern version of the doctrine supposed a trade barrier around the hemisphere, designed to keep European and Asian goods out and to provide American corporations with a secure environment in which to prosper. By the spring of 1993, NAFTA was complete except for convoluted "side deals" providing for weak sanctions or fines against nations that violated the environmental and labour provisions of the deal. These were not concluded until August 1993.

Only days before he left office, Prime Minister Mulroney watched with pleasure as Parliament approved NAFTA, his government using closure to force the deal through all its parliamentary stages. Again critics were furious. Migration of industrial jobs south had been speeded by the FTA; now NAFTA made it possible, even desirable, for Canadian (and American) businesses to relocate south of the Rio Grande, where wage rates approximated $2 an hour and social and environmental protections were still almost non-existent. Supporters of expanded free trade, much as they had done five years earlier, talked of Canadian exports cracking the large and growing Mexican market—in 1992 Canada exported only $616 million of goods to Mexico—and waited for the slow-to-develop economic upturn to showcase the benefits of the deal.

Whether the FTA and NAFTA will benefit the Canadian economy in the long term is still unclear. The only certainty is that Brian Mulroney in his years in power made more sweeping changes in Canada's relations with the United States than any other prime minister. Nothing could ever be the same again.

Empire to Umpire?

B Y THE TIME BRIAN MULRONEY left power in mid-1993, he had indeed achieved his goal of "good relations, super relations" with the United States. Despite continuous wrangling in the panels set up by the Free Trade Agreement to resolve disputes, trade relations were closer than ever before. Canadian foreign policy, as during the Gulf War, frequently seemed to march in lockstep with Washington; at least, critics claimed so. Canada was very different from just nine years earlier.

Yet much remained the same. Anti-Americanism abounded in the arts and in public discourse, and the media regularly drew unflattering comparisons between the two countries. The Canadian social safety net, for example, tattered as it had become by years of economic hard times, was always trumpeted as the mark of a "kinder, gentler" nation than the United States. As a hundred years before, the relative absence of guns on the city streets of Canada and the vastly lower murder rate were also held up to suggest that Canadian attitudes and behaviour were at striking variance to those of their American cousins. Even the reported increase in violent crime in Canada in the 1990s was statistically almost insignificant compared to the skyrocketing numbers in the United States.

Mulroney, despite his too-evident desire to bask in the smiles of Presidents Reagan and Bush, had continuous conflicts with the United States. His government engaged in arguments over acid rain, over control of the Arctic, over trade, over policy towards the former Soviet Union, and over the proper tactics to follow in the former Yugoslavia. Over the last of these, the United States predictably wanted to bomb

Serbian positions in Bosnia-Heregovina; also predictably, with peace-keepers on the ground, Canada usually favoured a moderate policy. The ordinary, regular dynamic of conflict and co-operation in Canadian–American relations went on much as before. The difference under Mulroney was to be found as much in tone as in content, though critics argued that the thrust of policy during these years tended more towards harmonization, a word much favoured by diplomats.

Still, for many Canadians, tone was crucial. They wanted their governments to have good relations with the United States but they did not like their leaders to look as if they were hand in glove with the Americans. In an era in which mass media blurred the line between appearances and reality, Mulroney behaved in a manner that made him seem too close to Reagan and Bush. Even Allan Gotlieb, the retired ambassador to the United States, noted harshly that Mulroney was perceived by many Canadians "as being too sub-servient to Uncle Sam, and as conducting himself in a manner demeaning to our national dignity."

Mulroney was gone by mid-1993, however, and Canada had a new prime minister in Kim Campbell. A British Columbian first elected to Parliament in 1988, Campbell had served as justice minister and

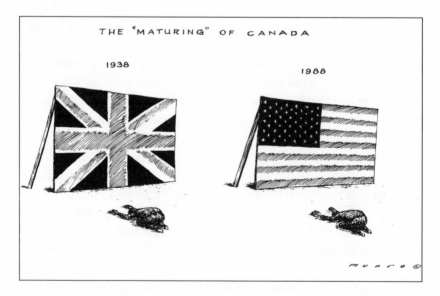

THE "MATURING" OF CANADA

1938   1988

From colony to colony? (Ken Munro)

briefly as minister of national defence when she took the helm in mid-1993. Like magic, her arrival on stage seemed to boost the opinion poll numbers, which suddenly showed the Progressive Conservative party, desperately unpopular while Mulroney led it, rising to the top. Campbell's first moves after becoming prime minister, such as slashing the size of Cabinet, were well received. When she attended the G-7 summit meeting in Tokyo, where she demonstrably held her own among the leaders of the world's most powerful economies, Canadians breathed a palpable sigh of relief. Campbell had substance along with flair and a penchant for cutting quips.

Campbell was not long for office, however. By the time she called a general election for 25 October 1993, her star was in decline. Serious questions were raised about Campbell's prior knowledge and her actions, or lack of them, as defence minister when Canadian Airborne Regiment peacekeepers serving in Somalia beat and murdered a Somali. That incident revealed profound command-and-control problems and racist attitudes in a crack Canadian regiment, all of which was troubling in a country where peacekeeping was regarded as a proud tradition. Many were also disturbed by Campbell's handling of the matter, believing that ministers should be accountable and not pass responsibility on to their underlings. More serious to the average voter than her evasions over the Somali affair, however, Campbell's sharp tongue seemed to suggest a distinct lack of compassion for the unemployed and poor. The carefully constructed image of a multilingual polymath began to crack as journalists probed ever deeper into her record.

The result was an astonishing sea-change in Canadian politics. The election saw Campbell defeated in her own riding in Vancouver and the Conservative Party simply crushed, reduced to two seats in Parliament. The Liberals captured a comfortable majority, while the separatist Bloc Québécois formed Her Majesty's Loyal Opposition and the Western-based Reform Party, a small-c conservative group, followed closely behind. The New Democratic Party, traditionally Canada's third party, was also devastated at the polls.

The new prime minister was Jean Chrétien, a federalist Quebecer, an experienced veteran of national politics, and a politician who had held senior portfolios under Pierre Trudeau and had been secretary of state for external affairs during John Turner's brief tenure as prime minister. In an election that centred on personality as much as anything, Chrétien persuaded the electorate that he was a compassionate man who could inspire hope.

Though it was not entirely absent from public discourse, foreign policy did not play much part in the campaign, as the victims of recession chose to look inward rather than out to the world. It was, *Maclean's* said, as if Canada had entered a period of "parochialization." There was no discussion of Bosnia, Haiti, India, Somalia, or Russia, "and that at a time when the bloodshed continued in Bosnia, [peacekeeper] Canadian Mounties were bobbing on an American boat in uncharted waters off the Haiti coast [having been turned away by the military regime], an earthquake had killed thousands in India, debate raged in the United States about attacks on u.s. forces in Somalia and Russia had a civil war, albeit a one-day wonder. Here, there was silence."

Instead, Canadians discussed NAFTA, which Chrétien claimed he would renegotiate. His promise suggested a new and tougher approach towards the United States. Another key election question centred on defence, specifically the fate of a $5-billion contract awarded by the previous government to acquire helicopters for the Canadian Forces. The Liberals argued that the deal was extravagant and pledged to cancel it, doing so at their very first Cabinet meeting. A Liberal campaign promise for full and complete reviews of defence and foreign policy was soon put into effect.

Chrétien appointed André Ouellet, another long-serving Quebec MP, to head the re-christened Ministry of Foreign Affairs. Without drawing attention to it, the new government had scrapped one of Canada's few remaining badges of symbolic colonialism. The term "external affairs" had been used to encompass relations with both foreigners and with British nations, which were thought to be family. Now, at last, Canada was to have a Ministry of Foreign Affairs and a foreign minister, like other adult nations. This departure passed almost without comment.

One change *was* noticed. The new prime minister travelled to Seattle for the Asia Pacific Economic Cooperation Forum, a gathering of Pacific leaders, to discuss trade questions. The highlight for

Chrétien, and for the Canadian media, was his first meeting with American president Bill Clinton. The differences in style between Mulroney and Chrétien were immediately apparent.

Instead of following Mulroney's adage that "you catch more flies with honey than vinegar," Chrétien took the position that "business is business and friendship is friendship and the two cannot be confused. . . . The president of the United States is not there to be your personal friend." As he told the media, "I used to make a joke that Mulroney would say yes before the telephone rings," adding, "Mulroney cares more about getting other leaders to like him than about getting the things Canada needs. Me, I understand that in politics there is no room for friendship." The prime minister made clear his understanding that Clinton's job was to protect the interests of the United States. "He will know that the Prime Minister of Canada has first in mind the interests of Canada. There will be clear lines there. I believe that Canada has to be independent. . . . It's not good if we are looked upon as the 51st state of America." He asserted that Canada "can play a useful role in many fields as a good friendly neighbour that is independent. Will that be very different from the previous administration?" Answering his own question, Chrétien said "probably."

Chrétien's approach indicated a certain new reserve in dealing with Washington, and the mood he fostered was much more in tune with the expectations of the Canadian public. Few expected Chrétien to secure the major changes to NAFTA that he had claimed to want; the deal was for all practical purposes done. Although he did fail to get those revisions, however, he at least achieved some small alterations that might prove beneficial in establishing rules to redefine what is and is not a government subsidy, a continuing bone of contention between the two FTA partners. Moreover, Chrétien issued a declaration of the Canadian national interest in secure energy supplies and made clear that water exports did not fall under the terms of NAFTA. None of this was essential, but again the tone was noticeably different.

American analysts were not wholly pleased with the new trends in Ottawa, which the knowledgeable American political scientist Joseph Jockel has said "will probably raise tensions" between the two countries "as striking an independent pose moves up the list of Canadian priorities." Jockel's phrasing is interesting; is "striking an independent pose" all that Canada can do in the 1990s? It seems so, for Chrétien soon allowed the United States to continue testing Cruise missiles over Canada, despite strong opposition voiced in previous Liberal positions and within his caucus. The United States, it appears, cannot be wished away.

More significantly for a country that has prided itself on its global vision, the Liberal government faces a Canadian foreign policy horizon that seemed to have shrunk to North America in the Mulroney years. Initiatives were made to Asia and Europe between 1984 and 1993, of course, but the follow-up was tepid at best. There is thus an opportunity for the Liberal government to look abroad, to seek a greater presence.

Peacekeeping, one activity in which Canada has expertise (and the United States notably does not), provides a useful underpinning for such a role, though the state of the deficit obliged the Chrétien government to slash at the armed forces in the February 1994 budget to such an extent that the capacity of the military for any overseas operations of substantial size is doubtful.

Similarly, Canada could pursue its foreign policies through multilateral agencies as a way to secure more elbow room in the too-close relationship with the United States. The Seattle meeting was about expanding trade around the Pacific Rim, for one thing, a high priority for the new government harking back to the contractual link with Japan negotiated, but scarcely acted upon, by the Liberals under Trudeau.

Any policy to allow Canada to strike more than an "independent pose" has serious limitations. The massive national debt and horrendous annual deficits that constrain the Department of National Defence also forbid daring new initiatives, even if they were desired. With the best will in the world, Canadian policy under Chrétien and Ouellet will not in all likelihood be very different in substance from what has gone immediately before.

The constant in Canadian policy has been the United States. The great power to the south historically has been a military and economic menace, a magnet attracting the best and brightest, a staunch ally, and a good trading partner. America has been both threat and promise for Canada and Canadians as they have sought to work out a relationship that preserves a measure of independence and all the benefits of the North American standard of living. This book has suggested that the task has always been difficult, though some governments handled the problem better than others.

Britain, however, did disappear almost completely from the Canadian consciousness. At the beginning of this volume, Britain was a great power to which Canadians clung for protection against Americans and aspired to emulate. Empire mattered to Canadians and in the world. The Commonwealth represented one attempt to change while retaining old connections, but Britain after the 1960s seemed more interested in the European Community than in the old or new Commonwealth nations. While the long process of British decolonization and decline was underway, Canadians found their own voice and became a nation. Today all that preserves the ancient links to the United Kingdom is the monarchy, and there can be no gainsaying that the royal family has little cachet or influence in Canada in the 1990s; no more, at any rate, than movie stars or pop singers, those other denizens of the gossip columns and supermarket tabloids. The old affection and loyalty have for the most part disappeared along with the empire.

France, Canada's other "mother country," similarly does not matter much, even in Quebec. French investment, French immigrants, went elsewhere, and despite a brief interlude of overt interference in Canadian domestic disputes under General de Gaulle, France has been scrupulous in keeping its hands out of Canadian federal–provincial squabbles.

The bickering will probably be resolved one way or the other in this decade. The rise in separatist sentiment in Quebec unleashed by the Meech Lake and Charlottetown constitutional debacles is likely to culminate in a referendum on independence. The implications for the country and for its global relations are profound. The Canada we have known since 1867 might disappear from the map.

Such a result is not unknown elsewhere. Canada's enemies in this century have vanished as well. Germany under the Kaiser, the Third Reich under Hitler, and the Stalinist Union of Soviet Socialist Republic are no more. World wars and cold wars preoccupied

Canada through much of the twentieth century. They swallowed Canadians in battle wholesale; they drained the national treasury; and, paradoxically, they led both to Canadian confidence in the skill of our military and our diplomats and to national industrialization. A mixed blessing, on balance, now the Cold War is over and new causes have to be sought.

The past suggests that it will not take long to find them. Moralism is one unifying thread running through the history of Canadian foreign policy. Canadians could always be found to prattle about the undefended frontier and to urge others to settle their disputes in the way that Canada and the United States did. Canada was the creator of the inter-racial Commonwealth, the leader in forcing South Africa out of that organization, and always one of the very few nations to pay its dues in full and on time to the United Nations. Canada was the real inventor of peacekeeping and its practitioner *par excellence*. Even our armed forces, in other words, were not the traditional "brutal licentious soldiery" but arbiters in blue helmets, umpires enforcing the world's rules on the unruly. Finally, Canada was the country of choice for refugees, a humane, liberal nation almost free of racist impulses, honourable in everything it touched. That is what we said. Canada, as one shrewd observer in New York said, usually acted like the United Church at the United Nations. Canada as a moral superpower? Had we moved in less than a century from empire to umpire?

Sometimes it has seemed that way. The streak of do-goodism in Canada is a useful impulse, to be sure, and idealism ought never to be dismissed. Nevertheless, the world has been and will continue to be a cold, heartless place much of the time, and nations must work to protect their interests, or else face being run over in the stampede. Most Canadians forget that their country may produce the best hockey referees, but it also breeds hockey players who go into the corners with their elbows up and frequently jab the other team's players in the ribs with their sticks. Canada has never been a choirboy in the concert of nations; it has fought wars and bargained for advantage like all the rest.

Still, if nations must have images, it is certainly better for Canadians to think of themselves as umpires, as morality incarnate, than as mass murderers or warmongers. Few Canadians would want their governments to sacrifice national advantage for the sake of international morality, but it serves a purpose to fret about the implications of every one of our actions abroad. For Canadians, it is also apparently essential.

Jaded Canadians also forget that, troubled as their country may be by division and economic problems, it is one of the world's few success stories. Domestic prosperity aside, Canada has a reputation for trying to resolve global problems, for contributing to world betterment, and for attempting to improve the lot of people in the Third World. We are not the world arbiter we sometimes pretend to be, unfortunately, but if the superpowers and mad-dog nation-states had exercised anything like the good sense that Canadians have shown over the last century then possibly, just possibly, the world might have been a better place.

As we move towards the twenty-first century, the global situation is as unpredictable as it has ever been. The collapse of the Soviet Union and its satellites has altered boundaries that had seemed to be set in stone. Old nationalities have suddenly found themselves with the chance to resume statehood, and, regrettably, to settle scores with their historical enemies. Eastern Europe and the Balkans are in flames, and the fire is unlikely to die down for years to come.

The North Atlantic alliance, its enemy having disappeared, thus faces the uncertainties of grappling with nationalistic hostilities in Eastern Europe. NATO must simultaneously reassure new, struggling democracies such as the Czech Republic and Hungary and persuade its reluctant member governments to maintain their defence budgets.

In Asia, China's ancient leaders must soon disappear from the stage, and it is by no means certain that the Communist centre can hold. Meanwhile, the "little dragons" of Asia have turned into economic giants whose production prowess threatens the markets that Canada has struggled to establish.

The boundaries on the map and in the mind seem to be in flux. Few things are sure any more, and there can be little doubt that Canadian good sense will continue to be needed in the world arena. The umpire will always be indispensable on the international playing field.

FURTHER READING

GENERAL

Valuable general studies of Canadian diplomacy are C.P. Stacey, *Canada and the Age of Conflict*, 2 vols. (Toronto, 1979–81); H.G. Skilling, *Canadian Representation Abroad* (Toronto, 1945); James Eayrs, *The Art of the Possible* (Toronto, 1961); and Kim Richard Nossal, *The Politics of Canadian Foreign Policy* (Scarborough, ON, 1985).

The Historical Section of the Department of Foreign Affairs and International Trade edits *Documents on Canadian External Relations* (Ottawa, 1967–   ) of which there are 16 volumes to date. John F. Hilliker, the section's head, is the author of *Canada's Department of External Affairs*, vol. 1, *The Early Years, 1909–1946* (Montreal, 1990). Volume 2, covering 1946–68, will appear soon. Another of the section's publications, *Canadian Heads of Post Abroad, 1880–1989* (Ottawa, 1991), is useful, as is the department's *Annual Report* and its *Canadian International Relations Chronicle,* issued since 1991. The official history of the Department of Trade and Commerce, then a separate ministry, reviews 1892–1939: O. Mary Hill, *Canada's Salesman to the World* (Montreal, 1977).

The *Canada in World Affairs* series of the Canadian Institute of International Affairs (CIIA) has 14 volumes covering most of the time from 1935 to 1973. These books, a straightforward record of Canadian policy, are unfortunately no longer published, but Carleton University has produced an annual volume, *Canada Among Nations,* on the years from 1984. The CIIA has long sponsored the quarterly *International Journal* (1946–   ) and *Behind the Headlines,* which has appeared several times a year since World War II. *The Canadian Annual Review,* brought out by the University of Toronto Press, and the *Canada Year Book* (Statistics Canada) are the source of much further contemporary data.

Compilations of readings on issues ranging over many decades are Don Munton and John Kirton, eds., *Canadian Foreign Policy: Selected Cases* (Scarborough, ON, 1992); J.L. Granatstein, ed., *Canadian Foreign Policy: Historical Readings* (Toronto, 1986; 2nd ed.,

1993); J.L. Granatstein, ed., *Towards a New World* (Toronto, 1992); Norman Hillmer, ed., *Partners Nevertheless: Canadian–American Relations in the Twentieth Century* (Toronto, 1989); John English and Norman Hillmer, eds., *Making a Difference? Canada's Foreign Policy in a Changing World Order* (Toronto, 1992); and B.D. Hunt and R.G. Haycock, eds., *Canada's Defence* (Toronto, 1993). Most of these collections have bibliographies of their own.

This book has argued that defence and immigration are an integral part of external policy. Desmond Morton, the leading military historian of Canada, gives an overview of defence questions in *A Military History of Canada* (Edmonton, 1985). James Eayrs has thus far carved out five volumes of his *In Defence of Canada* collection (Toronto, 1964–83), stretching idiosyncratically from the end of the Great War to the Vietnam War.

Surveys of Canadian immigration are Valerie Knowles, *Strangers at the Gates* (Toronto, 1992) and a Canadian Historical Association pamphlet by Reg Whitaker, *Canadian Immigration Policy Since Confederation* (Ottawa, 1991). Post-World War II developments are the subject of *Canada and Immigration* (Montreal, 1972), by Freda Hawkins. For an innovative examination of the relationship between foreign and immigration policy, see Angelika E. Sauer, "A Matter of Domestic Policy? Canadian Immigration Policy and the Admission of Germans, 1945–50," *Canadian Historical Review* 74 (June 1993).

There are three recent histories of Canadian–American relations, each with a distinctive viewpoint: Gordon T. Stewart, *The American Response to Canada Since 1776* (East Lansing, MI, 1992); J.L. Granatstein and Norman Hillmer, *For Better or For Worse: Canada and the United States to the 1990* (Toronto, 1991); and Robert Bothwell, *Canada and the United States* (Toronto, 1992). R.D. Cuff and J.L. Granatstein, *Ties that Bind* (Toronto, 1977) concentrates on Canadian–American relations in wartime and in the Cold War.

An excellent overall discussion of Anglo–Canadian links is provided in Nicholas Mansergh, *The Commonwealth Experience*, 2 vols. (London, 1982). This can be supplemented by Peter Lyon, ed., *Britain and Canada* (London, 1975) and J. L. Granatstein, *How Britain's Weakness Forced Canada Into the Arms of the United States* (Toronto, 1989).

Broad accounts of other bilateral and regional relationships include: John Schultz and Kimitada Miwa, eds., *Canada and Japan in the Twentieth Century* (Toronto, 1991); Klaus H. Pringsheim, *Neighbours Across the Pacific: Canadian–Japanese Relations 1870–1982* (Oakville, ON 1983); Frank Langdon, *The Politics of Canadian–Japanese Economic Relations, 1952–1983* (Vancouver, 1983); Paul M. Evans and B. Michael Frolic, eds., *Reluctant Adversaries: Canada and the People's Republic of China, 1949–1970* (Toronto, 1991); David Davies, ed., *Canada and the Soviet Experiment* (Toronto, 1993); Aloysius Balawyder, ed., *Canadian–Soviet Relations, 1939–1980* (Guelph, ON, 1981); Peyton V. Lyon and Tareq Y. Ismael, eds., *Canada and the Third World* (Toronto, 1976); Tareq Y. Ismael, ed., *Canada and the Arab World* (Edmonton, 1985); David Taras and David H. Goldberg, eds., *The Domestic Battleground: Canada and the Arab–Israeli Conflict* (Montreal, 1989); Brian D. Tennyson, *Canadian Relations with South Africa* (Washington, 1982); Brian D. Tennyson, ed., *Canada and the Commonwealth Caribbean* (Lanham, 1988) and *Canadian–Caribbean Relations* (Sydney, NS, 1990); J.C.M. Ogelsby, *Gringos From the Far North: Essays in the History of Canadian–Latin American Relations, 1866–1968* (Toronto, 1976); and James Rochlin, *Discovering the Americas: The Evolution of Canadian Policy Towards Latin America* (Vancouver, 1994).

CONFEDERATION TO WORLD WAR I

Among many sources on late-nineteenth-century external affairs are David M.L. Farr, *The Colonial Office and Canada, 1867–1887* (Toronto, 1955); Kenneth Bourne, *Britain and the Balance of Power in North America, 1815–1908* (Berkeley, 1967); John Kendle, *The Colonial and Imperial Conferences 1887–1911* (London, 1967); Donald Creighton, *John A. Macdonald: The Old Chieftain* (Toronto, 1955); and Robert Craig Brown, *Canada's National Policy 1883–1900* (Princeton, 1964).

Imperialism is illuminated in Carl Berger, *The Sense of Power: Studies in the Ideas of Canadian Imperialism 1867–1914* (Toronto, 1970) and his edited works, *Imperialism and Nationalism, 1884–1914* (Toronto, 1969) and *Imperial Relations in the Age of Laurier*

(Toronto, 1969). The latter reprints the seminal article by H. Blair Neatby, "Laurier and Imperialism," *Canadian Historical Association Report* (1955). The South African War finally has its historian: Carman Miller, *Painting the Map Red* (Montreal, 1993). John A. Munro, *The Alaska Boundary Dispute* (Toronto, 1970) and Paul Stevens, *The 1911 General Election* (Toronto, 1970) both collect documents and historical perspectives. Defence issues are dealt with by Roger Sarty, "Canadian Maritime Defence, 1892–1914," *Canadian Historical Review* 71 (Dec. 1990) and Michael L. Hadley and Roger Sarty, *Tin-Pots and Pirate Ships* (Montreal, 1991)

O. D. Skelton's *Life and Letters of Sir Wilfrid Laurier*, 2 vols. (New York, 1922) is still fresh (if partisan) after all these years. The indispensable resources on Borden are Robert Craig Brown, *Robert Laird Borden: A Biography*, 2 vols. (Toronto, 1975–80) and "Sir Robert Borden, the Great War, and Anglo–Canadian Relations" in *Character and Circumstance*, ed. J. S. Moir (Toronto, 1970). The dreams and disappointments of Borden's closest advisor are brilliantly depicted by Robert Bothwell, *Loring Christie: The Failure of Bureaucratic Imperialism* (New York, 1988).

1919–1945

British–Canadian relations from World War I to the late 1930s may be traced in Philip Wigley's *Canada and the Transition to Commonwealth, 1917–1926* (Cambridge, 1977) and in several articles by Norman Hillmer: "A British High Commissioner for Canada, 1927–28," *Journal of Imperial and Commonwealth History* 1 (May 1979), "The Foreign Office, the Dominions and the Diplomatic Unity of the Empire, 1925–29" in *Retreat from Power: Studies in Britain's Foreign Policy of the Twentieth Century*, vol. 1, ed. David Dilks (London, 1981), and "Defence and Ideology: The Anglo–Canadian Military 'Alliance' in the 1930s," *International Journal* 33 (Sept. 1978). For a British historian's view, consult Max Beloff, *Imperial Sunset*, 2 vols. (London, 1969–89).

There is a great deal of useful information on external affairs in the official biography, *William Lyon Mackenzie King*, 3 vols.

(Toronto, 1958–76). The first volume is by R. MacGregor Dawson, the second and third by H. Blair Neatby. C.P. Stacey demonstrates his light touch in *Mackenzie King and the Atlantic Triangle* (Toronto, 1976). Ramsay Cook studies the role of the influential journalist in *The Politics of John W. Dafoe and the Free Press* (Toronto, 1963). The life and ideas of O.D. Skelton are canvassed by Norman Hillmer, "The Anglo–Canadian Neurosis: The Case of O. D. Skelton" in *Britain and Canada*, ed. Peter Lyon (London, 1976).

Richard Veatch, *Canada and the League of Nations* (Toronto, 1975) is solid, but ought to be supplemented by Donald C. Story, "The Cahan Speech and Bennett's Policy Towards the Far Eastern Conflict 1931–33" in *An Acceptance of Paradox*, ed. Kim Richard Nossal (Toronto, 1982) and Robert Bothwell and John English, "'Dirty Work at the Crossroads': New Perspectives on the Riddell Incident," Canadian Historical Association *Historical Papers* (1972). These are the best studies of R.B. Bennett's foreign-policy methods.

Ian M. Drummond is the expert on interwar economics: *Imperial Economic Policy 1917–1939* (London, 1974) and, with Norman Hillmer, *Negotiating Freer Trade: The United Kingdom, the United States, Canada, and the Trade Agreements of 1938* (Waterloo, ON, 1989).

Robert Bothwell and Norman Hillmer, eds., *The In-Between Time* (Toronto, 1975) conveniently brings together the views of contemporaries and later commentators on the 1930s. As for all the periods up to 1948, C.P. Stacey, *Canada and the Age of Conflict* (Toronto, 1979–81) can be mined for ideas and references. *None Is Too Many* (Toronto, 1982), by Irving Abella and Harold Troper, is the sad story of Canada and the Jews of Europe, 1933–1948. J.L. Granatstein and Robert Bothwell, "'A Self-Evident National Duty': Canadian Foreign Policy, 1935–1939," *Journal of Imperial and Commonwealth History*, 3 (Jan. 1975) are sympathetic to Mackenzie King on his road to war.

The basic books on World War II are C.P. Stacey, *Arms, Men and Governments: The War Policies of Canada 1939–1945* (Ottawa, 1970) and J.L. Granatstein, *Canada's War: The Politics of the Mackenzie King Government 1939–1945* (Toronto, 1990). Selections from the prime minister's diaries are reproduced in J.W. Pickersgill and D.F. Forster, eds., *The Mackenzie King Record*, 4 vols. (Toronto, 1960–1970). Volumes 1 and 2 take in 1939–45; volumes 3 and 4 concern 1945–48.

Helpful on selected aspects of 1939–45 foreign policy are Robert Bothwell and William Kilbourn, *C.D. Howe: A Biography* (Toronto, 1979); Douglas G. Anglin, The St Pierre and Miquelon Affaire of 1941 (Toronto, 1966); Brereton Greenhous et al., *The Crucible of War, 1939–1945: The Official History of the Royal Canadian Air Force*, vol. 3 (Toronto, 1994); and two books on Newfoundland: David Mackenzie's *Inside the Atlantic Triangle* (Toronto, 1986) and Peter Neary, *Newfoundland in the North Atlantic World, 1929–1949* (Montreal, 1988).

It is also worth noting three articles by John Hilliker, editor of three of the wartime *Documents on Canadian External Relations* volumes: "Distant Ally: Canadian Relations with Australia During the Second World War," *Journal of Imperial and Commonwealth History* 13 (Oct. 1984); "No Bread at the Peace Table: Canada and the European Settlement, 1943–47," *Canadian Historical Review* 61 (March 1980); and "The Canadian Government and the Free French: Perceptions and Constraints, 1940–44," *International History* Review 2 (Jan. 1980). Two fresh perspectives on external affairs are Paul M. Couture, "The Vichy–Free French Propaganda War in Quebec, 1940 to 1942," Canadian Historical Association *Historical Papers* (1978) and Greg Donaghy, "Solidarity Forever: The Cooperative Commonwealth Federation and Its Search for an International Role, 1939–1949," *International Journal of Canadian Studies* 5 (Spring 1992).

SINCE 1945

The historiography of the period after 1945 is dominated by the writings of former diplomats: *Mike: The Memoirs of the Rt. Hon. Lester B. Pearson*, 3 vols. (Toronto, 1972–75); J.W. Holmes, *The Shaping of Peace: Canada and the Search for World Order 1943–1957*, 2 vols. (Toronto, 1979–82); Escott Reid's *Radical Mandarin* (Toronto, 1989), *On Duty: A Canadian at the Making of the United Nations, 1945–1946* (Toronto, 1983), *Time of Fear and Hope: The Making of the North Atlantic Treaty, 1947–1949* (Toronto, 1977), and *Envoy to Nehru* (Dehli, 1981); Douglas Lepan, *Bright Glass of Memory* (Toronto, 1979); Charles Ritchie's, *Diplomatic Passport: More Undiplomatic Diaries, 1946–1962* (Toronto, 1981) and *Storm Signals:*

Further Readings

More Undiplomatic Diaries, 1962–1971 (Toronto, 1983); George Ignatieff, *The Making of a Peacemonger* (Toronto, 1985); Arnold Heeney, *The Things that Are Caesar's* (Toronto, 1972); Arnold Smith, *Stiches in Time: The Commonwealth in World Politics* (Don Mills, ON, 1981); Chester Ronning, *A Memoir of China in Revolution* (New York, 1974); Robert A.D. Ford, *Our Man in Moscow* (Toronto, 1989); Arthur Andrew, *The Rise and Fall of a Middle Power* (Toronto, 1993).

J.L. Granatstein has written biographies of Norman Robertson, *A Man of Influence* (Ottawa, 1981) and of *The Ottawa Men* (Toronto, 1982), a group of distinguished public servants, many from External Affairs. There are two volumes in John English's portrait of L.B. Pearson: *Shadow of Heaven, 1897–1948* and *The Worldly Years, 1949–1972* (Toronto, 1989–92). David Bercuson analyses the work of Canada's longest-serving minister of national defence—1946 to 1954—in *True Patriot: The Life of Brooke Claxton* (Toronto, 1993). James Barros accuses Herbert Norman of Communist allegiances and worse in his *No Sense of Evil* (Toronto, 1986); Roger Bowen mounts a vigorous defence in *Innocence Is Not Enough* (Vancouver, 1986). Neither is wholly convincing.

Other accounts bearing on the early Cold War are Denis Smith, *Diplomacy of Fear* (Toronto, 1988); R.D. Cuff and J.L. Granatstein, *American Dollars—Canadian Prosperity* (Toronto, 1978); Joseph Jockel, *No Boundaries Upstairs: Canada, the United States, and the Origins of North American Air Defence, 1945–1958* (Vancouver, 1987); Robert Bothwell, *Eldorado: Canada's National Uranium Company* (Toronto, 1984); Shelagh D. Grant, *Sovereignty or Security: Government Policy in the Canadian North, 1936–1950* (Vancouver, 1988); David Bercuson, *Canada and the Birth of Israel* (Toronto, 1985); Melissa Clark-Jones, *A Staple State* (Toronto, 1987); Lawrence Aronsen and Martin Kitchen, *The Origins of the Cold War in Comparative Perspective* (New York, 1988); Reg Whitaker, *Double Standard: The Secret History of Canadian Immigration* (Toronto, 1987); Robert Bothwell and J.L. Granatstein, eds., *The Gouzenko Transcripts* (Ottawa, n.d.); J.L. Black and Norman Hillmer, eds., *Nearly Neighbours: Canada and the Soviet Union* (Kingston, 1990); and Joseph Levitt, *Pearson and Canada's Role in Nuclear Disarmament and Arms Control Negotiations, 1945–1957* (Montreal,

1993). Albert Legault and Michel Fortmann, *A Diplomacy of Hope* (Montreal, 1992), is another study of disarmament, extending from 1945 to 1988.

The study of Canadian foreign economic policy immediately after World War II is underdeveloped, but there are now some good books: B.W. Muirhead, *The Development of Postwar Canadian Trade Policy* (Montreal, 1992); A.F.W. Plumptre, *Three Decades of Decision: Canada and the World Monetary System, 1944–75* (Toronto, 1977); Frank Stone, *Canada, the GATT* and the *International Trade System*, 2nd ed. (Montreal, 1992); and Hector M. Mackenzie, "The Path to Temptation: The Negotiation of Canada's Reconstruction Loan to Britain in 1946," Canadian Historical Association *Historical Papers* (1982).

The standard monograph on Canada and the Korean War remains Denis Stairs' *The Diplomacy of Constraint* (Toronto, 1974). Robert Prince confronts the orthodoxy in "The Limits of Constraint: Canadian–American Relations and the Korean War, 1950–1951," *Journal of Canadian Studies* 27 (Winter 1992–93).

Geoffrey A.H. Pearson, *Seize the Day* (Ottawa, 1993), speaks good sense about his father's crisis diplomacy, 1948–56. Terence Robertson, *Crisis* (Toronto, 1964), claims to be the "inside story of the Suez conspiracy." Wm. Roger Louis and Roger Owen, eds., Suez 1956 (Oxford, 1989) has a number of relevant pieces, including one by Michael Fry, "Canada, the North Atlantic Triangle, and the United Nations." E.L.M. Burns, *Between Arab and Israeli* (Toronto, 1962) deals impressively the United Nations Emergency Force. On peacekeeping more generally, there is no better book than Alastair Taylor, et al., *Peacekeeping: International Challenge and Canadian Response* (Toronto, 1968).

Basil Robinson elegantly combines memoir and history in *Diefenbaker's World* (Toronto, 1989). The prime minister's relations with the Department of External Affairs are summarized in John Hilliker, "The Politicians and the 'Pearsonalities': The Diefenbaker Government and the Conduct of Canadian External Relations," Canadian Historical Association *Historical Papers* (1984). Donald Fleming, *So Very Near*, 2 vols. (Toronto, 1985) is the autobiography of the finance minister.

Further Readings

American author Jon B. McLin describes *Canada's Changing Defense Policy, 1957–1963* (Baltimore, 1967). On the Chief's fall, see Peter Stursberg, *Diefenbaker: Leadership Lost, 1962–67* (Toronto, 1976); Knowlton Nash, *Kennedy and Diefenbaker* (Toronto, 1990); and two articles by Jocelyn Maynard Ghent: "Canada, the United States and the Cuban Missile Crisis," *Pacific Historical Review* 18 (May 1979) and "Did He Fall or Was He Pushed? The Kennedy Administration and the Fall of the Diefenbaker Government," *International History Review* 1 (April 1979). The Ghent article on Cuba has been substantially revised with Don Munton in his *Canadian Foreign Policy* (Scarborough, ON, 1992). Peter T. Haydon's *The 1962 Cuban Missile Crisis* (Toronto, 1994) reveals important new research.

John English's *The Worldly Years* (Toronto, 1992) and vol. 3 of Pearson's own recollections (Toronto, 1975) give the outlines of Pearson's premiership. Five of Pearson's collegues have written their memoirs: Paul Hellyer, *Damn the Torpedoes* (Toronto, 1990); Mitchell Sharp, *Which Reminds Me. . .* (Toronto, 1994); Tom Kent, *A Public Purpose* (Montreal, 1988); Walter L. Gordon, *A Political Memoir* (Toronto, 1977); and Paul Martin, *A Very Public Life*, vol. 2 (Toronto, 1985). The uneasy relationship with France and Quebec is chronicled in Dale C. Thomson, *Vive le Québec libre* (Toronto, 1988) as well as Claude Morin's *Quebec versus Ottawa* (Toronto, 1976). Victor Levant's *Diplomacy of Complicity: Canadian Involvement in the Vietnam War* (Toronto, 1986) confronts the interpretation of Douglas A. Ross, *In the Interests of Peace: Canada and Vietnam, 1954–73* (Toronto, 1984). External aid is the focus of Keith Spicer, *A Samaritan State?* (Toronto, 1966). The nationalist flavor of the later 1960s is captured by books like Stephen Clarkson, ed., *An Independent Foreign Policy for Canada?* (Toronto, 1968).

The major work on Pierre Trudeau's foreign policy is J.L. Granatstein and Robert Bothwell, *Pirouette* (Toronto, 1990). There is also material in Mitchell Sharp's memoirs (Toronto, 1994); Richard Gwyn, *The Northern Magus* (Toronto, 1980); Stephen Clarkson and Christina McCall, *Trudeau and Our Times*, vol. 1 (Toronto, 1990); and Stephen Clarkson's excellent *Canada and the Reagan Challenge* (Toronto, 1985). Jean-François Lisée, *In the Eye of the Eagle* (Toronto, 1990) and Claude Morin, *L'art de l'impossible* (Montreal, 1987) have much to say about "la diplomatie québécoise" from the 1960s to the 1980s. Clyde Sanger recounts the law of the sea negotiations in *Ordering the Oceans* (London, 1986).

There is as yet no general assessment of the Mulroney government's stewardship of foreign affairs. A scathing, personalized, and not entirely convincing interim indictment is Lawrence Martin, *Pledge of Allegiance: The Americanization of Canada in the Mulroney Years* (Toronto, 1993). G. Bruce Doern and Brian W. Tomlin, *Faith and Fear: The Free Trade Story* (Toronto, 1991) is the best of many sources on the Canada–United States Free Trade Agreement. On NAFTA, a point of departure is Ricardo Grinspun and Maxwell A. Cameron, eds., *The Political Economy of North American Free Trade* (Montreal, 1993). The Carleton University *Canada Among Nations* series began with 1984, just as the Conservatives were taking office and provides a good guide to their policies.

For a good deal of rich material on recent policies, see Robert O. Matthews and Cranford Pratt, eds., *Human Rights in Canadian Foreign Policy* (Montreal, 1988); Allan Gotlieb, *"I'll be with you in a minute, Mr. Ambassador": The Education of a Canadian Diplomat in Washington* (Toronto, 1991); Mark W. Charlton, *The Making of Canadian Food Aid Policy* (Montreal, 1992); A. Claire Cutler and Mark W. Zacher, eds., *Canadian Foreign Policy and International Economic Regimes* (Vancouver, 1992); Andrew F. Cooper, Richard A. Higgott, and Kim Richard Nossal, *Relocating Middle Powers: Australia and Canada in a Changing World Order* (Vancouver, 1993); Tom Keating, *Canada and World Order* (Toronto, 1993); Donald Macintosh and Michael Hawes, *Sport and Canadian Diplomacy* (Montreal, 1994); and James Rochlin, *Discovering the Americas* (Vancouver, 1994). Finally, Denis Stairs and Gilbert R. Winham are the editors of three volumes on foreign economic policy in the research studies series of the Royal Commission on the Economic Union and Development Prospects for Canada (Toronto, 1985).

INDEX

Index